PENGUIN BOOKS

Michael Veitch hails from a family of journalists, but for years dodged his dynastic responsibilities, preferring instead to write and perform in television sketch comedy then, later, in stage productions. But blood will out, and after several years contributing to various newspapers as a freelance writer and theatre critic, he explored his life-long interest in the aviation of the Second World War in his first book, *Flak*, and now *Fly*. Michael Veitch lives in Melbourne and hosts ABC television's weekly *Sunday Arts* program.

FLY

MICHAELVEITCH

PENGUIN BOOKS

PENGUIN BOOKS

Published by the Penguin Group
Penguin Group (Australia)
250 Camberwell Road, Camberwell, Victoria 3124, Australia
(a division of Pearson Australia Group Pty Ltd)
Penguin Group (USA) Inc.
375 Hudson Street, New York, New York 10014, USA
Penguin Group (Canada)
90 Eglinton Avenue East, Suite 700, Toronto, Canada ON M4P 2Y3
(a division of Pearson Penguin Canada Inc.)
Penguin Books Ltd
80 Strand, London WC2R 0RL England
Penguin Ireland
25 St Stephen's Green, Dublin 2, Ireland
(a division of Penguin Books Ltd)
Penguin Books India Pvt Ltd
11 Community Centre, Panchsheel Park, New Delhi – 110 017, India
Penguin Group (NZ)
67 Apollo Drive, Rosedale, North Shore 0632, New Zealand
(a division of Pearson New Zealand Ltd)
Penguin Books (South Africa) (Pty) Ltd
24 Sturdee Avenue, Rosebank, Johannesburg 2196, South Africa

Penguin Books Ltd, Registered Offices: 80 Strand, London, WC2R 0RL, England

First published by Penguin Group (Australia), 2008
This edition published by Penguin Group (Australia), 2009

10 9 8 7 6 5 4 3 2 1

Cover design by Claire Wilson © Penguin Group (Australia)
Text design by Megan Baker © Penguin Group (Australia)
Cover photograph: Back at their base at Horsham St Faith, 114 Squadron airmen excitedly
discuss their recent attacks on the 'Scharnhorst' and 'Gneisenau', February 1942:
Bob Molesworth, private collection
Back cover photograph: Barney Barnett and fellow pilot Frank Wilding pose for a publicity
shot at their airfield in Burma: Barney Barnett, private collection
Author photograph by James Penledis
Typeset in Janson Text by Post Pre-press Group, Brisbane, Queensland
Printed and bound in Australia by McPherson's Printing Group, Maryborough, Victoria

National Library of Australia
Cataloguing-in-Publication data:

Veitch, Michael.
Fly / Michael Veitch
9780143011941 (pbk.)
Australia. Royal Australian Air Force – Airmen – Interviews
World War, 1939–1945 – Aerial operations, Australian.
World War, 1939–1945 – Personal narratives, Australian.

940.544994

penguin.com.au

CONTENTS

INTRODUCTION

It came as something of a shock to learn there was a German in town. Not just any German, either, but a living, breathing, highly decorated one-time member of Hitler's long-vanquished air force who, if the rumours were true, had flown an astonishing array of aircraft, had been shot down numerous times in various theatres, was awarded the Knight's Cross of the Iron Cross – the famous 'Ritterkreuz' – had cut a considerable swathe through the female population of Nazi Germany and had even managed to squeeze in a close encounter with Adolf himself. I didn't believe a word of it.

But here I was, standing once again outside a large and forbidding retirement complex, filled with gloomy thoughts of my own mortality, about to meet another octogenarian who I hoped would soon be revealing to me – a complete stranger – the terrible, traumatic, often exciting, but always compelling stories of the days of his youth spent in the cauldron of combat – flying in World War II.

With some trepidation – like visiting a relative for the first time since a dramatic incident – I stood at a big glass door, pressed a buzzer on a console and waited to be let inside. Beware: this is where an obsession can lead you.

I had spent the best part of a year tracking down men such as these and putting their stories into a book – the navigators, the pilots, the wireless operators and the gunners. The men – boys, really – who had flown the Lancaster and Wellington bombers into Germany; the fighter pilots in Spitfires and Hurricanes who had wheeled and turned and blacked themselves out in the skies over Britain and France and North Africa; the flying boat captains who had soared for countless hours over the glittering Pacific and grim grey Atlantic; the Dakota crews who dropped soldiers into the maw of battle and supplied voracious armies across warring continents.

Sometimes, when I look back over forty years, I'm bewildered as to where it came from, this companion that appeared at my side when I was a child, then stayed long past the time when such things usually wander off, or fade beneath the glare of everyday life. Instead, it accompanied me into adulthood, then middle age, and today sits with me still, just behind and slightly in the background, a permanent fixture, its origins as obscure now as the day it arrived. My own family's military heritage offers no satisfactory explanation. My only two relatives who served in the armed forces – a grandfather and an uncle, both of whom I barely knew – took their places not in the air force at all but in the army and navy, and about their experiences uttered not a syllable.

Beyond some brief lip-service as a kid, I harboured no serious ambition to join their ranks myself, knowing full well my fundamental unsuitability to such a life. Truth be known, I'm not even particularly fond of flying.

Recently, I scored a trip in a beautifully restored DC-3 airliner which regularly criss-crosses the evening skies over Melbourne, treating its passengers to a chablis and a wondrous view of the late-summer sunset. I sat amid chatty tourists, cramped and irritated, wishing instead that I could watch its stately progress from the ground, thinking how magnificent it must look, catching the sun's final glint as it banked, revealing its polished, seventy-year-old aluminium surface, accompanied by the fading throb of its twin Wright Cyclone engines.

Even as a kid, I preferred to be an observer. Model aeroplanes blocked out the isolation of being virtually an only child (my older siblings bolted the nest as soon as they could) as well as the racket of my parents' largely dysfunctional marriage. The money from several after-school jobs went towards little other than Airfix and Revell boxed kits, and I joined a select group of serious, school-uniformed regulars who, several afternoons a week, would descend on one of the city's several hobby shops as soon as the last bell had rung.

Sometimes it was a new model plane every week. I would bring it home – the tram ride spent savouring the dramatic illustration on the box – then excitedly show my father (who would feign interest for a moment) before breaking the seal and savouring the contents. Tiny bits of plastic, beautifully moulded to replicate rivets or canvas surfaces, and minute figures of the pilot and crew, complete with scarves and goggles, would tumble out of the box. Seated at a small table at one end of a draughty open-air landing, I went to work, surrounded by my glues and paints and brushes – a turpentine-soaked oasis. Light Tan for the leather helmet, Arctic White mixed with a drop of Aluminium for the glass goggles. In my hands the little aeroplanes took shape in glue and plastic, as in my head colours and sounds and stories exploded, carrying me deep into a world of knowledge where I felt secure, arming my early adolescent self with identity, teaching me a self-reliance that has equipped me to this day.

One by one, the planes took their place on my book shelf, or gathered in growing flocks on wires suspended above my head in my room. I went through mini love affairs with the different types – Hurricane, Mosquito, Wellington, Zero – devouring information on each of them in turn, until, sated, moving on to the next.

At twenty, I travelled to London on my first trip overseas. As I looked out from the descending airliner, the green mosaic of England and its myriad towns and villages rolled out below, but my gaze was fixed firmly on the sky, the same patch of blue and wispy-white where, I knew, the Battle of Britain had played out its twisting, monumental drama forty years earlier.

A few days later, I stopped short in front of a poster at Manor House tube station. In gaudy colours, painted images of First and Second World War aircraft wheeled around above the heads of the crowd. The annual summer 'Warbirds' airshow was barely a week away, a short train ride to the famous aerodrome at Biggin Hill in Kent. I could hardly believe my luck.

But, standing behind the crowd barrier in the tepid English sunshine as the PA system blared martial music and a commentator jazzed it up with one scripted cliché after another, it all felt strangely empty. Even the sight of the aircraft, restored to within an inch of their lives, varnished like aerial hot rods, left me disappointed. I'd had more of a thrill making them out of plastic as a ten-year-old, dirtying them up with simulated battle wear – stains along the cowling from the leaded petrol and scuff marks where the pilot's boots had worn away the paint on the upper surface of the wings.

On the train ride back to London that afternoon, I realised, perhaps for the first time, that it was not the sight and sound of machines I had hankered for all these years, but a time, a time long gone, though not for the people who had lived it. And getting them to tell me all about it was always one of my favourite pastimes.

As a youth, at assorted functions and gatherings both public and private, I would quite happily forego the usual merriment to sit with the greying fellow in the corner with the distinctive badge on his lapel, drawing him out, slowly at first, allowing him to set the pace as he spoke – sometimes for the first time in years – about his time in the war. I sat, mesmerised, and I listened. Occasionally I got the brush-off, but only occasionally.

Now, there are just a few of these men left, each with a tale of extraordinary personal experience from a war fought long ago, and a time long gone, but still real, vivid and alive to them. Before they all passed away, I wanted to speak to as many as I could, to paint the picture of what they did, not out of any sense of duty or honour or deference to some legacy in an era of dubiously revived jingoism, but simply for me.

I'd met Englishmen, Australians and New Zealanders – all now in their eighties – men once reticent but now eager to expound on that most extraordinary chapter in their lives, prepared at last to give it up to an interested stranger rather than letting their tales be lost forever. I'd met men who had told me extraordinary things I shall never forget. But I'd never met a German.

It's funny how it all came about. I'd told the story of Les Smith, a nuggety Englishman who had once been a turret gunner in the Royal Air Force, condemned to fly the truly appalling Boulton-Paul Defiant – a bizarre hybrid which saw a hydraulically powered turret shoved into the back of a single-engine fighter to scare the Germans with a radical new concept in aviation warfare. It didn't work. With no compensatory boost in engine power, the Defiant was heavy and unwieldy, and once the Germans recovered from their initial surprise that, with this bird, the guns fired backwards, they varied their attack and tore them to pieces in the daylight skies of France and England.

But Les somehow survived to be a more-than-sprightly old chap, especially on Anzac Day where, under the RAF banner, he marches up to the Melbourne Shrine and still today fits perfectly into his immaculate royal blue RAF uniform.

I'd written about Les in my first book, and at a lunch held sometime after its publication, organised so that a few of the blokes could meet each other, we all got talking. As we tucked into the fine fare, Les casually dropped to me that a friend of his – living right here in Melbourne – had been in the Luftwaffe flying all sorts of things: Junkers, Heinkels etc. He'd even had a spell as a courier pilot flying around some of the top-ranking Nazis. 'Nice chap, though,' he said.

Oh, and now he comes to mention it, what about his mate the Spitfire pilot, shot down attacking a Dornier during the Battle of Britain? 'Lives in Canberra. Did I mention him?' I just stared at him for a few moments, aghast. How many other tales had I missed? 'Good soup, this,' he said bringing another spoonful of minestrone to his lips.

But as luck would have it, I've been asked to do it all again, and who better than an envoy from the Dark Side to kick me off?

PETER ALEXANDER MEHRTENS

Pilot, Luftwaffe

The phone rang only once. He sounded friendly. Perhaps Les had tipped him off to my calling, but no, Peter was simply an affable bloke expressing not the slightest hesitation about my wanting to come over and poke around in his past. 'Yes, sure, anytime. Come, sure,' he said keenly in an odd mixture of educated European corrupted with an Australian twang. I didn't want to sound pushy but was, er, tomorrow morning too soon? 'Yes, yes, of course, of course, tomorrow, anytime,' he assured me.

Where he lived was a rabbit warren with several wings and complicated floor plans on boards. I asked a small Vietnamese woman clutching an enormous vacuum cleaner which of the many lifts and stairwells I should take to get to the third floor. She deciphered the address in my hand and sent me down a passageway. On the way I passesd items of strange Masonic regalia in glass cabinets as well as the latest efforts of the village knitting circle: colourful tea cosies and something in cream for a new grandchild.

I had no idea what to expect from talking to a German airman from World War II. I had never thought I should ever meet one. I had grown up obsessed with the victorious Allies, but my interest in the defeated Germans was comparatively small.

I knew what they flew, of course, and at age seven could bore people senseless with long explanations of the differences between the Messerschmitt 109 'E' and 'G' variants, or expound on such oddities as the Blohm und Voss 141 (as far as I know, the world's only asymmetrical aeroplane). From time to time, I would even embark on minor love affairs with some of the German aircraft, such as the Luftwaffe's stalwart early-war bomber, the Heinkel 111, revering its camouflaged splinter-green form in photographs and lovingly constructed model kits (although goodness knows why – this heavy, antiquated bus of a thing was one of the ugliest aeroplanes ever built). But all in all, I never had the same feeling for the 'enemy' as I did for the 'good guys'. I suppose the poison of the Nazi regime had a lot to do with it, but I had little notion about how the men themselves felt about flying, fighting and, in their case, losing.

Peter's door was open. I knocked and walked into a room that seemed to be full of people. It was a tiny space – functional with a small bathroom, space for a bed, a little desk and shelf and that was it. Cat-swinging definitely not recommended. I introduced myself to three people simultaneously. A cacophony ensued. 'Yes, we know, seen you on the telly!' announced a middle-aged woman to another man who kept insisting we had already met. 'No, the *telly*, he's been on the *telly*,' she reiterated. The man was still unconvinced. 'What's he doing here?' someone asked.

Peter, who I had come to see, sat a few feet away in a chair and chuckled quietly at the scene. 'Goodonya, My-gel,' he said in a friendly way, perspiring slightly and offering his hand like we were old friends. With my added presence in the little room, I began to recall the cabin scene from *A Night at the Opera*.

There was nowhere to sit other than on the bed alongside the others. 'Sure we haven't met?' asked the man once again – Peter's stepson Gary, as I later discovered. He and his wife eventually gave up trying to unscramble the incongruity of my presence, and it all became quite jolly.

Peter, I could soon tell, was a pleasant man, but not well. He looked already exhausted by the time I arrived and explained that his blood sugar levels had of late been high. 'Way, way high,' he said, lifting his hand for emphasis. Without another word he reached for a pile of books on a shelf and passed one over. It was a homemade work of eighty or so typed A4 pages slipped into plastic page protectors and bound by hand: *Such is Life – the good times and the bad times – autobiography of Major Peter Alexander Mehrtens (retd)*. I thanked him and began flipping through his short autobiography as a conversation about family matters evolved around me.

The cover showed a series of pictures of various German aeroplane types, the stylish pilot's badge, an Iron Cross, and in the centre, an image of an extremely handsome young man – beautiful almost – with large soft eyes and a high forehead, dressed in the uniform of a Luftwaffe officer: Peter, in his youth, over sixty years ago. Time, as they say, is a terrible thing.

Not to be trumped, I handed over a copy of my own book, a professional and slickly produced effort by comparison, then instantly regretted it, feeling like a show-off. I told him it was a gift. He glanced at it, a little awkward, then put it aside.

'Gary started to rewrite it,' said his wife, 'but someone suggested we leave it the way it is to give it more character. Oh well, we'll leave you to it,' and they all stood suddenly, giving Peter an affectionate farewell. On his way out, Gary tapped the cover of Peter's book. 'Not a bad story either,' he said. Peter gave a small chuckle. There was a moment's silence as we two strangers sat and contemplated each other.

'I'm not too hot at the moment, you know,' he tells me, dropping the armour of good humour he had been holding up for his family. I offer to postpone the conversation but he will have none of it. I suggest a cup of tea or a glass of water but that too is waved away. 'Forget it, forget it,' he says in his affably mangled accent.

A few words of introduction about me, and then, to business. Let's get the ball rolling with an easy one. 'What part of Germany are you from?' I ask.

'Berlin!' he announces with something like a flourish. 'A Berlin boy – baptised with water from the Spree,' and so he proceeds to tell me the fascinating story of his life.

Peter's father was a major in World War I, wounded by shellfire at the front while serving in the Pioneer Corps. Exactly which front Peter is a little unsure. Then again, his memories of the old man don't exactly ring with tenderness. 'One of my sons will serve the Fatherland!' was the paternal decree to his children, and the honour fell to Peter. 'He was tough. He really was,' he says. 'One of the old Kaiser's men.'

As a child growing up in the suburbs of Berlin, Peter remembers the chaotic years prior to the Nazis taking power. 'I'd go down into the street and watch the different parties marching around with my sister, Eva,' he says. He can still see the badge vendors supporting whichever group was marching that day, noisily parroting 'Red Front!' or 'Heil Hitler!' to whoever would buy their wares.

I turn on my tape recorder, at which he looks momentarily askance. I remember my manners and ask him whether he minds. 'You tape record as much as you like!' he adds with another dismissive wave.

Then he bolts ahead, tantalising me with fragments of stories from the Russian Front, or flying over England and being forced down in the English Channel. He points to a large scar on the centre of his left hand, then mentions the nurses who looked after him, and something about a gorgeous female officer in Hamburg. But we wouldn't want to get ahead of ourselves.

'I was thirteen when I first started learning to fly,' he tells me. It was the same year Hitler came to power, 1933. Peter was packed up and sent to live in Berlin's prestigious Lichterfelde military cadet school, a grand old Prussian establishment built by the Kaiser in 1873. It was expensive and sounds utterly Dickensian. Visits from friends and family were forbidden. Only once was the rule broken, when his mother came to see him as he lay ill with diphtheria. Despite this, and visits home being restricted to two a year, Peter loved it.

Once Hitler became Chancellor, in January, the teachers could openly wear the Nazi Party badges they had been concealing for years under their lapels. Cadets like Peter were given a choice of which service they wanted to join. 'Ever since I was a kid I wanted to fly, fly, fly,' he says. Some of his earlier chuckle begins to return.

Officially at least, Germany still had no air force, banned as it was under the Treaty of Versailles, so Peter was required to join the Hitler Youth flying school to learn the basics in gliders, then powered aircraft. 'The instructors were tough, really tough,' he recalls. Peter, though, was a natural, perfectly executing his solo examination flight in a Henschel biplane and earning his pilot's wings in 1937.

To gain wider knowledge of the aircraft he would be flying, cadet pilot Mehrtens was sent to Bremen for a stint at the Weser Flug factory constructing the famous Junkers 87 dive-bomber, the Stuka. Here he was put to work as an electrical fitter, installing some of the fifteen kilometres of wiring that went into every aircraft, as well as learning instrument-making, a skill he would be thankful for in a later life. It was here though, that it all so nearly came undone.

One morning after a birthday party, Peter awoke with a hangover and decided to stay in bed without calling in. Nazi Germany, however, had little tolerance for sickies, especially in the military. Clocking on the next day, Peter was promptly arrested and interrogated by the resident SS officer, one Hauptsturmführer Wiesler. A shocked Peter was charged with sabotage: failing in one's contribution to Hitler's Germany was seen as tantamount to conspiring against it. As he stood to rigid attention in a small office, his file lay open on the officer's desk. Above it, a pen was poised ready to wipe out years of hard work and the dreams of a lifetime. It appears, however, that a decent grovel and the hint of a tear could, even in that macabre atmosphere, occasionally work wonders. Peter was let off with a severe warning. He never missed a day again.

After swearing personal loyalty to the Führer, 'and other nonsense like that', he says, Peter passed out as a nineteen-year-old Luftwaffe lieutenant in April 1939 – five months before the start of the war.

Like most young pilots, he hankered to fly fighters. It was not to be. Peter was instead sent to Bavaria for yet more training at Kampfflieger Schule for bomber, transport and long-range aircraft. Here he learned to handle the cumbersome Heinkel 111 and Junkers 52 tri-motor transport, an aeroplane for which he still holds affection. 'I fell in love with that big plane,' he says. The ones he flew were ex-Lufthansa, still with their peacetime fittings. 'I even had thoughts of becoming an airline pilot after the war,' he says, and chuckles darkly.

He also tried out on the Stuka, but the 90-degree dives just didn't agree with him. To pass the test, you were made to sit back-to-back with the pilot who executed two dives in quick succession then landed immediately. 'Then I had to jump out of the plane and stand to attention in front of the doctor. If your eyes were still spinning after a minute or two, you were out. I, unfortunately, was out.' I doubt he could have remained disappointed for long: over England, Stuka losses were horrendous.

Despite a conviction that the war would be over before his training was completed, Peter was eventually posted to the famous Kampfgeschwader (bomber squadron) 53, the 'Legion Condor', so named during its time fighting alongside Franco's forces in the Spanish Civil War. In late 1940, he arrived at an aerodrome at Vitry-en-Artois near Lille in northern France, ready to take part in air operations against England.

First, though, he was treated to some spoils of war: part of the vast hoard of equipment left abandoned on the beaches of Dunkirk by the British in June. The squadron was given three railway wagons, still locked and ready for looting.

'One was full of cigarettes and booze, the other fine cloth. But the third was full of golf balls! Can you believe it? I didn't even know what golf was!' Several towns in northern France soon became inundated with the things.

Thus, in the latter stages of the Battle of Britain, Peter commenced his long and eventful combat flying career. He piloted the Heinkel in daylight, attacking places like Bristol, Southampton and London. They were shot at and hit many times, but not seriously. 'The English were not very accurate then,' he says. He encountered the Spitfire and Hurricane pilots of the RAF but made a habit of putting his aircraft into a sudden dive when they came close, which he reckons saved him on several occasions.

Once he saw a Hurricane passing close to him, probably out of ammunition. 'I could see the pilot quite clearly. I waved . . . he waved back!' he chuckles. Then over the Isle of Wight one day, he caught a shrapnel splinter above his eye – the first of many wounds he was to survive. Back at Vitry, the surgeon simply grabbed a pair of pliers and yanked it out. 'I will never for the life of me forget the pain,' he says.

One day over Kingston near London, Peter's wireless operator and friend, Willy, a veteran of the Spanish campaign and obviously a man at the end his tether, gave in to his frayed nerves and simply jumped out of the aircraft. Back in France it was the source of much amusement. 'Better strap your boys to their seats,' the other officers joked. 'Who's going to want to fly with you now?'

Peter also took part in a night raid, his first ever and one he can never forget: the devastation of Coventry, 14 November 1940. He hardly needed his navigator – the firestorm could be seen a hundred kilometres away. 'It was a frightful sight,' he remembers. 'We had no specific target, just the area northeast of the city. When I saw it had already been flattened, I asked over the radio if I should target another area. I was simply told, "Bomb according to plan." I will never be able to forget it.'

I'm unsure whether it's the subject matter, but Peter at this stage abruptly stands and mumbles an apology about having to get to lunch. He pulls on an old reefer jacket that has seen better days and with both hands grabs hold of a movable walking device he keeps by the door. I realise only now that movement for him is neither easy nor comfortable. I stand to thank him, and ask if we can possibly reconvene sometime over the coming week, as I feel we've only just got started. 'Anytime, anytime,' he mutters.

Then, without even turning to look at me, he suggests I might like to simply wait there till he gets back. I accept his trusting gesture and settle back into the seat, alone in the old airman's modest room, wishing I had something to stem a sudden feeling of melancholy. I pick up his book and, for the next hour, read.

When Peter returns, he looks even worse than before. I just let him sit there for a moment, catching his breath. Eventually, he looks up and sees his book open in my lap. 'Such is life,' he mutters. 'The good times and the bad.' I agree that it's not a bad title. 'I was a career pilot for a while, too. Flying all the big shots around. Ha,' and he shakes his head.

In March 1941, on his 42nd mission over England, at about four in the afternoon, Peter discovered that not all English anti-aircraft gunners were rotten shots. After dropping his load of bombs over Southampton harbour, he passed over the Isle of Wight in his Heinkel, and caught a big burst of anti-aircraft fire between the starboard motor and the cockpit. The perspex in the nose shattered, the engine caught fire and Peter suddenly noticed that he could see bones sticking out of his bloodied right hand. Next to him sprawled out on the cockpit floor, Werner Moos, the co-pilot and most experienced of the crew, lay dead, his head split open by a shell fragment. Peter was covered with blood – his own, as well as his friend's.

'He was a terrific guy,' he tells me. 'One of my best friends. I remember his strong Cologne accent and his lovely wife – she'd just given birth to a baby daughter.' Peter did his best to trim the aircraft but the big ungainly Heinkel, an aircraft not renowned for its gliding characteristics, ditched in the Channel, a hundred or so kilometres from the English coast. The three remaining men scrambled into a life raft and bobbed around in the sea for a couple of hours before being picked up by a German destroyer. 'We just had to ditch Werner in the sea,' says Peter, who was patched up, spent a few weeks in hospital, and was sent back to the squadron.

The day he arrived back at Vitry, his hand still heavily band-aged, the place seemed deserted. Only a single private was on duty, with some advice that he might like to quickly make his way to the parade ground where the rest of the squadron had assembled to honour an important visiting general. As Peter approached the group, he thought he recognised a loud and familiar voice. 'I could hear someone saying something like, "We've got England on her knees" and "push harder!" etc.' Like a skulking schoolboy at assembly, he tried to hide up the back. To no avail. His commander caught his eye and thrust him forward into the presence of Reichmarschall Hermann Goering himself.

'I never liked the fat bastard,' says Peter. Even after a clean, Peter's uniform still looked ghastly from its spell in the sea, and his officer's cap was missing. 'You look shocking,' Goering said to him. After what he had been through, Peter was not in a particularly reverent mood. 'Well, I *have* just been in the water,' he said and proceeded to explain. His candour obviously impressed Goering, who conferred on him the Iron Cross Second Class on the spot and promoted him to first lieutenant. 'You will go to hospital in Bremen, have three weeks holiday and a new uniform on my account,' he pronounced.

And so he did, making particular effort to seek out the most expensive tailor he could find, and forwarding the bill to 'Luftwaffe Headquarters, Berlin', marking it, 'Attention: Goering'. As far as he knows, it was paid.

A little later, Peter and his crew, though not yet officially back on flying duties, made one brief, highly irregular trip: a return to the spot in the sea where they had committed their friend Werner to the deep. Spirited inside the aircraft that day was an extra passenger, Werner's wife. 'Just so she could see the spot where he died,' he tells me. Peter is a little vague on what, if any, permission had been received for this poignant unofficial funeral flight.

I look at Peter curiously. Once or twice I have to remind myself that the air force days of which he speaks, laced with anecdotes of individualism, and a less-than-solemn respect for authority, took place on the German side. He still looks pale, and occasionally stops for gulps of breath, as if walking up stairs, before launching back into his story once again.

One morning a few months after Peter ditched in the English Channel, the officers of the squadron were ordered into the mess at 7 a.m. to hear the voice of Goebbels on the radio. It triumphantly declared, 'By our Führer's command, our victorious troops, at five o'clock this morning, crossed the Russian border to smash the Soviet Union and Stalin!' According to Peter, this announcement of war in the east was met with dead silence as the men huddled around the set. 'Is he going mad?' someone asked, the question seeming to catch the general consensus.

Now began a very different kind of war for Peter Mehrtens. A few weeks later, he found himself in Russia, flying the three-engine Junkers 52 transports to supply the trapped Second Army Corps, surrounded by the Red Army at Demjansk near Leningrad. Despite it being dubbed 'the corrugated coffin', Peter liked the big Ju52. It was slow but reliable and, covered in its unique ribbed skin construction, highly robust. Just as well, as running the eight-kilometre gauntlet on supply drops to the besieged German army was dangerous work.

He was shot at constantly, and avoided the big anti-aircraft fire by flying perilously close to the ground. 'After thirty-two missions and a plane full of gunshot holes, we knew it was not all fun and games,' he says with an odd chuckle. Then, around October that other enemy began to arrive – winter. 'At that time, I had no idea how bad things were going to get,' Peter says. The snows began, and then cold such as he'd never known.

Even at 20 below, they were still expected to fly. Simply

keeping the aircraft airworthy was a nightmare. 'One sergeant came up with the idea of throwing petrol on the exhaust stubs to warm the engine.' The theory was that once the engine started, the propeller would extinguish the flames, hopefully before the aircraft blew up.

There were days when the mercury plunged to minus fifty-two – too cold even for war. 'We couldn't leave our huts even for the twenty metres to get food,' he says. 'All we could do was stand in front of our heating drums, warming our backs while our fronts would freeze, and then rotate,' he says.

One bright day the temperature registered a balmy minus five, and flying was back on. It was only a distance of ten kilometres, and Peter had a war correspondent along for the ride. Overflying the Russian lines, he felt 'a hard bump. I thought I'd hit a tree.' In fact it was a mortar shell which had exploded behind the cockpit and left a gaping hole in the fuselage. Peter's elevator controls were dead and all he could do was put the aircraft down, crash-landing safely in the snow, close, he thought, to his own lines. Five men piled out and started tramping towards their own positions, only to be greeted with heavy bursts of machine-gun and rifle fire.

Every conceivable obscenity they could think of was screamed, but to no avail. The war correspondent stripped off his white winter overalls to reveal his German uniform underneath and, handkerchief in hand, boldly led the wary procession over to the 'friendly' lines. Once there, the correspondent asked to see the officer in charge, and promptly punched him in the mouth. 'He felt a lot better after that,' says Peter. German-speaking Russians, it was explained, were a favourite ploy of the enemy.

This incident provided Peter with another wound courtesy of a bullet he failed to even notice until someone pointed out the blood pouring from his leg. It earned him another stint in hospital, a promotion to Hauptmann (captain) and another Iron Cross – this time First Class.

I can soon see why Peter was compelled to write a book of his own, but even that, he tells me, barely scratches the surface. I read between the lines on some pages, and press him to fill me in on other matters. At the start of the great retreat from the east, he was ordered back into the air making several trips to Kiev to pick up wounded soldiers in his Junkers painted with the red cross. 'It made no difference,' he says. 'In Russia a red cross meant nothing.'

'Lines and lines of wounded men,' Peter remembers, some screaming, some hysterical, all desperate to get out. On several occasions the plane was mobbed. 'Even as we taxied to the runway, guys were hanging off the wings and even the wheels. The military police had to shoot them so we could take off. On one flight we took out 200 wounded. The whole thing was absolutely shocking – a nightmare.' He points to a page in his book, a rough photo taken at the time. 'There, that's me,' he says. 'I'm that skinny kid.'

Then came an order to report to Field Marshall Milch in Berlin who, by coincidence, happened to be a friend of his aunt. This was, however, no social call. For his services to the Reich, Peter had been decorated yet again, this time given permission to wear around his neck the Knight's Cross of the Iron Cross. He was also given what can only be described as a dream job – official courier pilot attached to Luftwaffe Headquarters flying generals and other Nazis all over the Greater German Reich. It's hard to believe his auntie's influence didn't play its part, but Peter was given a natty little single-engine Messerschmitt 108, and carte blanche to stay in the best hotels across Europe. Understandably, he speaks of these few months as his happiest of the war: paradise compared to what he had seen of it so far. 'Yes, I flew all the big shots around all over the place,' he tells me. 'I even had Himmler in the back once,' although not a word, he says, passed between them. His proximity to people such as these would later land him in deep trouble.

Once, he thought his number was surely up when, carrying a general to somewhere in France, he watched as two RAF Spitfires dipped their wings to attack from above. Armed with nothing but a flare pistol, Peter calmly thought, 'Goodnight, general, we are dead.' But not a shot was fired. The attacking aircraft wheeled around and simply went home. Peter still doesn't know why.

Then there was the time he was ordered to Augsburg to pick up a certain Lieutenant Reiner to take him on to a Luftwaffe training camp in Hamburg where he was to spend a few days lecturing the recruits. Arriving, he found no one who fitted the description, until a stunning uniformed blonde held out a hand. 'I'm Lieutenant Reiner,' she said, admiring his Knight's Cross. 'Ah, young Irma,' Peter remembers with a definite sparkle. 'Warm, bubbly and wonderful.'

The camp, as it turned out, comprised 800 young women undergoing intelligence training. 'I was the only male,' says Peter. 'Walking to the dining room was torture.' It doesn't exactly sound like hardship though, particularly when he explains that 'young Irma' knocked quietly on his door later one night with a bottle of champagne and a couple of glasses in her hand.

It was only very gradually that Peter began to appreciate the nature of the regime for which he was fighting. As we talk, surreal and nightmarish anecdotes drop into his narrative which, he fully admits, he did not comprehend at the time. At an aerodrome outside Riga, he approached the extraordinary sight of a group of young women working on the runway with shovels, dressed in what appeared to be their Sunday best: high heels, some even wearing furs. Peter stood by, innocently suggesting they would be better off in work clothes. 'We are Jews,' one woman said in a strong Berlin accent. Probably fleeing with what wealth they could carry on them, the women had made it to Latvia, only to be picked up there when the Germans invaded. An SS guard approached and warned Peter not to talk to them, 'For their sake,' he said, 'and yours.'

Later, waiting to enter the main gate of the old citadel in Torgau, he was approached by an old man who 'sort of saluted' and spoke politely. 'Herr Hauptmann, do you see that little string of bullets on the side of the wall?' Peter remarked that it looked like machine-gun fire. 'Yes,' said the man. 'That is where they stood. Women, children and old men, mainly Jews.' Uncomfortable, Peter told the man not to talk such nonsense. Then the man pointed across to a freshly dug field. 'That is where they buried them. It looks like a potato field doesn't it? But the potatoes are already out this time of year.' And with that he was gone. 'I thought about it,' says Peter, 'but it took me a long time to believe that he was right.'

One day in March 1944, Peter found himself on a train heading south with a group of other officers, all of whom, like him, were already wearing the Knight's Cross around their necks. At the station, they were picked up by two big black Mercedes and driven through 'the most beautiful countryside in Germany' to Berchtesgarten, then to the Berghof – the private residence of Adolf Hitler. 'We could see SS guards all over the place,' he tells me. 'We were guided to a big hall where we were asked to salute Hitler, who was standing there with an army general.'

Here, I have to draw breath. It's not every day that you meet someone who has come face to face with the most infamous person in history, and I must have looked a little tongue-tied. 'Did you . . . speak to him?' I ask. 'Oh yes,' says Peter, quite casually. Standing in line, the officers one by one received their clasp of oak leaves and swords to their Knight's Cross as well as the announcement of their new rank, straight from the mouth of der Führer. Peter at just twenty-three, was now 'Major der Luftwaffe'.

'He made a little speech about bravery and all that stuff,' Peter tells me dismissively. There is another pause in our conversation. I remember reading accounts of people who had met Hitler and the extraordinary aura he was said to exude. 'What was he, er, like?' I venture, feeling a little foolish. 'Nothing,' he answers. 'Just nothing. A little man. He shook my hand and made a speech. I thought he looked pale and he was twitching. That's all. None of this . . . you know, power.' So, I suggest, was he even a little . . . dull? 'Dull! Yes, very dull,' he says emphatically, like he'd been searching for the word. Then he pauses for a bit. 'But Eva Braun was lovely!'

Now I feel dizzy. Eva Braun? It seems the Führer made an excuse at the end of the brief ceremony and left to resume his work of devastating Europe and slaughtering its inhabitants. 'Eva Braun will look after you,' was the perfunctory announcement.

'She really spoke our language,' says Peter, and he, evidently, was not shy about speaking hers. What apparently followed had me gobsmacked, and were I able to think of a reason Peter had to invent it, I think I would have remained highly sceptical.

There is some very famous colour footage of Hitler up at the Berghof (in fact being afraid of heights he disliked the place and seldom went there) on a large outdoor terrace overlooking the Alps towards his native Austria. Eva Braun can be seen, posing to the camera like any vacuous twenty-something. Guests and other uniformed Nazis mingle around self-consciously admiring the view. The whole place was bombed to bits on Anzac Day 1945 (many Australian airmen took part) and the remains were finally demolished in 1952. But one Spring afternoon eight years earlier, Peter Mehrtens sat there, helping himself to the buffet and flirting with Adolf Hitler's mistress.

As he tells it, she was sick of the war and wanted it to end. 'This bloody war! I've talked to Hitler and told him he should just finish it up,' she apparently said. Just like that. 'Yes, I liked her,' Peter tells me. They seemed to have hit it off. 'I had a long chat with her.' What on earth about, I ask him, and he smiles a little sheepishly. 'Well, I said to her, "How on earth can you get into bed with a guy like Hitler?"'

'You said *what*?' I almost shout out loud. He repeats the claim. 'Peter,' I ask him, 'what on earth made you say that?'

'It just came to me, you know. I was feeling a little bold, I suppose.' And her reply? 'She just laughed and said something like, "Ah well, you know, he's just a guy like anybody else."' The really frightening thing is that were it not for the fact these two kids were discussing the greatest mass-murderer in history, they could have passed for any pair of gossiping teenagers. At the end of the day, he thanked Eva for being 'such a lovely girl', and went back to the war. It's at this point I need a break and go and look for a cup of tea. First, I use his small bathroom to splash my face with water.

The cushy courier job didn't last, and Peter was sent back into action. He was shot down and wounded for a fifth time when attacking American positions at Arnhem, this time in a Junkers 88. Again, it was his right engine which caught fire and he put the plane down in a paddock between German and American positions. Having to clamber out over the burning engine to avoid the American fire, he swam across a canal to reach the safety of his own lines, collecting another bullet – in the backside – in the process.

Then in late 1944, Peter, now in command of a group, was ordered to report to a hotel room in Hamburg for an important meeting with some high-ranking officers, including a general. There they sat making small talk and smoking in big leather arm-chairs, when the bombshell was dropped. With Peter's experience, he was told, it was decided that he would be perfect to lead an attack on shipping in Glasgow harbour – a mission they wanted carried out the very next day. Appalled, Peter jumped out of his seat. 'I told them that such an attack was barely possible back in '41, but to attempt it now was suicide.' To placate him, they promised him two squadrons of escorting fighters. Not that he really had a choice. He was told to pick twelve of his best crews for the job.

The next afternoon, with a heavy heart, Peter sat on the run-way, about to lead his formation to Scotland. Perhaps, he thought, if the fighters protect us and if we can get in and out quickly via the quiet west coast, it may just work. He took off, but at the appointed rendezvous, the promised Focke-Wulfs and Messersch-mitt 110s failed to appear. 'I got on the radio and asked where all our fighters were. *"Please let me know where we stand!"* But I soon realised that what they had told me was all lies.'

It started well. The run in to Glasgow went smoothly, 'like in peacetime', without a shot being fired. Peter's formation, in two close groups of six, made a sharp dive from 6500 metres to just under a thousand and bombed. He thinks he hit some of the ships but isn't quite sure. Gaining altitude to rejoin the rest of the formation, then heading out to sea, Peter was attacked by American P-47 Thunderbolts. One sharp loop got him out of the firing line, but then, quite surreally, he saw openings – 'like razor slashes' – appear in his flying suit, just above the knee.

Two Thunderbolts appeared either side of him and his star-board engine burst into flames. Then he felt the pain. 'It was unbelievable. I think I was screaming,' he says. He has no idea how he managed to put the Junkers down, but remembers coming in over a field of sheep 'way too fast'. Then, the tail caught some powerlines, and was ripped clean away, but this washed off enough speed to get them down in one piece. 'Lotar and Heinz, my co-pilot and radioman, grabbed me by the shoulders and threw me out onto the wing. I was half dead.' A minute or so later, from bushes twenty metres away, the men heard the aircraft catch fire and explode. Peter had three bullets in his leg and his broken bones were clearly visible. He clutched his trousers to stop the bleeding and asked if anyone had anything to stem the pain. They didn't.

The first person on the scene was a lone Scottish policeman. In their flying suits, their nationalities were not obvious, and as Lotar had studied at Oxford, he spoke perfect English. The bobby assumed them to be RAF. It was only when Peter undid his jacket and revealed his Knight's Cross that the policeman went pale. 'Are you . . . Germans?' he asked nervously. Calmly, Lotar took out his pistol, offered it by the barrel and said in his perfect Oxbridge accent, 'Yes, and if you want to shoot us, please feel free to use this.' The policeman declined, disappeared, and returned soon after with a doctor.

Peter was still in hospital at war's end, but was repatriated back to his shattered country soon afterwards. 'There was nothing to eat, nothing to wear, nothing at all.' Then, on his first week-end home back with his parents in Bremen, he was arrested and charged as a war criminal. Apparently his time flying around the 'big shot' Nazis in his little Messerschmitt 108 connected him a little too closely with some of the top criminals of the regime. It took Peter years to shake the charge, but finally they believed his claims of being simply a driver, and in 1952, he turned his back on Europe forever to come to Australia.

He indicates his wounds – eye, right leg, left leg, back, hand – and, chuckling, rolls up his trouser leg to show me the ghastly scar on his thigh, courtesy of the US Air Force. He also rummages around on a shelf and hands me a rectangular black box. Inside is his Ritterkreuz – the real thing, complete with swastika in the centre. It occurs to me also for the first time that I have actually shaken a hand that has been shaken by Adolf Hitler. It's all a little disorienting.

'Come back anytime. Anytime,' says Peter, who seems to have recovered a little of his colour, and I believe he means it.

It would take more than just a couple of meetings to answer some of the burning questions I still wanted to ask Peter, the only member of the Luftwaffe I had ever met. He makes no bones about admiring Hitler – at least to begin with. 'We all hated him, but only after he was gone. In the beginning, we loved him,' he says candidly.

I believe Peter when he tells me he was never a Nazi, and the old photographs of him show no tell-tale party badges. At times, his poor health and the subtleties of language were obstacles to my gaining a deeper understanding of how he felt, but on reflection I was probably kidding myself that I could achieve that anyway.

That Peter survived the war at all is truly astonishing. He flew hundreds of missions and was shot down an amazing six times. There was no concept of a 'tour' in the Luftwaffe. Pilots simply flew until killed or captured, and Peter beat the odds dozens of times. His life since, though, has been marred by the pain of wounds which would have broken the spirit of a lesser man years ago.

Ironically, having nearly died several times for the Nazi regime, he discovered after the war that he was in fact part Jewish, on his mother's side – a fact she had successfully concealed for many years.

He told some amusing stories too: playing ping-pong with Adolf Galland, and a wartime affair he once had with Hanna Reisch, the famous, diminutive female aviator who became one of the Luftwaffe's top test pilots. 'Yes,' says Peter smiling broadly. 'She already had another fellow, but she was my girlfriend for three days. She was a tiger!'

But the story he keeps coming back to is one of a little orphaned French girl who was found by the side of the road during the chaos of the invasion in 1940. Beside her was her dead mother, most likely strafed by pilots from Peter's own air force. She was spotted by a small group of officers. 'I think you should come with us,' they said. 'No, I will stay with my mother,' the little girl replied. 'No, it's time to come with us,' they said. And so she did.

'Monica', as she was known, became something like the squadron mascot for a time, living on the base at Vitry until being taken in by a local French family. 'She became our interpreter and ran my office, telling everyone how to salute,' says Peter. He kept in touch with her for a while, but lost contact eventually. For the girl's sake, it was safer that way.

In the end, Peter's story was a strangely familiar one, that of a young man who wanted to fly, caught up in extraordinary times. Sadly, it was the similarities rather than the differences with the people he was fighting that stood out for me the most.

NEVIN FILBY

Pilot, RAAF

I have never been one, sadly, for getting things finished. I blame my parents, because it's easy, and besides, they're not around anymore. Take music, for example. My mother came from a family that loved music, and she dreamed one day of having one of those families whose visitors would enquire about the sweet sound of, say, a cello wafting from behind closed doors in a distant part of the house. 'Oh, that's so-and-so,' she would dearly love to have answered. 'He/she has an audition next week for the Melbourne Symphony. I think his/her *Bourrée* is coming along rather nicely, don't you?' The reality was very different. My oldest brother dabbled with the guitar for a week or two, the other, to my father's fury, screeched endless selections from The Beatles' *Double White* album in the shower, and my sister seems to have been born tone deaf.

My mother's greatest disappointment, however, was reserved for me. Far from being a write-off from the start, I at least had good pitch, an early interest in classical music and a passable singing voice which, for a few years, served to shave a fraction off the school fees when I grudgingly agreed to be corralled into the school choir. What she really dreamed of, however, was a child who played the piano. Not to concert standard, mind, but at least passably. At considerable expense, she found the best teacher she could afford, bought a very nice German upright and, as an incentive to practise, placed it squarely next to the main door of my bedroom. It was all, of course, a complete waste of time and money, in a family where money, or the lack of it, was a constant, brooding presence.

For years I thumped away on the damned thing, managed to learn the odd chord here or there, sometimes even a whole tune. But I was hopeless, and I knew it. (Years later, I learned my old piano teacher committed suicide. I still wonder whether I was a contributing factor.)

I also tried the trumpet. After a year or two of bruising both my embouchure and the neighbours' ears, I packed that in too. In more recent years, I bought myself – of all things – a banjo, which, after many fruitless lessons, was commandeered by my son William who, in about three minutes, was strumming the opening chords to 'Old Joe Clark'.

There were also my attempts to write a children's book, a novel, a couple of film scripts and a play. All destined to die withering deaths in the bottom drawer of shame.

So imagine how pleased I was when a courier delivered to my house a box filled with advance copies of my first book about the men who flew the aircraft of World War II. My initial feeling was one of relief, but it was a bittersweet victory. Even as my hands crunched down through the plastic foam packaging to extract the first sweet-smelling volumes, I thought of the pile of cassettes on my desk, full of rich and interesting stories which time and space had excluded, and the notebooks dotted with tantalising contacts from the sisters, wives, sons and neighbours of gunners, bomb aimers and navigators who I hadn't even spoken to. Take Nevin's case, for example.

His was a name written cryptically on a piece of notepaper in strange handwriting and pinned to a manila folder: 'Nevin Filby. Pilot – Spitfires, Lancasters'. For weeks it tantalised me. Who on earth had written it? Where had it come from? And most intriguing of all, who on earth had managed to pilot both single-engined Spitfires and big Lancaster bombers? I couldn't even think of a scenario whereby this could be possible but I was dying for the opportunity to find out.

So, when the go-ahead came to proceed with the next project, Nevin's was the first number I rang.

What, I wanted to know, were the particular circumstances that led him to fly both fighters and bombers, and which had he spent more time on, Spitfires or Lancasters? The answer was simple: he hadn't flown either. The note was one of those well-intentioned errors in communication via a well-meaning relative who had apparently buttonholed me at a function and shoved the note into my hand. I couldn't remember a thing.

But what did that matter? Because when Nevin told me what he *had* flown, and with whom, my heart soared. Nevin Filby, it transpired, had spent his war at the controls of a mighty North American B-25 Mitchell medium bomber, flying with the fire-men, the quick-fix, dial-an-air-raid boys of the Second Tactical Air Force. He'd also had a go at much smaller aircraft. I couldn't wait to meet him.

'Now, what is it you want, exactly?' Nevin asks pointedly as we sit down at his 'office', a large oak table in the living room piled with papers and books. After goodness knows how many interviews, I still find this a tough one. 'Well . . .' I stammer, 'I would like to hear some of the . . . be very interested to learn . . . the experiences . . . of your, er, flying career.'

It was enough for him. 'Righto. That's easy,' he says in a firm, slightly gravelly voice, as his wife Mary places in front of me a cup of tea to accompany a tempting array of homemade goodies.

I take a closer look at some of what constitutes Nevin's office. Many of his books have pages marked with little coloured pieces of paper. I also notice a great deal of handwriting crammed into exercise books, on small notepads and in the margins of books and photocopied pages. Among it all I notice my own modest tome.

Nevin hails from Grenfell in New South Wales, birthplace of Henry Lawson, and former haunt of Australia's second-most famous bushranger, the oddly revered Ben Hall. His is genuine pioneer stock, and when war came in 1939, it was only natural he would get involved.

Unlike most of the country at the time, Nevin had been carefully following the advance of the Japanese through China and Manchuria in the years before the war.

'I don't think I joined up for any great reasons of patriotism,' he tells me plainly. 'I could shoot, I'm strong, I can knock over a few Japs – I thought I might as well get in to do my part.'

By 1942, however, the closest he'd got to the Japanese, or any other enemy for that matter, was sitting under a 3.7-inch anti-aircraft gun behind Sydney's Balmoral Beach. I can personally think of much worse places to spend a war, but Nevin was far from happy.

'My next-door neighbour was a lecturer at [RAAF Initial Training School] Bradfield Park. I told him that what I was doing was pretty bloody useless, and perhaps there was something more I could do in the air force.'

Nevin must have impressed the man. Straightaway he suggested he apply to be a pilot. But for Nevin, the mere word struck within him a deep chord of fear.

As a sixteen-year-old, he had watched one day as a barnstorming

Gypsy Moth biplane arrived to put on a show. With his sister, he was looking forward to presenting his shilling and going up for a spin the very next day. That afternoon, however, over the town, the upper wing of the little aeroplane failed, and it ploughed into the main street, killing both passenger and pilot. 'We all rode up on our bikes to see the crash,' says Nevin. 'I saw a man kick a dog who had grabbed a bit of meat – I thought it was an old cow. He replied, "That's not a cow, son, that's the pilot." I vomited in the street. It's a wonder I ever flew at all.' So, unlike most boys of his day, Nevin grew up devoid of the usual fantasies about flying aeroplanes.

I wonder if, a few years later, he was struck by a certain irony as he strapped himself into the cockpit of a Lockheed Ventura in faraway Canada, about to graduate as a bomber pilot. Here again, at his chilly New Brunswick Operational Training Unit, he witnessed another omen that would have scuttled the ambitions of a lesser man, when he saw a twin-engine Ventura touch down at the end of the runway then cartwheel into the ground as an engine failed. Helplessly, everyone dashed to the scene, pathetically clutching fire extinguishers. 'I saw the blokes still strapped into their seats through the perspex, and the fire licking around them. I saw them shrink from about six feet to three feet. Horrible, horrible.' Again, he had leaned over the fence and vomited. 'It should have put me off flying,' he says, 'but it didn't.'

After arriving in England on the *Queen Mary* with thousands of American servicemen on their way to D-Day and the Normandy campaign, Nevin found his way to Brighton's appropriately titled Grand Hotel, or to give it its wartime name, No. 11 (RAAF) Personnel Dispatch and Reception Centre. It's nicely ironic that this symbol of Victorian-era opulence, for decades the haunt of English society's most well heeled and powerful, was, during her darkest hour, the home to thousands of grubby colonial airmen from the farms and cities and suburbs of one of the Empire's most far-flung possessions.

Nevin could rightly have expected, along with thousand like him, to be channelled into the heavy Lancasters or Halifaxes of Bomber Command. Instead, he joined No. 2 Group, which had recently become the bomber contingent of the Second Tactical Air Force. 2TAF had been formed out of the experience of North Africa, where it was seen that a quick-response, army cooperation air strike force was an extremely useful thing to have when fighting Germans.

Heading up 2TAF's bombers was the very colourful Air Vice-Marshall Basil Embry, a man whose life reads like the pages of a *Boy's Own*. Embry joined the RAF at nineteen, flew in Iraq, Turkey and India, rose meteorically through the staff officer ranks, then pleaded to be put onto operations when war came in 1939. It could have all ended for him over Dunkirk when he baled out behind the German lines from a burning Blenheim bomber and was taken prisoner. While being marched into captivity, he spotted a sign, 'Embry . . . 3 km', and took it as an omen. He rolled down a bank, escaped, was recaptured, escaped again, spent several weeks on the run having all sorts of adventures, and eventually found his way back to England, where he was given a few weeks 'sick leave' before plunging himself once more into the action.

Embry won just about every medal going, including the DSO an amazing *four* times, but could never quite keep his mouth shut, and this tended to hamper his career. He was passed over for command of the Path Finder Force, and was handed 2TAF instead. Still, he insisted on ducking away from the office from time to time to fly with his men under the highly imaginative pseudonym 'Wing Commander Smith'.

After the war, he got jack of it all, headed to, of all places, Western Australia and became a sheep farmer in a middle-of-nowhere place called Boyup Brook. Embry, like very few military commanders, imbued his organisation with his own maverick personality. It seems he never met a junior officer from New South Wales named Filby, but I've no doubt they would have hit it off famously. As I spoke to Nevin, more than a few similarities emerged.

Twelve squadrons of Mosquitos, Bostons and Mitchells comprised 2TAF's bomber force, and prior to D-Day in mid-1944, Nevin joined one of them, 98, based at Dunsfold in Surrey. Called in at quick notice by the army fighting in Normandy, Nevin would fly not at the high altitudes of the heavies, but low, and often in broad daylight. 'We could bomb accurately but we made ourselves a bloody easy target!' he says.

I ask him if he remembers his first operation, 'Yeah,' he tells me. 'I was scared stiff.' At this point, something rather odd happens in my conversation with Nevin. Picking up some of the papers from a neat pile beside him he announces, 'When I read your book, I found it rather bland,' and, by way of contrast, proceeds to read from his own account of his flying. And it is certainly anything but 'bland'.

'On my third operation to the Hague, the flak was intense and very accurate,' he recounts, reading slowly and with complete objectivity, like a man reading a statement in court. 'The main starboard wing spar was virtually cut from a shell going through it without exploding. Other shell fragments had cut the rudder control wire. The wing was wobbling to the extent that I considered baling out . . .' He continues like this for a while, the calmness in his voice belying the drama in his words. But, impressive or not, I'm not content to be read to from a prepared statement, and interrupt like a badgering child. 'Tell me more about the damage to the aircraft!' I demand.

He puts down his notes, picks up a blank sheet of paper and a pen and begins to draw. The long, thick steel and aluminium spar connected the wings through the fuselage. His sketch shows an enormous bite taken out, almost cutting it in half. As he flew home after the raid, he thought to himself, 'How am I going to do this?' Handling the aircraft as gingerly as possible, with no sudden turns that would put too much pressure on the wings, and with deft use of engines and flap, he made it back to Dunsfold. 'People don't believe me that you can control an aeroplane like that, but we got home,' he says.

A week later, incredibly, it happened again. This time it was the other wing spar, again nearly severed by another miraculously non-exploding shell, which this time also took out the elevator control. Nevin's going too fast and I have to sometimes gently wrestle him away from his manuscript. I'm glad I do. It was regarding one trip – to Bonnieres in France – that he elaborates on his one and only wound from operations, one that could so easily have killed him.

'We'd just been given these American flak jackets and helmets, and I wouldn't wear them,' he says. 'On this particular day, Keith, my navigator, went crook at me. "For God's sake, Chief, put the bloody thing on!" And I did.'

So, looking like a soldier from a later war, rather than an airman from the Second, Nevin flew with an oversized helmet and flak jacket. It was only a piece about the size of a thumb – but with the strength of a bullet, the hot steel fragment tore through the windscreen and into the big steel helmet that had only recently adorned his scone, hitting square above the temple. It hurt like hell, and he was stunned a bit, but that was all. 'I've still got a little indentation on the left side of my temple,' he says, and shows me to prove it. We agree that without his navigator's commonsense, he would certainly have been killed. 'That's how lucky you can be. Thank God for Keith.'

But back to his recitation, and as for his literary critique of my work, I'm not out of the woods yet. 'The feelings of aircrew who knowingly flew into dangerous barrages of flak with no option than to fly a straight and level course while their bomb aimer lined up the target' were not, in his opinion, adequately dealt with in my initial literary effort, etc., etc.

Sufficiently humbled, I ask him if he would be so kind as to plug some of the gaps in my obviously inadequate narrative. He has already written his response, according to what he witnessed with his own eyes. '*Red balls, black smoke and the pinging and clatter of bits of exploding shell hitting the aircraft fuselage. I couldn't seem to shrink down small enough when I flew through it*,' he continues. I have to admit, it's not bad. The point, though, that Nevin is at pains to convey is that he was *scared*, extremely so, and a good deal of the time. 'Everyone was,' he says. 'You'd be mad not to be when you think of some of the things we had to do. We were all of us scared stiff – but hardly anyone talked about it.'

Indeed, approaching a heavily defended target must have been truly terrifying. Looking forward through the windscreen, the hundreds of puffs of bursting blackness – pricked for a deadly instant with a dark red heart – seem like a barrier that you have no choice but to crash through. You hold the column tight in your hands, fighting the instinct to turn aside. The only movements you make are the ones ordered by the voice of the bomb aimer in your ears – tiny incremental adjustments as he lines up the target in his sight. 'Left, left . . . left a bit . . . steady . . .' The calmness in his voice is infuriating. Rushes of adrenalin course hot and cold through your body making it tingle. You sweat and take quick, deep breaths, like you're about to dive underwater, sucking in as much oxygen as possible to keep the senses alert, and suppress a rising wave of panic.

'When we were low enough for the twenty- and forty-millimetre guns, the sight of the stream of projectiles was like a string of fireworks, terrifying but quite beautiful. And in between every one that you could see was another nine that you couldn't,' he says.

Occasionally, they'd have to go around a target again. Nevin tells me about 22 June 1944. The squadron was sent to attack the heavily defended steelworks at Colombelles near Caen, which had halted the progress of the 51st Highland Division, just 1000 yards away.

On the ground, the Scots of the Black Watch and Seaforth Highlanders had been told this was going to be the easy bit, but had instead become stuck in a bloody door-to-door struggle with a hardened enemy that had been fighting just such a war for three years in Russia. Now they faced a fortified factory, preventing access to Caen, the city which needed to be taken and around which the breakout was to pivot. It was close, bloody fighting. Any lack of accuracy in the placing of Nevin's bombs, therefore, would have dire consequences.

Referring to his logbook, he tells me it was a small target on the edge of a large city. Some of the men in other aircraft had already been wounded by the flak, but to hit the target, and nothing but the target, they needed a closer look, so around they went again. *'The German gun crews were very well prepared. The smoke from the bursts on our first run was still hanging in the sky when we came around for our second. It was one of those times we gritted our teeth a little bit harder and flew into the colourful, thick maelstrom,'* he reads, then looks up, abandoning his text. 'You know, we never got the credit for that that we deserve.' Later they discovered just what it was they were running into: seventy 88-millimetre and ten 120-millimetre anti-aircraft guns in an area the size of two house blocks. 'We virtually had to put our landing lights on for that second run, it was so dark with the flak,' he says.

Nevin's first tour in Normandy was an eventful one. I can well imagine that the more unpredictable nature of the Tactical Air Force suited his individual temperament. 'It was the closest thing you could get to being a fighter pilot, without actually flying one,' he says. Early on, Nevin decided that being caught by a fighter from underneath was not a way he wanted to go, and so decided to fly low, sometimes under 1000 feet. The crew didn't like it much to start off with. 'For God's sake, Skipper, get up a bit, we're level with the tops of the bloody trees!' said Joe Kerry, Nevin's nervous top gunner one day. 'It's alright, Joe,' he replied over the intercom, 'we're in a valley!'

As well as supporting the army, Nevin would do night-time flare drops, pinpointing targets for the fighter-bombers. On the way home from one such trip, having already been caught in searchlights and holed by flak, Joe called up again. 'Hey, Skip, there's a P-Plane coming up behind us.' 'P-Plane' was one of the many names given to the infamous Fieseler Fi 103, more commonly known in wartime parlance as 'Buzz Bomb', 'Doodlebug' or simply 'V1'. The Nazis fired about 10 000 of these pilotless precursors to today's guided missiles at southeast England, killing or injuring nearly 20 000 people and creating, for a few months in 1944, a second terrifying Blitz. The noise of them sounded like a car with a broken muffler, but more chilling was when it cut out – the point at which it fell to the ground detonating the near ton (1870 kilograms) of amatol in the nose.

'Have a shot at the bastard,' Nevin replied to his gunner as the small ramjet-powered craft came up alongside and began to overtake them at a mere seventy yards. Joe fired away with his two half-inch guns and tried to score some hits as it passed. 'He should have bloody well hit it,' says Nevin, chuckling, 'but I'm glad he didn't.' Indeed. At that distance, had it exploded, it would certainly have taken Nevin and his crew with it.

Nevin seems to have used every one of his nine lives. Once, his was the only crew to locate a bridge the army wanted destroyed behind the German lines. They circled the night sky for a while, considering how to attack it, then dropped their thousand-pound bomb so low the explosion tore holes in their own wings and fuselage. 'I thought it felt a bit sluggish on the way home,' he says.

On another occasion, Nevin led a box of six Mitchells at night, flying wingtip to wingtip with no lights. He is still today aghast at the very notion of it. 'Imagine it. Someone only had to sneeze and two aircraft would have gone in.' At the debrief, his comment to the top brass was typically direct: 'Well if you want to help the enemy, you'll do this again.' It went down 'like a lead brick', and was one of several instances of outspokenness that he says contributed to his remaining a relatively lowly Flight Lieutenant till war's end.

Having been indirectly responsible for a great many holes in several of His Majesty's aircraft, Nevin completed his first operational tour of thirty-five trips and was sent to the Group Support Unit at Swanton Morley to cool his heels while the air force decided what next to do with him. 'I had nothing to do but sit around, winning at poker and losing at craps,' he says.

He now faced a spell as an instructor, a job which suited him not one little bit. By chance he became friendly with a 'bloody mad English Wing Commander', who Nevin still doesn't want named. 'This bloke had been a jackaroo in Australia and seemed to have the run of the place,' he says. 'There were aircraft of all sorts up there, and he and I got on well.' So well that, one day, the 'mad' Wing Commander made a rather 'mad' suggestion.

'Ever flown a Mosquito?' he asked. Nevin hadn't, but was keen to have a go at this already legendary all-wooden machine. 'Well, we'll go and get one then.' He signed a form, and the two men treated themselves to a flight through the Midlands in a very fast, very manoeuvrable de Havilland 98 Mosquito. Nevin could instantly see what all the fuss was about. 'It handled like a peregrine falcon,' he says. The Wing Commander was also enjoying himself – so much so, that he didn't want to come home. 'Come on,' he said, 'Let's go over to France and do a raid. Unofficial. Find a train to shoot up. We'll tell 'em we're just going down to the south coast.'

'And like a ruddy fool, I went along with it!' Nevin says today, shaking his head at the madness of it. Like a couple of kids taking Mum's car out for a spin, they headed off to German-occupied France to look for trouble. Where exactly they got to, Nevin was never sure because this was one trip that didn't make it into his logbook.

At 3000 feet, they spotted a train pulling out of a station somewhere or other, and Nevin put the nose down. But this was no B-25 he was flying, and almost as soon as he'd lined up the locomotive and pressed the gun button, it came roaring up in his windshield and he was virtually on top of it. He had to pull up sharply to avoid hitting it, and the engine shot by just beneath him. 'I wasn't aware of how fast it was. Like a fighter. I bloody near wiped myself out!'

Then from nowhere, flak came up and one of his engines caught fire. Nevin thought the aircraft was lost. 'This thing's made of wood!' he thought to himself. Thankfully, normally unreliable internal fire extinguishers worked, and the wing was saved.

The hydraulics, however, were shot – no flaps, and no brakes.

'When we landed, the only way we could stop it was by my steering it into a field at the end of the runway and doing a ground loop,' he says.

In a lather of sweat, Nevin emerged and surveyed his very expensive, very damaged aeroplane. 'What the hell are we going to do?' he asked the Wing Commander, who seemed curiously unruffled by the whole business. 'Don't worry about it,' he said calmly. 'I'll get the erks to fix it up.'

'And he did,' says Nevin. 'I never heard another word about it.'

Obviously impressed with the young Australian's zest for adventure, the Wing Commander oiled the wheels and saw Nevin transferred to the 2 TAF communication squadron operating near Brussels. 'I flew everything there: Austers, Magistars, Ansons. You name it, I flew it.'

Flying the small, lightly constructed Taylorcraft Auster was as radically different an experience from the B-25 as a pilot could get, but Nevin enjoyed his new job as a dispatch courier and 'odd-job' man, ferrying around orders and personnel from his aerodrome at Evere, codenamed B.56. Having previously carried several tons of bombs, Nevin's only armament now was, he says, 'a .45 and a flare pistol'.

B.56 was situated right near the present head office of NATO, which in 1944 was just one of hundreds of Allied aerodromes – some requisitioned, others newly constructed – beginning to dot the French and Belgian landscape as the Germans were pushed eastwards. Ironically, it was while flying the relatively tame Auster that Nevin came closest to killing himself.

He continued his habit of flying low, sometimes at a mere forty feet. This ruled out fighter attack from below, but gave itchy gunners – even 'friendly' ones – little time to identify you.

It all happened very quickly. On a trip one morning from Eind-hoven to B.56, Nevin remembers flying alongside some trees next to a field, when suddenly his engine cut out. Later he found out that the fuel line had been severed, most likely by a bullet – exactly whose was never discovered, but he suspects it was not German. He did his best to quickly wash off some speed on the way down, but his wheels hit hard. Rather than tangle with a fence which he thought would flip him over, he chose to hit the trees at sixty knots.

When he woke up on a table in a farmhouse, someone was cleaning blood off his face. 'A doctor came along and told me I'd broken my nose and teeth but not my back or neck,' he says. His knees, wrists and skull were heavily bruised, and the aircraft was a wreck. Nevin's clearing mind returned to the leather dispatch pouch which still had to be delivered. 'They told me some Ger-mans were still wandering about the place, cut off from their unit and making a nuisance of themselves,' he says.

After explaining the urgency of his situation, some aviation petrol was siphoned from the Auster, mixed with some kerosene and poured into an old truck that was started up for the first time in ages. Later that night, looking like something out of the Old West, Nevin was put on the truck with some hay bales, and a posse of locals clutching shotguns provided a homemade escort to the front gate of the base. It was midnight by the time he arrived, and if he thought it had been bizarre up till now . . .

Sore, and slightly dazed, he wandered into what appeared to be a party, with everyone, as he says, 'as full as a boot'. He asked what was the occasion, and someone blithely replied, 'Old Filby got the chop today.' Faces saw him, and the party stopped. Nevin Filby had walked into his very own wake.

'Someone offered me a drink. I said, "No thanks, I'm going to bed.'" He was given an aspirin, spent the next day in bed and was flying again the one after that.

One wake is enough for anyone's lifetime, and Nevin was determined not to be brought down again. In his unarmed Auster, avoiding a fight was the only sensible option. Just once did a Messerschmitt decide to pick on him, and Nevin displayed a highly original instinct for survival. Slowing down to 100 knots, he spotted a church steeple and circled it as tightly as he could fly, frustrating the German pilot's aim. 'He had a shot, then he went up and had another shot, and then he nicked off,' he says. There were more shots to come.

On a very chilly New Year's morning, 1945, Nevin drove out to check his Auster before a quick flight to Ghent. It was quiet, with some on the base still nursing sore heads from the celebrations the night before. It had been a big one, as everyone knew this would be their last wartime New Year's Eve. This is just what the Germans had counted on.

'Bodenplatte' (Base Plate) was the Luftwaffe's last throw of the dice: a massive surprise attack to regain the momentum of the Battle of the Bulge, now faltering in the Ardennes. Over a thousand fighters and fighter-bombers, many flown by barely trained pilots, were, that morning, thrown into the attack. Their targets: the Allied forward airfields of Holland and France.

Nevin had been up early. After an ugly episode in Canada when he had endangered himself and his crew when throwing up in the cockpit on take-off while hungover, he had vowed never, ever to drink the night before flying – including New Year's Eve.

After giving the aircraft the once-over, he went into the shed next to the main hangar to complete the pre-flight paperwork. 'I was in there and heard a very loud, very close burst of automatic fire,' he says. Rushing out, he was confronted with the sight of several Messerschmitt 109s tearing across the airfield at low level, lines of machine-gun bullets hitting the ground everywhere. He jumped into an already occupied slit-trench, his only armament being a Webley revolver. 'Bullets were ricocheting all over the bloody place,' he says. 'I've still got chip fractures on my knees from them knocking together.'

Rather bravely, Nevin popped his head up and witnessed one of the most remarkable displays of flying he'd ever seen, and of which he still today speaks with awe. Just behind the hangar, a 109 was making a very steep turn, its port wing almost touching the ground.

'We could see him,' Nevin tells me. 'He passed us and gave us a look. If he'd had time, he would have waved.' The German flattened out and lined up on a row of conveniently parked Spitfires, tearing through them with his guns. Still amazed, Nevin watched as he then fired into the door of an open hangar, 'fishtailing' his aircraft with the rudder to spray his fire. 'When you can do that and not kill yourself, you're a bloody good flyer,' he says. 'If I'd taken off five minutes earlier I would have been shot down by him.'

'Him', it later transpired, was one of the Luftwaffe's great aces, Oberleutnant Adolf 'Addi' Glunz who finished the war with seventy-one kills, the last of which he achieved that very morning. Nevin reckons that, but for a few minutes, he would have been number seventy-two.

It all lasted about a quarter of an hour. As impressive as it looked from the ground, 'Bodenplatte' was a pyrrhic victory for the Germans. Several hundred Allied aircraft had indeed been destroyed, but they were easily replaced, while the Luftwaffe endured their largest single-day loss of the war: over 250 pilots, many to their own anti-aircraft guns who had known nothing of the operation, such had been the level of secrecy.

After things had quietened down, Nevin spotted a single undamaged Auster and, with a corporal, went up for a look. 'Smoke everywhere,' he says. 'Every airfield for thirty miles around had burning aircraft on it.'

VE Day found Nevin in the middle of the ocean on his way home. It was a strangely sombre affair with just one small bottle of scotch to share around. He had completed at least fifty-two official operations, and a few more unofficial ones besides. His individualism and lack of fear in expressing an opinion, still undiminished today, probably held him back in terms of promotion, not to mention a Distinguished Flying Cross (DFC), which a Group Captain once told him he thoroughly deserved.

However, not fitting in with the ways of the air force was something that, I suspect, bothered Nevin very little, even when it came to going on leave. 'I couldn't get out those gates fast enough,' he says. But instead of hitting the bars and fleshpots of London, Nevin headed down to the same little farm in England's southwest, found a couple of cartridges to shoot grouse, ate homemade cheese and went for walks through the green fields. Paradise.

Nevin is sharp, and likes to talk. As we wind up after interviews that extend over a couple of days, Nevin hands me some more of his handwritten thoughts and recollections, many of which I have quoted here. Writing, he tells me, is cathartic for him, even more so as he gets older. With some amazement he confides in me, 'About month ago, I had a very vivid dream about one of the ops I had from go to whoa. Sixty-four years after the event!'

Never though, he says, has he actually spoken to anyone about the war in such detail and, perhaps, with such honesty. He apologises for his bluntness in critiquing my own work earlier, but I assure him I'm truly grateful, and that it is his candour I've come to hear. Even now, it's rare for me to meet a former flier so willing to talk about the fear that he and others underwent, a fear that I, with half a lifetime of obsessive imaginings, cannot even begin to comprehend. Then he pays me perhaps his greatest compliment.

'I think it's admirable what you're doing. Most of us fellas are at the age now when we're going to die fairly soon. After that, the real stories are gone forever. You were there to fight a war. You were there to kill as many people as you could. You were there to do as much damage as you could. You were there to do all the things that horrify you as you look back.'

ARTHUR CUNDALL
Navigator, RNAS

There were many ways airmen coped with the stresses of operational flying. The most common was alcohol, with every penny of their by-no-means meagre air-force pay frenziedly spent in pubs and clubs both near the base and in the larger cities on leave. Some sought gentler outlets, and found secret boltholes where they could soothe their nerves for a week or so in the tranquillity of the English countryside. Others were simply resigned to the statistics and considered themselves already dead. A few – amazingly few, really – reached their own private breaking point, declaring their refusal to fly and bringing the stigma of disgrace, humiliation and court martial crashing down upon their heads. Thousands more have, for decades, paid their own price in haunted night-time hours and terrifying visions, endlessly relived.

But for the vast majority, it was simply the fear – eclipsing that of death itself – of being seen to be letting down your friends that kept them going, bonding them with a strength seldom replicated in peacetime. That, to me, is one of the saddest aspects of war.

One of the things that helped Arthur Cundall survive a near-fatal crash and thirty-six operations against the Japanese was an unwavering faith in a higher power. Although now retired, Arthur still has something of the Baptist minister about him, a gentle aloofness, a slight wonderment at what he achieved and how he made it through a three-and-a-quarter years' service career culminating in flying off the decks of aircraft carriers in the Fleet Air Arm.

On a cold day, Arthur invites me into his home – a little pool of England in a retirement estate on the outskirts of Melbourne. Despite the tall eucalypts, it reminds me of the Cotswolds, particularly on a chilly day such as this. Rows of azaleas line the front gardens, and a song thrush fossicks through the last of the fallen leaves.

Arthur is a unique find for me. Although he flew in aeroplanes, it was not the air force he joined at all, but the navy. It was, after all, something of a family tradition. Arthur's father served in destroyers in World War I and was called up from the reserve at the beginning of the Second. In the Norwegian campaign in 1940, he happened to be on deck when a German torpedo struck the side of his destroyer, and he watched as the front half of his ship separated from the rear. He survived, but it's an incident that might explain his son's preference for aircraft.

Arthur's childhood sounds like a ghastly one. Some years before the sinking, his father had absconded with the funds from a ship's library, run off with another woman and left his family destitute. TB carried off his mother soon after and Arthur was left to be brought up by an archetypical wicked stepmother. As soon as he could get out of home he did so, at seventeen finding a protected job in the meteorological office of a RAF bomber station.

It was the stories of Japanese atrocities in the Far East that pricked his conscience and made him put his hand up for active service. This, Arthur decided, was the war he wanted to be a part of, and he wanted to fly. But the air force would be ages finding its way out there to wreak vengeance on the Japanese. Far better to travel with a mobile airfield, and so it was for the Royal Naval Air Service he volunteered, better known as the Fleet Air Arm.

Arthur had high hopes of being a pilot and faced his big test after just five-and-a-half hours of training. 'I messed it up,' he says. The Tiger Moth had a drift to the right on take-off that needed to be compensated for with a little left rudder. 'I was pressing down on the left alright, but forgot to take my foot off the right.' With that gentle, terribly English self-effacement that suddenly reminds me of John Le Mesurier, Arthur describes himself taking off in a 'rather erratic line'. It was politely suggested he might instead like to try his hand at becoming a navigator. The good news was that he would get to do so in exotic, faraway Trinidad.

For a young man from Yorkshire, the contrast could hardly have been greater. Certainly, the weather was a far cry from a grey and miserable wartime Britain, but in fact Arthur nearly didn't make it through alive. Over the sea one morning in a Supermarine Walrus – a superannuated biplane given such apt nicknames as 'Shagbat' or 'Steam Pigeon' by its wary crews – he gave up trying to contact base with his archaic radio set, reeled in the trailing aerial and strapped himself into the co-pilot's seat to enjoy the rest of the flight. Just then he remembered the bar of chocolate he had stashed in a drawer in his little navigator's desk and went aft to retrieve it. Returning to the cockpit, the sight that greeted him was a ghastly one: the pilot distracted and the sea rushing up alarmingly in the windshield.

He could barely blurt an ineffectual 'Look out!' before the nose hit the water and his unstrapped body was hurled straight through the cabin roof. After this he remembers little except the gurgle of the sea around him, a gentle sense of oblivion, and an overriding desire to simply 'let go'. Roused to semi-consciousness by intrusive voices that demanded to know if he was alright,

Arthur muttered an 'I think so,' but really just wanted to be left alone. 'Well you'd better come up here then,' he heard them say urgently. 'There are sharks around!'

That seemed to do the trick and up he clambered onto one of the capsized aeroplane's floats, forcing it to tilt and releasing the trapped air within the fuselage with a noisy 'glug'. The whole thing then immediately sank beneath them, leaving three crewmen bobbing in the water forty kilometres off Port of Spain.

The sharks stayed away long enough for them to be picked up, but Arthur had a large hole in his leg above the knee and burns to his abdomen after being exposed to the petrol and battery acid in the water. He had an agonising recovery and for years suffered nightmares in which the sea rose up to swallow him.

From the jalopy of the Walrus, Arthur graduated to a true thoroughbred – the magnificent Fairey Firefly. The Royal Navy looked long and hard to find a replacement for the slow and antiquated Swordfish biplanes, before choosing one that was even worse – the truly terrible Albacore. The less said about this disaster the better, but sadly it was just one in a long line of failures. There was, for example, the turret-armed and entirely useless Blackburn Roc, the slow and clunky Skua (a fighter-bomber in name only) and possibly the ugliest aeroplane ever built by anyone anywhere – the Fairey Barracuda. This high-winged monoplane monster was designed to carry torpedoes, but no one thought of giving it an engine that was up to the task. The only times it seemed to manage it was when posing for propaganda shots for the press, and in some of these the pilot can be seen looking distinctly nervous. Arthur trained on Barracudas and, like everyone who had anything to do with them, hated them. There was even a song about it sung, Arthur tells me, to the tune of 'As Time Goes By':

The Barracuda Two will be the death of you,
On that you can rely
No matter what their Lordships say
It still can't fly.

The navy even tried a maritime version of the Spitfire, the Seafire, but its flying characteristics and narrow undercarriage made it extremely difficult to land on the pitching flight deck, and its accident rate was enormous.

Just when all hope seemed lost, the Fairey Aviation Company, which had so far produced a string of aviation lemons, came through with a masterpiece in the Firefly. Although a piston-engine aircraft, the Firefly always looked ahead of its time, a fact borne out by its continued employment with the Royal Australian Navy until the mid-1960s. It was fast, powerful and armed to the teeth with four 20-millimetre cannons, and gutsy enough to carry both bombs and rockets. Their two-man crews adored them.

Arthur joined No. 1770 Squadron, Royal Naval Air Service. Its home: the 32 000-ton *Implacable*-class aircraft carrier HMS *Indefatigable*. In November 1944, he was granted his longstanding wish and steamed out of Portsmouth Harbour heading to the Far East.

Landing and taking off from the deck of an aircraft carrier seems a near-impossible task at the best of times, but in rough seas with a rolling deck, it seems positively superhuman. With gentle patience in keeping with his more recent profession, Arthur explains to me the technique his pilot used: brakes on, full throttle then release, taking off with a 'whoosh', and hurtling at full speed towards the end of the very short-looking flight deck. Then, suddenly, you're off the edge and over the sea, with the nose making a terrifying 'dip' before picking up enough speed to keep going. ('I used to look *up* at the flight deck,' he says). The pilot then makes a sudden 'jink' to the right, just in case the aircraft decides it wants to hit the water. This at least would spare you from being run over by 32 000 tons of ship, though not necessarily from drowning. 'All quite fascinating really,' muses Arthur. It's not quite the word I would have used. I ask him if he said a little prayer every time he took off. He just laughs at that one.

0615 hours on the morning of 24 January 1945. *Indefatigable*, along with three other carriers of the British Pacific Fleet, turned into the wind to launch its aircraft. Its target was the largest enemy-held oil refinery in the South-West Pacific – Palembang in eastern Sumatra. At the briefing, Arthur was told it would be the most heavily defended target outside the Japanese homeland, protected by veteran pilots in four fighter squadrons, and over 400 heavy anti-aircraft guns. It was to be his first real combat operation.

The British Pacific Fleet was, and remains still, the most powerful armada the Royal Navy has ever put to sea – a massive force of seventeen aircraft carriers, four battleships, ten cruisers, forty destroyers and dozens of smaller vessels, all determined to return the white ensign to the Far East, avenging the humiliations of Burma and Singapore three years earlier. For Arthur, it was quite a debut. As well as the Fireflys and Seafires, American-built Corsairs, Hellcats and Avengers made up a force of over a hundred aircraft. The flight plan took them on a 240-kilometre overland journey to the target, through a mountain pass and low over the jungle. Then a climb to their operational height of 8000 feet and a dive to attack at 2000.

'The Corsairs had come in earlier to shoot up the fighters on the ground but we were the first ones in to attack the actual target,' says Arthur, remembering the morning vividly. They'd been told to expect the fighters and anti-aircraft defences, but as Arthur's pilot, Dave Hebditch, heard the attack signal 'Lights Out!' over the radio, an entirely unforeseen obstacle came rushing up to meet them. Barrage balloons, hanging in the air on long steel cables. 'I'd been in London during the Blitz and I knew they could shear the wing off an aircraft like a knife,' he says. The cables were also nearly invisible and Hebditch, from the West Country and, says Arthur, a fine pilot, had to thread his way through them at over 300 miles an hour.

'Our target was the cracking point right in the centre where the oil is converted into petrol,' says Arthur. 'I remember all the pipes and tubes and cylinders and all sorts of things.' Then the sky erupted around them as the Japanese put up a carpet barrage of flak. 'That was hairy,' he says. They came in and poured their four cannons into the maze of metal at the centre of the refinery and up it went, he says, 'in great sheets of flame'.

After two such runs and an attack on a radio station, their job was then to protect the bombers. 'There were aircraft of both nationalities going down in flames or out of control all around us,' he says. At this point, he was soothed by a verse he recalled from the psalms: '*Be still and know that I am God.*' 'Just to know that, whatever happened, God was in control was enough,' says Arthur calmly in his living room today. I wonder if it was words quite so divine that came to him as an unknown twin-engine fighter turned towards them on their starboard beam. 'Beaufighter,' thought Arthur in a flash, before realising the nearest one of those was in Burma over a thousand miles away. 'Break left!' he yelled to Dave at the controls. 'We tried to get onto his tail but lost him in the melee of weaving aircraft,' he says.

Ammunition spent, Arthur and Dave escorted some of the returning bombers back to the carriers. Seven British fighters had been lost at Pelambang that day, as well as two bombers, and a number of damaged aircraft were forced to ditch. However, the biggest Japanese oil refinery in the South-West Pacific had been reduced to 30 per cent of its capacity.

Two months later in March 1945, *Indefatigable* formed part of the massive endgame on Japan, the assault on the homeland island of Okinawa. Its job, to cover the southern flank of the invasion. Standing on deck, Arthur was awestruck by the scale of the armada: 'The most amazing spectacle I have ever seen,' he says. His job for the next few weeks was to continually attack Japanese bases on the Sakishima Gunto, three small islands southwest of Okinawa. The daily routine varied little: shoot down Japanese aircraft; bomb their runways; attack anything that floated and which might be bringing in reinforcements, including junks. The junks were so flimsy that Arthur remembers seeing his armour-piercing rockets pass through their wooden sides without exploding, leaving a long visible wake under the water.

The Japanese defences, however, were not so flimsy, and losses mounted steadily. Arthur tells me that No. 1770 Squadron lost roughly 20 per cent of its strength over the brief campaign. Low-level attacks could be particularly deadly and one squadron leader gave the strict instruction: 'Never, ever, attempt a third strafing run.' 'You could get away with two,' says Arthur, 'but by the third the Japanese gunners would find their aim, and it was nearly always fatal.'

One afternoon after strafing anti-aircraft emplacements, Arthur's aircraft was hit by a shell fragment. 'We felt the bang and our engine became irregular,' he says. 'Our main concern then was to get clear of the enemy coast as quickly as possible.' Everyone knew the Japanese did not take prisoners and reserved a particular loathing for the Fleet Air Arm, none of whose captured airmen survived the war. 'They just didn't like us at all,' he says, 'and we knew it.'

Limping back towards the fleet, the Firefly's engine began to shudder, and the temperature gauge went into the red. Dave and Arthur discussed the prospect of it holding out long enough for their ship to turn into the wind and allow them to land, but decided it was a remote one. 'We're not going to make it,' said Dave, and Arthur suggested they ditch. 'Right,' he replied. 'Let's do it.'

The drill was to fly into the wind at just above stalling speed, catch the tail on a wave, wash off some speed, then hit the water and hopefully not sink before getting out. With the cockpit hoods open, radio leads and parachutes disconnected, Dave Hebditch executed a textbook emergency water landing. Arthur felt the whack of the tail, then a big solid bump as they flopped onto the sea.

'It all went perfectly,' says Arthur. 'I even had time to get out onto the wing, inflate my dinghy and step into it without getting my feet wet.' Dave, however, banged his head on the compass and must have been a little dazed. 'We had always trained for this in water, so he instinctively reverted to the drill, jumping straight in, inflating his life raft, then climbing into it, all soaking wet!'

Bobbing in the water in their little yellow inflatable, the two men watched as the 40000-ton battleship *Howe* steamed imperiously past without so much as noticing them, then decided it might be an opportune moment to set off a distress flare. In due course they were picked up by the Australian destroyer *Quiberon*, where the Medical Officer was waiting on deck to greet them. 'Are you alright?' he enquired eagerly. When they replied in the affirmative he seemed almost disappointed. 'Damn. I've had nothing more serious than piles since I've been on this fucking ship!' This, we agree, is the moment Arthur's love affair with Australia began.

Both men were back on board *Indefatigable* the next day and flying again that very afternoon. 'They were pretty tough,' says Arthur. 'They didn't give you a chance to get any "twitch".' There was, however, in typical British bureaucratic style, the inevitable paperwork to be completed, in particular the 'A-25 Loss and/ or Damage of Aircraft' form which awaited Arthur and Dave on their arrival. There's even a song about it, and in a particularly fine voice, refined no doubt by years of Sunday choirs, Arthur treats me to the following to the tune of an old Irish folk ballad:

They say in the 'Raff' that the landing's okay
If a pilot can get up and still walk away.
But in the Fleet Air Arm the outlook is grim
If you prang in the drink and the pilot can't swim.
Cracking show! I'm alive!
But I've still got to render my A-25.

He assures me there are far bawdier versions.

Not nearly so jolly were the Kamikaze attacks, which erupted around Arthur as the campaign began. It's surprising just how extensive the Kamikazes were, and at Okinawa they reached their zenith. Figures vary a little depending on sources, but it is estimated that in a ten-month period beginning late-1944, the Japanese sacrificed nearly four thousand young pilots – nearly half of those at Okinawa. Flying everything from dilapidated trainers to specially designed flying bombs – impossible to land and with fuel only for a one-way trip – most of the young Shinto warriors had received barely enough training to fly in a straight line before being given a final cup of rice wine and sent off on their flight to oblivion. Nonetheless, they managed to sink around eighty Allied ships causing over six thousand casualties.

High on the deck, Arthur witnessed them hitting everything

around him. 'They hit all the carriers and all the battleships,' he says. 'It was quite terrifying.' When they came for his own ship, however (the *Indefatigable* was the first British vessel to suffer a Kamikaze attack), he was safely in his cabin under the quarter-deck. Arthur remembers it well – April Fool's Day, 1945. 'I heard what seemed to be just a bump,' he says. Emerging up top, he saw a large hole in the steel bulkhead at the base of the control tower and a scar in the flight deck. A Kamikaze had crashed into the aircrew ready room, killing seventeen men, including a friend, a young Salvation Army steward. 'I had the job of writing to his wife and telling her what happened,' he says. 'She wanted to know if she could ever visit his grave but there was absolutely nothing left of him, not even his identity disc. He was a non-combatant. It would have been fair if it had happened to me but not to him.' The unknown Japanese pilot died for little – five hours later, *Indefatigable* was operational again.

One afternoon, when not on flying duties and manning one of the many light anti-aircraft guns that studded the ship, Arthur witnessed one of those awful little tragedies of war that simply vanish amid the wider calamity. At the height of the Kamikazes, *Indefatigable* reported one of its Seafire pilots shot down while pursuing an enemy suicide bomber. 'It was nothing of the kind,' says Arthur adamantly. 'I was there and I saw it with my own eyes.' The pilot, who Arthur knew, was in the circuit to land when, from the port forward side of the carrier *Formidable* sailing a mile to stern, 'a stream of tracer opened up', hitting the Seafire and sending it spinning out of control straight into the water. 'There was an alert on,' he tells me, 'but there were no Japs about at the time.' In impotent distress, Arthur watched the aircraft and pilot disappear beneath the water. 'I was so angry I wanted to spray *Formidable* with bullets. Some trigger-happy gunner on that ship who hadn't boned up on his aircraft recognition shot that aircraft down,' he says with an enduring bitterness. 'I didn't report it to anyone. There would have been no point. "Friendly fire", we call it now. It was a very unpleasant moment.'

'Come and have a look at this,' he says to me, brightening deliberately and drawing me over to a place on the wall where a large frame hangs, a watercolour of four Fireflys over the ocean with a carrier beneath them. I'm not usually much of a fan of this kind of aviation art, but this is certainly one of the better ones I've seen and a source of obvious pride for Arthur. 'It was painted by one of our observers for the fiftieth anniversary of the formation of the squadron,' he says, pointing to one of the aircraft bearing a '277' on the fuselage. 'This was my very aircraft,' he says. It's a handsome work, and so is the squadron emblem emblazoned close by. '"To See is to Destroy",' quotes Arthur. 'Very good for a minister of religion!'

Then he brings out a small parcel of souvenirs, reverentially handling the contents. He passes me over something folded in a clear plastic sleeve. It's a large yellowish triangle of material inscribed with some homemade artwork. 'The back panel of my Mae West,' he says. 'The one that saved me when I had the crash in the Walrus. It's never been washed.' I unfold it gingerly and try to picture it on Arthur that day in the sea off faraway Trinidad, supporting his unconscious head and saving his life. At some stage, someone has decorated it with a cartoon and the somewhat incongruous word 'Crusher'. 'I used to play rugby,' he explains a little sheepishly. 'Left wing three-quarter. They reckoned I never went around anyone, so they called me Crusher.' This humble man of God is full of surprises.

Then he hands me two photos: one of a beaming boy in a fresh naval uniform; the other of a face still young but devoid of youthfulness, eyes glazed with a distant hollowness. 'These were taken a couple of years apart,' he says. 'That's me as a young midshipman, and then later, with all the troubles of the world.'

Arthur indeed saw his fair share of violence and destruction but, ironically, it was not fighting in his Firefly that he came closest to a premature meeting with his maker, but deep within the ship, lying on his bunk in his cabin speculating with a friend as to what might be on offer on the evening's dinner menu. Above them, through several walls of steel, a Grumman Avenger torpedo bomber, recently stowed in the hanger, suffered a mechanical malfunction – possibly an overheated round exploding in the breech of one of its .5-inch machine guns, or simply an electrical fault – but somewhere up top they could hear all hell breaking loose as the un-manned Avenger began firing off its entire 450-round belt of armour-piercing and incendiary ammunition.

At nineteen, Arthur's friend and fellow observer Sub-Lieutenant J. A. Ross McIntyre RNVR – 'Mac' to his friends – was, says Arthur, the baby of the squadron, 'a cheerful likeable fellow full of fun and humour'. Barely had he had time to mutter something about 'some clot having his finger stuck in' when the shower of bullets burst through the walls of their cabin. The aircraft, its wings folded, and its armament pointing straight down, was aiming straight at them.

'I dived from the top bunk to the floor,' says Arthur, 'but Mac didn't move and was hit by several bullets in his stomach.' He rolled onto Arthur, covering him with blood. Mortally wounded, Mac pleaded with Arthur not to leave him. The ship's doctor soon arrived, but could do nothing with his bloodied, mangled stomach, and in a few minutes the young man was gone. He was buried at sea within the hour.

A deeply shaken Arthur was taken in hand by a fellow officer and walked around and around the flight deck. He was not allowed to attend the funeral. 'If I hadn't moved it would have been me too. He was nineteen,' says Arthur, shaking his head at the waste of it still. Another awful little tragedy of war.

In his little parcel of memories, he rummages again, pauses, then sighs quietly and hands me a small knob of twisted metal in a plastic envelope – one of the bullets he dug out of the wooden frame of his bunk, which nearly killed him deep within the bowels of the great aircraft carrier *Indefatigable* sixty years ago.

'Yes, one way or another I had a few hairy moments,' he says. But Arthur believes he was spared by the atomic bombs that brought the war to an abrupt close in August 1945. Had it gone on, Arthur doesn't believe he would have survived. 'The atomic bombs were terrible, terrible weapons, but I just look at it statistically. Sooner or later my number would simply have come up. I remember when peace came there was this strange feeling of relief. A feeling of "I'm going to live, I'm going to get an ordinary job – I might even get married!" – the very things you hadn't dared let yourself focus on for years.'

Arthur went on to do all this, and much more.

FRED PHILLIPS
Pilot, RAF

It was a little ironic that when trying to find the home of Fred Phillips, a Pathfinder pilot who flew his Lancaster at night over thousands of blacked-out miles to pinpoint the targets for the rest of the bomber force to attack, I became hopelessly lost. Despite the most detailed of instructions, I was foiled by an old map, a dead mobile and a muddy country lane which, only on the third circuit, began to suspiciously resemble another country lane I had already travelled not once but twice in the last half-hour. No wonder that farmer on the tractor shook his head and seemed to grin as I came around, yet again, in my seriously muddied hire car.

Not that Fred seemed to mind. He lives an hour or so out of Sydney in an exquisite 1880s-built heritage home, amid delightful rolling countryside teeming with the ghosts of early settlers. It was a cold but sunny winter's afternoon, and despite my being well over an hour late, Fred cheerfully unwrapped the sandwiches he had prepared and sat me down next to the heater overlooking an old and sculptured garden. Just as well – I was starving.

The Pathfinders were an elite. Which is precisely why the head of Bomber Command, Arthur Harris, wanted nothing to do with their establishment. But in 1941, a quiet bespectacled civil servant in the War Cabinet Secretariat named D. M. Butt took the time to study hundreds of actual bombing photos taken of targets the morning after raids and compare them with the results claimed by the aircrews. The report he handed the British Government was, well, a bombshell. In it, he claimed that, far from Bomber Command's ebullient confidence in winning the war single-handedly, 90 per cent of its aircraft were in fact missing their target by between five and one hundred miles, and that almost half their bombs were falling in open countryside. Only when the moon was bright could targets be found and attacked, he said, but when dark, barely one aircraft in fifteen bombed within five miles of the intended aiming point. The *Butt Report* was a bucket of iced water in the face of those who were running Britain's war effort, and caused many to never quite trust Bomber Command again.

The problem was navigation. It was simply not possible to pluck people from civilian life, train them up for a few months then expect them to deliver an aircraft to a pinprick on a map in the middle of a blacked-out continent in wartime.

So, in August 1942, amid much protest, Bomber Command's five Groups – similar to an army's Divisions – were each made to surrender a squadron to form the nucleus of the brand-new No. 8 Group, which would henceforth become known as PFF or Path Finder Force. The crews of this special outfit were selected (one could not volunteer) for their skills in navigation and bombing accuracy and were immediately granted an increase in rank and, after a few trips, the permission to wear a unique silver eagle on their tunics, just under the medal ribbons. It was the very least they would deserve. Instead of the standard thirty operations, the 'Pathfinders' would have to complete the almost impossible feat of fifty. So much for Harris's attempts to avoid the creation of an elite.

Instead of bombs, the Pathfinders were required to drop coloured flares, or Target Indicators (TIs), and drop them with incredible accuracy. Pathfinder navigators bore the responsibility not just for their own crew finding the target, but the entire bombing force as well. In preparation for a raid, they would pore over the myriad photographic details of the target – the aiming point, the approaches – and took into account predicted wind directions and other meteorological concerns that would be brought to bear on the course they would ultimately tell their pilot to fly.

To command the Pathfinders, Harris selected one Donald Clifford Tyndall Bennett, a Queenslander, and one of those true freaks of command that war sometimes throws up. His career reads like an adventure book. A grazier's son, Bennett had joined the RAAF as a twenty-year-old cadet in 1930 and transferred to the RAF the following year. His prodigious skill as a navigator was soon noticed and in almost no time at all he was instructing at a flying boat base. In 1934, he became only the seventh person ever to pass the extremely rare First Class Navigator's licence and even began lecturing on the subject. He then seemed to tire of the air force, joined Imperial Airways and quickly became a sensation as a civil pilot, entering the Centenary Air Race from England to Melbourne, becoming a test pilot and breaking the record for an Atlantic crossing from east to west.

When war broke out, he rejoined and was quickly given a squadron of Halifaxes to command. In 1941, attacking the German battleship *Tirpitz* in a Norwegian fjord at 200 feet, he was shot down with a wing ablaze, baled out and, with his wireless operator, trekked across the Alps for three days to Sweden. A month later, with a new DSO ribbon sewed to his tunic, he was back in England again, flying. Not that he thought his exploits were anything out of the ordinary. His attitude was that if a downed pilot hadn't escaped and been flying again inside a month, he wasn't really trying.

His reputation within the RAF, particularly as a navigator, soared. It was said that he wrote the book on the subject in three parts: one for beginners, another for advanced students, and the last for himself – which he alone could understand. At thirty-two, he was, indeed still is, the youngest person in the British or Commonwealth air forces ever to have held the rank of Wing Commander. But the swashbuckling hero image was not a perfect fit. The highly intelligent Bennett was cold and aloof, and suffered fools not at all, particularly those of higher rank who tended to sneer at 'colonials' of any description, talented or otherwise. After the war, it was an attitude that seemed to cost him, when he became the only Group Commander to miss out on a knighthood. He entered politics briefly but quickly lost his seat and somewhat bitterly turned his back on it forever.

Harris, it is said, appointed Bennett with an eye to controlling him, only to discover that malleability was not one of his traits. Bennett thought nothing of tormenting his superiors, badgering constantly for new and better aircraft and striving continually for ways to avoid casualties among his airmen, who adored him. He would in time transform his handful of crews and mismatched, obsolete aircraft into a highly efficient, highly deadly force. Despite the unlikelihood of surviving a tour on Pathfinders, the greatest fear amongst its members remained being sacked from it and posted back to an ordinary unit.

But Fred Phillips didn't know any of this when he volunteered for the air force in Melbourne, trained in Canada and Britain, and eventually found his way to a Heavy Conversion Unit at Strad-ishall in Suffolk, where he learned to fly Stirlings. Coming in to land after a night cross-country exercise, the war found him.

Fred was flying astern of his friend Ken Gilkes, both of them lining up with the runway a mile-and-a-half apart. 'Just then my mid-upper gunner called out, "There's a 190 just gone over the top of us!"' The Germans were known to make regular hit-and-run visits to RAF airfields, both training and operational, slipping in behind a returning bomber undetected, and shooting it down while coming in to land before vanishing into the night. 'Actually,' says Fred, 'he was wrong. I think it was a Ju-88.' For some reason Fred will never know, the German pilot selected Ken in the aircraft ahead of him, and not himself. 'He overshot me and then straight-away began firing. I saw all the tracer going into Ken's plane.' Fred watched Ken's Stirling crash, then break in half. Ken was thrown out of the cockpit into a pool of burning petrol, unconscious. 'We had been together right through training. Even come over on the same ship. He was terribly, terribly burned.'

Fred and his crew paid a visit to Ken in hospital a couple of days later. 'He was completely bandaged up in a saline bath with sprays going all over him,' he says. 'The only thing he could see was his fingers. They didn't give him a mirror. Two of my crew fainted when they saw him.'

Ken spent the rest of the war in hospital, came home and married the girl who had stood by him. He is still alive and active today and he and Fred are still friends. But thinking back to that dreadful night of the crash, Fred knows it could very easily have been him. 'We were pretty arsey,' he says. I can but agree.

Unlike Ken, Fred continued his piloting career and was posted to RAF Mildenhall where he commenced operations on the now-obsolete Stirlings. 'I was on the last bombing operation where they used them,' he says. 'We lost an engine and hit a warm front. I could barely keep her from stalling with the weight of the ice building up on the wings.' Not many mourned the Stirling's passing from operational bombing – losses were appalling. The Stirling's abysmal ceiling meant that when attacking short-range targets such as in the Ruhr, it was impossible to climb to any significant altitude. 'We'd be down about 9000 feet and they'd pump the 20- and 40-millimetre cannons up at you. It looked like someone holding a hose. Sometimes we'd get the incendiaries falling through the wings being dropped from the Lancs and Halifaxes at 20 000 feet above.'

Fred has prepared quite a bit of documentation for me to look at, including a small book he has written about his life which he intends to rewrite and expand upon. He speaks extremely softly but precisely, and I can sometimes find it hard to hear him above the whirring of the heater which, thankfully, is keeping me warm. Fred sits away from it and doesn't seem to mind. He insists I finish up the sandwiches, which I do greedily, while he prepares tea. The way he speaks, the way he conducts himself tells me that it is no surprise that he was once part of an elite. There's still something of it about him today.

Fred completed nine trips in Stirlings, four in Lancasters, every one a drama. 'Some kind of disaster went on every time,' he says. 'We'd have holes in the wing tanks, we'd be running out of juice, we were shot at . . .' But he knew he had a good crew, as well as an exceptionally good navigator. 'I think they had us fingered from early on,' he says.

Talent was a precious commodity in Bomber Command and gifted navigators stood out. After only a couple of trips, Fred's navigator, Dave Goodwin, was being requested to report back the wind variations he was finding en route to the target, which were then forwarded to the other aircraft in the main force. So it came as little surprise when Fred and his crew were asked to join the Path Finder Force. I had imagined the request to be something dramatic – a secret meeting, a sealed envelope or a summons to Bennett himself – but in fact it was all rather unexciting. Just a quiet conversation and a request. 'I had to put it to the crew that it meant doing fifty trips with Pathfinders, not including the ones we'd already completed. All of us agreed we'd do it.'

The Pathfinders had their own airfield at the appropriately named venue of Warboys in Cambridgeshire. Here, for a month, Fred and his crew went back to school. They were drilled in extra navigation courses, and bomb aimers in particular were taught to hone their skills. They were also introduced to the concept of dropping not bombs but the coloured flares that would mark the target for other aircraft. They were to be the first aircraft to arrive on target, and the last to leave. And they would have to do it night after night, fifty times. Their chances of surviving were negligible.

Fred was posted not far away from Warboys to Oakington, flying Lancasters with No. 7 Squadron, one of the original four Pathfinder squadrons. As soon as he arrived on station, Fred knew just what he was in for. 'There was a board with all the names of the crews written in chalk. They were rubbing out the buggers that hadn't come back the previous night.'

The details of some of the many individual trips Fred carried out are a little sketchy, but he conveys to me the general sense of the work of the Pathfinder, not to mention the dangers.

At briefing, Fred's bomb aimer was told the colour of the Target Indicators for that night, as it changed daily. From his bomb selector panel beside him he could choose which flares to drop, and keep dropping, as the target would need to remain visible for the duration of the raid. As well as the flares, they would also carry a load of bombs which they would drop after the target was marked.

'The one place where no one wanted to be was in the target area,' says Fred. Every bomber pilot would shudder for that two minutes when he would have to hold the aircraft steady for the bomb aimer to line up the target below with a little illuminated cross on the bombsight, press the release button, then wait an interminable thirty seconds for the photo flash which would take the verifying aiming point photo. 'Then they'd tear off as quickly as they could to get away.' No such luxury could be afforded the Pathfinders. The target flares would burn out, be destroyed, or become obscured by smoke, and Fred would need to go in again to drop another. 'Sometimes we'd make three separate runs at the target,' he says.

Remaining in the target area for so long – sometimes up to twenty minutes – magnified the dangers tenfold. There were searchlights – 'We had more than our fair share of being "coned"' – night fighters and, flying against the flow of the main stream, the ever-present risk of collision.

Even natural elements conspired against their chances of survival. Fred came to hate the aurora borealis, or northern lights, as it would silhouette his aircraft against the night sky.

In a typical Pathfinder-led raid, the so-called Master Bomber would, like an orchestra conductor, fly in wide circles deciding whether the aiming point had been accurately marked, then, over the radio, direct and correct the often hundreds of aircraft and their bombing patterns as a grim dialogue ensued between them. 'Slipping back from target – correct aiming point is two widths to the west – ignore yellow TIs – bomb on the green – dropping green TIs to reposition aiming point . . .'

'It was a pretty high chop rate among Master Bombers. You can imagine – sticking around the target like that. Quite often we'd appreciate anti-aircraft shells coming up because at least you knew that the night fighters weren't moving in.' Fred's crew took over from their New Zealander Master Bomber, Fraser Baron. In a single night both he and his deputy were shot down over the target by night fighters.

But the longer one survived, the more one learned. Fred was given the job of Deputy Master, and eventually Master Bomber himself, carrying out no fewer than seventeen operations just 'hanging around the target, telling them where to drop the bombs. You could hear the anti-aircraft fire rattling on the sides of the aircraft like hail. After one trip, our Flight Engineer counted 320 holes from the shrapnel. They called us the "lucky crew".'

I ask him whether he thought he'd make it through alive. 'No. Not at all,' he says quite matter-of-factly, as if the very idea was an absurdity. It all came down to luck, he says. 'You could be flying along coming home at night. You'd see a tiny little spark moving along in the distance. Then it would burst into full flame. Somebody had been shot down. It could have been you.'

They coped, says Fred, by playing hard. Alcohol was the universal remedy administered by most aircrew to deal with levels of stress almost impossible to comprehend. How any of them survived a day without cracking up is completely beyond me. It has often been said that it was the strange, disjointed nature of bomber flying that made the job so difficult. In the army, one was able to adjust to the reality of the situation over a period of time. In Bomber Command, it was far more schizophrenic. In the morning, an airman would wake up between clean sheets, shave, have breakfast, watch the rabbits gambolling amongst the hedgerows in the pretty English countryside, all the while knowing that this very night, you would be flying into a hell on earth where there was a high prospect of being shot at and killed.

On nights off, the crews would frequent the many pubs

and dancehalls of the university town of Cambridge and its surrounds, an area they shared with the United States Eighth Army Air Force. 'We were a fairly wild bunch. You needed to be to get through it psychologically,' says Fred. The greater the losses and the more of their friends who simply didn't turn up the next day, the harder the partying. The Americans, though, had a different approach. 'When they'd had a bad day, there wouldn't be one in town. Didn't make any difference to our mob. We'd be there regardless,' he says.

After the beginning of the Normandy campaign, Bomber Command, much to Harris's disgust, was taken off the attacks on German cities and industrial centres and used as a tactical strike force for the army. Fred suddenly found himself operating in daylight, and it was a shock.

'That's when we got to see just how many aeroplanes there were in the sky. It was amazing,' he says. One day, he was taken by a staff driver to be briefed by the 8 Group commander, Air Vice-Marshall Bennett himself. 'First of all I have to swear you to absolute secrecy,' was Bennett's rather sobering opener. 'I want you to get over tonight and observe the shellfire of the Germans – then tomorrow go over again and control the raid. And make sure you really control it,' he added emphatically.

Later that evening, Fred was flying over Normandy, observing the distinctive orange shellfire of the German guns. Twenty-four hours later, he returned, this time directing over a thousand aircraft at a very low 3000 feet to bomb a tiny restricted area of French countryside to prevent the surrounded Germans from escaping through the Falaise Gap. It was this he was detailed to hit. 'It was a very, very precise piece of bombing,' he says. A little less precise, and it could have meant killing his own troops. For his efforts, Fred became one of only nine Australians in World War II to be awarded the French Croix de Guerre, quite the thing to go with his DFC, of which he also became a worthy recipient, along with his entire crew.

Then, with an abrupt, 'I think you've got enough now,' my interview with Fred is concluded. Perhaps I have been prying a little too deep; perhaps there are memories in his head he is happy to have remain dormant; perhaps he is just sick of me. But the tape recorder is switched off and I thank him for his time and his hospitality. He then takes me on an extended tour of his lovely home. We talk about other things for a while, trees and books and birds and antiques, as well as his many happy years as a senior airline pilot for Qantas. He seems to cheer up, as if these happier, life-affirming subjects wash away the gloomy spectre of war and death. He tells me of the finches and fairy wrens that delight him as they dart about in the hedges of his garden and points out an unusual pine tree some distance off. Still fit and very active into his eighties, Fred shows me the old cellar under his house, and like two adventurous boys we clamber down some steps into the dank but exciting subterranean atmosphere.

A little later, refreshed by the cold outside air, I thank Fred and drive away, my head spinning – my first and only encounter with a Pathfinder.

JOCK McAULEY
Pilot, RAAF

I could soon tell that Jock McAuley is a man who prefers to waste neither time nor words. Over the course of our afternoon together in his suburban home, I had the impression that it was not he but myself under the spotlight. Arriving at the appointed time, I was greeted courteously and we sat down to talk in a rather formal front section of the house that I could see was reserved for guests. All very professional. Somewhere, the sounds of some other visitors enjoying a meal could be heard – family, perhaps, or friends – but Jock's focus never wavered from the task I had set him: to cast himself back more than half a century to his time spent flying one of the most famous aeroplanes of all time in the latter stages of the European war.

A few days after his eighteenth birthday, in January 1943, Jock and a mate boarded the train to Melbourne from his home in Horsham in western Victoria. Alighting at Spencer Street Station, they walked up the hill to the RAAF recruiting office in Russell Street. A year to the day later, he walked up a gangplank onto a ship that would take him to fight overseas. In the meantime, he had achieved every young air force recruit's dream job – selection to be a fighter pilot.

Before all this, though, there had been basic training to contend with, and an instructor Jock found less than congenial. He was a bloke he'd known back in Horsham. The idea of being taught to fly by someone he knew was something Jock found a little unsettling, so in the first few weeks when still on ground duties, he did his best to avoid him. 'It didn't work,' says Jock. 'He found *me*.' No concessions were made to familiarity either. 'This bloke did everything he could to stir me up.'

'*Get that bloody stick back!*' was one of his favourite sayings, and Jock can still hear his voice, yelled loud enough to be heard on the ground by the other students when coming in to land in a Tiger Moth. '*A child of two could fly an aircraft, providing they have a bit of commonsense, and I doubt whether you have any!*'

He survived the humiliation, completed the course and progressed to Number 7 Service Flying Training School at Deniliquin for pilot training on Wirraways. 'The Wirraway was a . . . self-respecting aircraft,' says Jock cautiously. I've heard it called far worse. 'One of its worst features,' he says, 'was that if you let the speed get down on landing, it would stall and flip. Just like that!' He illustrates with a dramatic flick of the hand. 'We had a number of pilots killed that way.'

He also continued his run of eccentric instructors. At three a.m. one morning, he climbed into the two-seater Wirraway to commence his scheduled hour of night flying. 'Circuits!' was the perfunctorily grunted order from the back seat. Jock taxied, took off and landed again, thinking he must have done rather well for a change, judging by the silence from the rear. He did another circuit, then another after that, still without a word. At the end of the hour, he climbed out of the cockpit and went to bed. Later that morning, the instructor rushed into his hut looking a little bleary. 'Did I fly with you last night?' he asked anxiously. 'I've got to fill in me logbook and I was as full as a bull!' It seemed he'd been sound asleep the whole time.

Speaking with Jock in his suburban home, there's still something of the fighter pilot sharpness about him. He chooses his words carefully and wastes not a single one. We proceed methodically through his logbook in sequence, and he politely lets me know when, in my rambling, style, I have repeated a question or missed a detail he's already told me. It's meeting men like Jock that brings home to me the fact that despite my childhood fantasies of doing what he did, I would have most likely never made the grade.

Jock, however, did make it. After 168 flying hours and a rigorous final air test, he stood to attention in front of an Air Commodore who happened to share his surname. A brief conversation concerning the semantics of genealogy later, the man with the big ring on his sleeve handed him his wings.

A few days later, departing from Port Melbourne at the height of summer, Jock froze his way across the icy waters below Tasmania – en route to South Africa then God knows where. In Durban, he and a mate were billeted for a few days in a private home, waited on by Zulu houseboys roughly their own age. 'Both of us treated those boys as equals,' he remembers. Such consideration did not go down well with their white hosts. 'Look,' they were told, 'you can hit them over the head, you can kick them, you can do anything you like to them, but please don't be *civil* to them.' It's an incident that left an indelible impression on the young man and Jock has retold the story many times. 'As a nineteen-year-old it was the greatest awakening I could have had,' he says.

After eventually landing in Scotland, Jock headed south by train. Passing through London, they were held up at Clapham Junction by an air raid. He and his mates peered out the carriage windows at the aircraft overhead as the wailing sirens signalled their introduction to the realities of war. At a Brighton hotel they were sorted out. 'What do you want, son?' asked the officer on the category selection board. 'Fighters, sir!' replied Jock with the standard answer, to which he received the standard response: 'Well, you're in luck. We have a nice line of four-engine night fighters: you can have a Lanc, a Halifax or a Stirling. Take your pick!' In the months before D-Day, bomber pilots were in demand. And Jock was lucky not to be summoned into their ranks.

Instead, after some weeks waiting around, he was posted to an Advanced Flying Unit in the Midlands where he trained on single engine Miles Masters, then joined a convoy headed to the Middle East. At Fayid in Egypt, he flew over the Suez Canal's Great Bitter Lake, cutting his teeth on some decrepit P40 Kittyhawks that had seen far better days in the desert, then on to Salerno in Italy to convert to the mighty Mustang.

'It was like going from a Holden to a Rolls Royce,' says Jock. 'With the Kittyhawks, if there were trees at the end of the runway, we'd have to go over them, then put the nose down to get more speed. The Mustang could do a climbing turn off the deck, even with bombs on. It was a delight to fly.' And Jock would fly them with a very special unit indeed: the all-famous, all-Australian 3 Squadron RAAF.

There is a photograph of No. 3 Squadron taken during its stint in the North African desert in 1942. It shows a group of smiling Australian airmen sitting on and under one of their Kittyhawks, wearing an array of clothing that may or may not be a military uniform. Some wear hats, others do not, some are in odd shirts or topless or in little other than a pair of shorts. They sit happily, draped over their aircraft as if in a living room, while behind them the moonscape of the desert stretches endlessly to the horizon. I have seen other images of airmen at play but it's hard to imagine one quite so comfortable and unconstructed. There is a spirit to this photograph that's hard to look at without smiling, a spirit in no way undermined by the knowledge that this happy-go-lucky bunch of young airmen accounted for no fewer than 217 enemy aircraft destroyed, making theirs the highest kill rate of any Royal Australian Air Force squadron in World War II.

The pedigree of No. 3 Squadron exceeds that of the RAAF itself, having been formed at Point Cook in 1916 when still part of the Australian Flying Corps. It distinguished itself on the Western Front flying RE8s till the end of World War I. In 1940 it sailed as a complete unit to the Western Desert to meet the Italians. They jumped around the Mediterranean from Africa to Malta, the Middle East, Sicily and Italy, then zigzagged up the Adriatic coast to Cervia, south of Venice where Jock McAuley joined them for the last few months of the war. By this time, No. 3 Squadron had re-equipped from Kittyhawks to the truly amazing North American P-51 Mustang.

The Mustang epitomises the gutsy, unconquerable all-American fighter aircraft of World War II and it's no coincidence that there are more of them still flying today than any other type from the era. But it's actually the English who were responsible for its conception. It began as a cry for help from the British whose industry by 1940 was already stretched to the limit. The logical step was to look to the limitless capacity of the United States. The British would have been happy to increase their order of P-40s and Airacobras, but in California, the North American Aviation Company, which until then had produced little more than trainer aircraft like the Harvard, had an idea for a new aeroplane the Brits might find more interesting. They were right. Despite it existing only on the drawing board, they took a punt, and just 102 days later, the first prototype, 'NA-73X', rolled out of the Inglewood factory into the Los Angeles sunshine. The sleek, powerful and disarmingly simple-looking new aeroplane would henceforth be known as 'Mustang'.

Initially, however, the Americans themselves weren't much interested in them, and were quite happy to see them all go to the RAF. It was a full year before they got wind of their performance, then started to make a few for themselves. With its Allison engine, the Mustang was a good aeroplane, but not a great one, especially at high altitude, where its performance dropped off considerably. Then one day, an English test pilot had the inspired notion of marrying the airframe to a Rolls Royce Merlin, the same engine that powered the Spitfire, and an aviation superstar was born.

The new Mustang was fast, robust, had an incredible range and was armed to the teeth with six half-inch machine guns in the wings. In the European air war, it accounted for nearly half of all American victories in the air and in ground strafing, and nearly 16 000 were produced. It could escort a bomber from England to Berlin and back and still have fuel enough for a couple of circuits of the airfield, the only impediment to its endurance being pilot exhaustion. It could carry bombs under the wings and was deadly in ground attack, and it was in this role that Jock McAuley would be privileged to fly them.

'Dive-bombing and strafing' is how he economically describes his few months flying Mustangs in combat in the northern Adriatic. It was an uncomplicated procedure. From their base at Cervia in Italy, No. 3 Squadron would wait to be called up by army units to clear a road junction or a river crossing which lay in the line of their advance. A spotter aircraft would sometimes fly with them, directing their fire onto pinpoint targets.

Jock's extensive logbook is open across his knees and in a low monotone he reads a couple of extracts. '*Six aircraft led by*

"Tubby" Shannon bombed first. Flak nil. All bombs fell on target area. Made strafing run. Army waiting to cross river after we finished.' Or the next day, *'Four aircraft led by Ken Richards bombed motor transport parked under the trees near a house. Excellent bombing. Started two big fires. Between us accounted for two flamers, two smokers, four damaged. And a stampede of horses. Congratulatory message from the army.'* Like the horses, the Germans on the ground came to dread the Jagdbombers, or *Jabos*, but they could also hit back, and at low level Jock had to contend with all manner and all calibres of ground fire.

Once near Venice, he was flying number two behind another Mustang flown by a fellow pilot from Perth. All of a sudden, he noticed liquid stream out of his friend's aircraft. 'Don, your glycol's gone!' he radioed urgently to the unsuspecting pilot. 'You're going to have to get down.' Small-arms fire from the ground had scored well, and without coolant, the 12-cylinder Merlin had about two minutes before it seized. His friend made a wheels-up landing on a beach. 'I flew down and watched him emerge from the cockpit, then run like hell!' Assuming he was now a prisoner, Jock after a day or two packed up his downed friend's possessions. 'On the third day, he came in and shouted, "Where the hell's my gear?!"' Jock gives a dark chuckle.

There are reports I have read of strafing pilots becoming strangely mesmerised by the sight of the ground rushing up towards them, and even in an aircraft as manoeuvrable as the Mustang, a second's delay could be fatal. In dual-seat aircraft, the navigator would sometimes have to hit the pilot's arm to remind him to pull up from the dive. Jock, all alone, needed all his wits about him.

Occasionally, he would adopt the very dangerous practice of duelling with a large gun as it was attempting to shoot him down. Like a deadly game of chicken, it was a question of who would blink first. Dive-bombing an 88-millimetre on one trip, it fired a couple of times and Jock watched it grow bigger in the windshield, his finger poised on the bomb release button on his control column. At the last instant, he watched the gun crew break and run for cover, then hit the switch. 'It was amazing how accurate you could become by just aiming the aircraft at what you saw through the windshield,' he says. Accurately placing a bomb at that speed was an art, and Jock had to be careful not to pull out too early, making it 'skid' over the target. It all sounds rather hair-raising, but in the short time Jock was operating, he dropped 16000 pounds of bombs.

Anti-aircraft fire usually came up in a pattern of four, and the pilots would anxiously count the explosions around them. 'If you saw one puff, you knew there were three more. If you saw three, you knew there was one more.'

In the final chaotic weeks of the war, the trapped German armies in Italy sought to escape north through the Alps into Austria. Here, the Allies believed – wrongly as it turned out – the Germans intended to regroup in the so-called National Redoubt, where they could hold out for years. This obsession with a Redoubt – for which the Germans had never seriously planned – is one of the more curious aspects of Allied policy during the war's latter stages, and even led to the large diversion of forces which facilitated the Russian desire to take Berlin.

However, whilst they remained a threat – perceived or otherwise – it fell to Jock and others like him to stop them. Strafing runs would be conducted as low as fifty feet. The techniques were simple but effective. A mobile German column would be located and bridges either side would be knocked out, causing a massive traffic jam and turning two or three hundred vehicles into almost stationary targets. 'That made it pretty easy,' he says. First the Commanding Officer or flight commander would go in, and at intervals of just a few seconds – making sure the aircraft ahead of you was on the way up before you fired – half a dozen Mustangs with their six machine guns would wreak havoc.

Trains, motor vehicles, tanks – anything that moved was shot up. 'You had to be very careful about hitting an ammunition truck. It could blow up in front of you,' says Jock. It was grim work, and he doesn't give too much away about what it must have looked like at low-level. He doesn't have to. I've read enough reports on what he must have seen through the windshield as the deadly, decapitating storm ripped its way in lines through wood, steel and flesh. I press him a little on the detail, but he gently deflects my line of enquiry. I can't really blame him.

We return to his logbook. I can see it's been a while since he's examined it closely. He's on a journey of remembrance all his own. Long pauses develop where Jock is simply absorbed as the memories rush back. From his living room, the lunch guests emerge and say farewell. Doorbells ring and a yapping dog makes a ruckus. Jock barely notices.

There was obviously a tremendous pride in operating in an all-Australian fighter squadron in Europe. No. 3 distinguished itself by painting the stars of the Southern Cross on a blue background on the rudders of its aircraft, an emblem which still adorns its jet fighters today. With their uncamouflaged, all-metal finish, the Mustangs were quite a sight. Their aerodrome was in close proximity to the American 79th Fighter Group flying Thunderbolts. Occasionally, they would hear the Americans talking on their radio frequency, and it was often the cause of some amusement. 'Hey, guys,' they would hear an American pilot say to his formation. 'I've only got twenty gallons left. I'm going home.' At which the Australians, unable to resist some one-upmanship, would break in, 'Yeah, well I'm showing empty and I'm staying!'

The Australians' ways also differed from those of the RAF. 'We had a pilots' mess,' says Jock, 'irrespective of rank.' The class-conscious English still adhered rigidly to the separation of officers and 'other ranks', despite them all performing the same job and often relying on each other for survival. 'The RAF were disgusted,' says Jock, with a distinct note of pride.

At war's end, the squadron found itself still flying, but often in 'showing the flag' patrols over the Balkans, which were already wracked by another regular episode of fratricidal bloodletting. Soon after VE Day, Jock received an unusual request from his Commanding Officer. 'There's a job to go to Klagenfurt. We'd better toss for this one.' Klagenfurt was the location of a Luftwaffe base over the Alps inside Austria, a place Jock had 'visited' several times in the recent past. But with the Cold War already in play, it was the Russians who were now regarded as dangerous, and the map on the ops room wall was marked with red-lined 'no go' areas over their positions. The flight path had to be flown between the just-defeated Germans and the suspicious, trigger-happy Russians. It was a toss Jock would have been quite happy not to have won.

It was only a courier drop to pass on some documents, but as he says, 'It was eerie landing on a German airstrip a couple of days after the war.' He flew in and taxied. Across the tarmac, he could see lines of Luftwaffe aircraft, still in their black cross and swastika livery. He stayed in his aircraft, alone except for the silent gaze of hundreds of uniformed Germans. 'I was scared stiff that one of them was going to do something. They'd seen a Mustang before, but not this close up.' He chuckles and gives me one of those steely, fighter pilot looks. 'Well, that's about all I can give you. Is it enough?' The interview, I realise, is over, and Jock rises. Job done, it is time to go, and I thank him.

PAT KERRINS & NOBBY CLARKE

Pilot, RAAF & Air Gunner, RAF

One wet 25 April many years ago, I stood as a soggy fourteen-year-old at the bottom of the wide expanse of concrete that leads up to Melbourne's Shrine of Remembrance on Anzac Avenue, right where the annual parade has to make an awkward dogleg only to bottleneck as it contemplates the final leg up to the hallowed ground itself. Back then, there were still a handful of World War I blokes on show, looking grateful, if a little bewildered, and long past their marching days, waving weakly from inside an old black Bentley that looked like it was earmarked for a wedding later that afternoon.

As I watched the parade, the sole spectator for yards around, the air force fellows paused in front of me just as the heavens really opened up in sheets of water that made one former officer's original 1940s blue service uniform (it still fitted him) turn suddenly black. He was holding up his old squadron banner and having trouble keeping it aloft. As it began to topple, I instinctively stepped forward, took one of the poles and attempted to right the soggy depiction of a Lancaster, just as the march took off again.

'You might have to stay with me, son,' the man muttered. So, swept up with the inexorable momentum of several thousand ageing veterans eager to get to their reunions, I did just that.

These days every man and his dog seems to march on Anzac Day (sons of servicemen, widows, grandsons and daughters, neighbours, possibly – who knows who they are), but back then it was a strictly 'participants only' affair. I felt so awkward walking alongside the former pilots, navigators and gunners of 467 Squadron – past the row of cypress pines and scattered groups of old ladies enthusiastically applauding in their plastic raincoats – that all I could do was look straight down at the ground, or up at the wavering pole. We reached the end of the march a few minutes later, and my friend was immediately buttonholed by an old colleague and caught up in the crowd. I snuck off without a word. It was the first and, in all likelihood, last time I would ever march on Anzac Day.

Exactly thirty years later, in a rather depressing illustration of how little my youthful dreams of a life spent living in different parts of the globe have been realised, I found myself just a short march from that very same spot, outside the Victoria Hotel in Little Collins Street. On this day every year, it is filled to the brim with the men and their families who once again have travelled from places far and wide to rekindle the indelible friendships forged in the terrible conflagration of their youth.

This was one interview I was particularly looking forward to. I had met men who had trained together, flown in the same squadron, and the same type of aircraft, but never two men of the very same crew. As I walked up the stairs that led from the lobby to the mezzanine to meet Nobby Clarke and Pat Kerrins, that was going to change.

'You're writing a story about us old blokes, are you?' asked Pat. 'Why didn't you get onto us fifty years ago when we could remember something?'

'Sorry about that, Pat,' I replied. 'So when did you join up?'

'26 June 1942,' he rattled off in a flash. Somehow I didn't think his memory would present too much of a problem. I'd got onto Pat via his mate, Max Durham, who I'd spoken to some months earlier. Max had been awarded the DFC for his tour as a Lancaster pilot but never wore it, in deference to the many others who, in his words, deserved it at least as much as he did. And one of the most deserving, he says, was Pat. It was quite a recommendation.

I'm glad we agreed to meet in the Victoria Hotel. It has always been one of my favourite spots in a city where favourite spots abound. As its name suggests, this old hotel has long been favoured by country people coming down to the city, who contribute, I think, to its unpretentious atmosphere. It began its days in the 1880s as a respectable monument to the teetotalling temperance movement and, minor updates aside, its decor has remained unchanged for decades. It's full of brass and terrazzo, big staircases and all sorts of odd little nooks, including a tiny upstairs bar that brings to mind a cruise ship in the 1960s. For years I have been waiting for, dreading, the day they knock it all down, or transform it into another steel and white-marble monument to functional blandness. Although perhaps now, at last, the Victoria has survived just long enough to come back into itself, an inviolable oddity in its own right. I'm ever the optimist.

But back to Pat: 'I did transport driving for a while, then initial training at Somers where we were categorised. I was fortunate enough to be categorised as a pilot . . .'

'And a bloody good one, too!' adds Nobby, leaning forward.

We sit around a low table and order tea as Anzac Day eve evolves around us. 'Stan, ya bastard!' shouts one man to another as they encounter each other in a corridor, followed by the sounds of hands slapping on the backs of woollen jackets, then laughter which fades after a moment, replaced by the serious murmur of plans for the morrow.

Nobby and Pat are laughing too. Nobby speaks with the deep rounded tones of south-west England. 'He won't tell you, but I will,' he says, indicating his friend. 'He passed top of his course in aerobatics and was going to be a fighter pilot.'

'That's right,' says Pat. 'But by the time I got to England I got the message that if I wanted to see some action, I'd better go onto the bombers.'

The two men, from opposite sides of the world, talk in, over and around each other like an old married couple. They first met in the summer of 1944 at their Operational Training Unit at Leighton Buzzard in Bedfordshire when crewing up to train on Wellingtons. They are at complete odds as to how it actually happened.

'A couple of cheeky gunners came up to me and declared they were the best in the RAF,' says Pat.

'Hang on,' says Nobby, 'I distinctly remember you coming up to us at the table and saying, "How would you blokes like to be my gunners?"' 'No, that was after . . .' and on it goes until they both concede the other is probably right.

Nobby joined up later than Pat, sewing his Air Gunner brevet onto his sergeant's tunic two days after his nineteenth birthday. 'I didn't have the ability to be a pilot,' he says. 'I was offered an air gunner's job and I took it.' As a boy, he'd watched Messerschmitts being chased low over the rooftops of his home town of Portsmouth by Spitfires during the Battle of Britain, and had even been an auxiliary firefighter when it was heavily bombed. 'I remember being called down to the docks once,' he says. 'There was a destroyer lying on its side on the quay, virtually intact. The bomb blast had lifted it clean out of the water.' Perhaps this is what made him choose the air force over the navy.

Pat, Nobby and the rest of their crew were posted to No. 115

Squadron at Witchford, just outside Ely in the Cambridgeshire fens. 'The whole place was as flat as a pancake,' says Nobby. 'Ideal for airfields.' Airfields, indeed, were everywhere. Witchford's next-door neighbour was the New Zealand No. 75 Squadron, located at another temporary wartime base, Mepal. At one point, the perimeters of the two aerodromes converged, and on more than one occasion, incoming aircraft would mistakenly land at the wrong one, then have to wait hours before being allowed to take off again and land over the fence. We chat about the area, the famous Ely Cathedral, and I show off by mentioning it was also the home of Oliver Cromwell.

'Yes, that was name of the pub we used to go to,' says Pat. 'You remember, Nobby, Ely Brown Ale. I can see all the bottles lined up.' Nobby nods towards Pat.

'Thursday was our drinking night down there, but if we were on ops that night, he'd do a low pass over the pub to let them know we weren't coming.' The young men of Bomber Command were good customers.

Pat has brought along his logbook for our meeting, and we pore over it, careful to avoid falling drops of tea and cake.

As always, I try to get them to start at the beginning. Ably assisted by Nobby, Pat has no trouble recalling the details of his first operation, flying as second pilot to an experienced crew on a daylight to Oberhausen. 'I heard this pilot call out, "Scarecrow, starboard bow," and saw a huge explosion in the sky.' For much of the bomber war, the RAF crews believed the Germans employed these so-called 'scarecrows' – aerial explosions designed to shake airmen's nerves by simulating the destruction of a large aircraft. It was perhaps some comfort to the crews, feeling they hadn't been taken in by the ruse. Only after the war was it revealed that no such weapon existed, and what the men were seeing was in fact exploding aircraft, usually a result of the thinly cased 4000-pound 'Cookie' blast bomb being hit by flak. 'I saw it as plain as anything,' says Pat. 'It just disintegrated. My first trip.'

Nobby's start to his tour was also a fiery one, a trip to Vohwinkel in the Ruhr Valley. 'On my first night trip I saw four Lancasters go down,' he says. In the closing stages of the war, the diminished German night fighter force employed inventive tactics to compensate for its lack of fuel and numbers. 'We were in the stream, and about half a mile behind I saw them drop their flares,' he remembers. Slow-descending parachute flares would illuminate the bomber formation, giving the German pilots time to duck underneath and pick the bombers out, silhouetted against the light. 'Just half a mile to starboard. Four of them went down at a rate of knots. I don't think any of them would have got out,' he says. 'It was quite a popular tactic towards the end of the war.'

The jollity drops away a little as the men remember darker moments, and I can see in their eyes a slight faraway look, as they recall visions unspoken.

I ask Pat about the Lancaster from a pilot's point of view. 'A four-engined Spitfire,' he tells me, brightening up. Just to show off its remarkable flying characteristics, he tells me that sometimes they would sidle up alongside the Americans in their B-17s and feather first one, then two and finally three engines in a show of one-upmanship that no doubt had the American crews in their underpowered Fortresses agog.

'What was the conversation among the crew?' I ask. It's one of my favourite questions. They both think for a moment, each giving the other the opportunity to answer. Nobby obliges by recreating some of the instructions he gave to his pilot, now beside him again sixty years on. 'Mid-upper to pilot. Fighter, fighter – thousand yards, port quarter up. Prepare to corkscrew.' He holds up a hand as if focusing on something in the middle distance and explains to me the illuminated gunsight. 'I've still got the aiming point in my mind. A circular orange ring outside with a point in the centre. You'd get the graticule on the centre of the enemy and open fire when you thought the range was 600 yards.'

'There was no unnecessary chatter, was there, Nobby?' asks Pat.

'Well, you were concentrating that hard, weren't you?' he replies. Returning from a trip, though, with the friendly coast of England in sight, they could relax a little. 'I remember the rear gunner calling up to me on the intercom when we got close to home, "How you going up there, mid-upper?" It was like meeting a friend again.'

This jogs something else in Nobby's memory. 'And I'll tell you another story about this man . . .' Awkward at the prospect of adulation, Pat screws up his face and looks away. It was a night raid somewhere – Nobby tries, but cannot remember where. On the run in, the bomb aimer called up to say that he was unable to get a clear sight of the target. 'Right then,' said Pat over the intercom, 'we'll go round again.' Turning into the oncoming stream of anything up to several hundred bombers – risking collision as well as giving the anti-aircraft gunners below a second bite at the cherry – was, to say the least, not a popular option among the crews.

'Now me being an abject coward,' says Nobby, 'I said, "Look, we're over Germany, let's just drop the bloody things and go home!" But Pat was right. We were there to do a job, and so we did it.' Pat hasn't forgotten the incident either. 'I think we were only on three engines for that one, too,' he says. I ask him how he managed to avoid collision. 'You just have to use your judgment,' he says. 'And hope the others move a bit to let you in.'

The two men meander in and out of their conversation, feeding each other's memories. At times I feel like I'm just eavesdropping but know my presence is providing some kind of catalyst. They argue briefly about small details, competing for the sharpness of their recollections. At one point, they can't decide which particular Lancaster they finished their tour on in March 1945, arguing over the aircraft's registration numbers

'It was PB 786, wasn't it? No, 686. 686, was it?'

'No, 796 we finished in, Nobby . . .'

'Are you sure?' Then they speak about some crews who didn't finish at all – faces and personalities briefly known and who one morning were simply absent from the mess at breakfast.

'I always remember another young air gunner. Terrific piano player, he was. I came in one morning and found out he'd got the chop the night before.' Pat remembers him too. 'He was in Bill Long's crew. Yes, C Flight. I think he was a navigator.'

'Oh, perhaps he was. Could have been. Yes.' What, I ask, was their most dangerous moment. Nobby is first to answer.

'The closest I came was a God almighty "crack" in my turret and piece of shrapnel the size of a walnut that finished up in my ammunition tanks. Frightened the hell out of me,' he says. 'They'd get your height and then chuck as much as they could in the hope of getting something.'

'I got one under me seat. Big piece of flak,' says Pat. 'They said that when you could see the flame in the explosion, it was close.'

Both of them, however, admit to feeling cloaked with the seeming invincibility of youth. 'It was never you that was going to get it, was it, Nobby?' says Pat. 'You're bulletproof when you're young. It was always that other bloke, way out there on the edge of the stream who was going to be killed. "Bloody idiot, what's he doing out there?" we'd say.' Nobby nods quietly. They're both quiet now.

Nobby remembers the enormous fire started on a big raid to Munich, one of seventy-one carried out on the big city during the war, which left 6500 people dead and half a million homeless. 'There were sparks and embers flying around us from the fire below, and we were at 20 000 feet!' remembers Nobby, with awe.

Pat and his crew completed thirty operations, including one 48-hour period in which he did three, a sombre way indeed to celebrate his 21st birthday. I look again at his logbook. There it is. One trip on the 5th, then two on the same day, 6 March 1945. 'We finished at daylight and there was a notice on the board, "All crews go to bed immediately." We knew something was on for that night.'

Then one morning after a big raid on Potsdam near Berlin, Pat, Nobby and the rest of the crew were ordered to assemble on parade and told officially that they had finished their tour. 'An enormous cheer went up,' says Pat, but then they experienced a strange, empty feeling. 'It all happened so quickly, and we all thought, "What's going to happen now?"' Soon, the whole crew would disperse and go their separate ways.

Around us, in the dignified mezzanine lounge of the Victoria, more groups of people meet and settle close by. Country men with ruddy faces and pressed grey trousers sit with their wives and families, and the noise level rises. An old naval officer, already wearing his medals – the Atlantic Star and the distinctive blue and white ribbon of the Distinguished Service Cross – hobbles by on a frame, assisted by a son, who is old himself. It's getting onto beer time and Nobby and Pat are getting a little restless for their pre-march rendezvous with some others at a nearby pub.

Tomorrow, they will once again take their place among the

ABOVE The war over, and nearly six years of fighting behind them, 3 Squadron lines up at Campoformido in Italy, May 1945, just before a final victory flight and the handing over of their aircraft.

LEFT The war in sunny Italy. Jock McAuley dwarfed by the prop of his 3 Squadron Mustang at his base in Cervia.

TOP Jock and his Mustang. Note the distinctive Southern Cross on the rudder – still used by the jets of 3 Squadron today.

BOTTOM The front end of a well-worn RAAF P51, Cervia, Italy 1945.

TOP A 3 Squadron Mustang taxis along a runway of 'Marsden Matting', Italy, 1945.

BOTTOM The dashing young airman. Barney Barnett beside his 136 Squadron Spitfire in Burma.

TOP Somewhere over New Guinea, Ray Riddell in the seat of his
75 Squadron Kittyhawk, 'O-Orace', so designated in honour of his
father, Horace.

BOTTOM A 136 Squadron Hurricane takes off from a former Burmese
paddy field near the front. It was so dusty, formation take-offs were
abandoned.

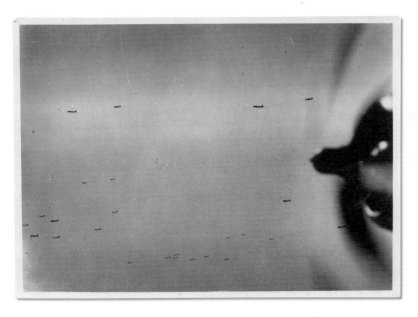

ABOVE 'The crowded sky' – Ralph Proctor's view as glider-towing Stirlings make their way to Arnhem and disaster, October 1944.

ABOVE Enemies everywhere. The crew of this late-mark Halifax look on, amused, as some local experts deal with a swarm of bees which have found their way into the rudder.

LEFT The rearward view as Ralph Proctor's Albermarle tows a Horsa glider in training over England.

TOP Ralph Proctor at the controls of his Albermarle, in which he flew clandestine supply operations for SOE.

BOTTOM Ralph Proctor and his crew underneath their 295 Squadron Stirling. Note the complex undercarriage designed to increase the angle of incidence for take-off.

TOP Even training was dangerous. The result of a ground collision between two Harvards in Canada.

BOTTOM Bob Molesworth greets an unexpected visitor at Horsham St Faith, Winston Churchill.

ABOVE Bob Molesworth, DFC, a veteran of 74 operations.
He would happily be back on his Victorian farm by war's end.

LEFT Back at their base at Horsham St Faith, 114 Squadron airmen excitedly discuss their recent attack on the 'Scharnhorst' and 'Gneisenau', February 1942.

ABOVE After his tour fighting the Japanese with the British Pacific Fleet, Arthur Cundall stands beside his 1770 Squadron Fairey Firefly at Maryborough, Queensland, 1945.

29 TBS555 D.114 12-8-41 F2.

26 TBS555 D.114 12-8-41 F2.

TOP Across the North Sea to Holland, Bob Molesworth snapped this view from his 114 Squadron Blenheim.

BOTTOM Another photo from a low-level raid, Holland 1942.

ABOVE Roy Riddel beside his 'lopsided' 66 Squadron Spitfire 11a, fitted with its long-range 40-gallon fuel tank under the port wing.

LEFT Palm trees and Marsden matting. One of 75's Kittyhawks at its tropical aerodrome at Milne Bay.

ABOVE Roy Riddel enjoying a cigar with fellow 66 Squadron pilot Ted Spradley, Perranporth, Cornwall. Soon he would swap the skies of Europe for the jungles of New Guinea.

OPPOSITE A fine shot of an RAAF Kittyhawk, Number 2 Operational Training Unit, Mildura.

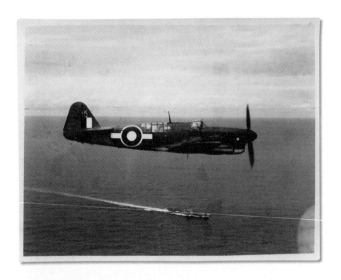

TOP Not a big place to land on. Somewhere over the Pacific, a 1770 Squadron Fleet Air Arm Firefly overflies its 'home', the aircraft carrier, HMS 'Indefatigable' – part of the British Pacific Fleet, 1945.

BOTTOM Arthur Cundall's view of the burning Japanese oil refinery at Palembang, Sumatra, during his first major combat operation, January 24, 1945.

ever-thinning ranks of those making the long march up to the Shrine of Remembrance, watched by crowds of enthusiastic onlookers, as if at one of those curious Medieval theatre pieces continually re-enacted on the same spot every year.

I think back to the Anzac Days of my youth, as that overly-serious fourteen-year-old, clapping solemnly as the thick ranks filed past, vastly outnumbering the scattered patches of onlookers. Not so today.

As the resonance of the World Wars – and even later ones like Vietnam – fades, an entire generation who has been spared the prospect of war can relax about it, and feel free to enjoy one of its colourful trappings.

Sentimentalist as I am, I think I would have nonetheless been quite happy to see Anzac Day quietly fade away, dying gracefully along with its original players. Instead, every year it transforms into something else, something a little more forced and hollow, a plat-form for politicians and flag-wavers and jingoism, of which I never believed it guilty in its more dignified years. I have never really thought Anzac Day to be a glorification of war, but the question was always a worthy one, perhaps even vital. These days, no one even bothers to ask it. I wonder what the men who were there think?

I turn to the boys – there is something decidedly boyish about them still as they sit together – and ask them. They think care-fully. I'm not sure if it's Pat or Nobby who answers, but I like to think he speaks for a great many. 'You know,' he says, 'I don't think it's really *possible* to glorify war. Not when you've been in one and seen what it's like.'

The characters of these two men, I decide, fit perfectly with the positions they held in their aircraft in the skies over Europe. Pat, the pilot and captain, quieter but with an understated air of authority; and the more independent Nobby, sharp and enthusiastic, the archetypical gunner. I ask Pat whether he has any regrets about not becoming the fighter pilot for which he trained. Not a bit, he says.

'Going through that experience alongside these other men,' he says indicating his friend, 'well, it's worth a hell of a lot to me. That's one of the reasons I never regretted not staying on fighters. It's a unique experience – if you're lucky enough to get through.'

Unused to articulating emotion, the two nod for a bit in agreement. Little more needs to be said. Besides, the Victoria Hotel is getting busy, and these two have another engagement. 'We're going up to the Irish pub to meet some blokes for a Guinness. Come along if you like,' they offer, but I decline. I figure this one really is a 'participants only' affair.

RALPH PROCTOR

Pilot, RAAF

I would have been happy with just a look at Ralph's logbook, and a couple of flying stories. Instead, I got a whole museum.

To the east of Melbourne, near the outer suburb of Lilydale, is a charming old pioneering estate named Mont de Lancy, built in the 1880s by a family called the Sebires. Today, it's a quaint tourist attraction where people eat scones, admire roses and tie the knot. According to the brochure, it boasts many original features including hand-made bricks, twelve-foot high ceilings and 'a wide verandah taking in panoramic views of the Yarra Valley and surrounding ranges'. And while you're there, you can inspect the small local museum, lovingly set up in an adjacent room to highlight the district's history. Here, amid the usual array of bits of old ploughs and sepia photos of grey-whiskered pioneers (who were probably about thirty), you can't help but notice the somewhat incongruous 1:72 scale Airfix plastic model of a four-engine Short Stirling bomber. A strange addition to a pioneer museum. Next to it is an open logbook, some bits of what looks like an aircraft instrument panel, an RAAF uniform and sundry other assorted items relating to World War II aviation, all stemming from the personal collection of Ralph Proctor. As I was to discover, Ralph is more than just a former glider tug pilot who operated on D-Day and throughout the Battle of Arnhem, he's a local treasure: a living, breathing museum piece all on his own.

No sooner had I arrived at Ralph's unit on the outskirts of Melbourne than I was bundled into a car with him and his mate Herb and taken up for a private inspection. Here, I was to receive a personal guided tour by the man himself. I felt decidedly honoured.

Born in Hay in rural New South Wales, Ralph spent ten years before the war on outback cattle stations until coming down to Melbourne to join the RAAF with a bunch of other jackaroos. He trained mainly in Canada, and would have liked to have flown single-engine aircraft but doesn't seem to have been too fussed when a decree was passed preventing anyone over the age of twenty-five from becoming a fighter pilot. Ralph had just celebrated his twenty-fifth birthday.

'What's that, Ralph?' I ask, pointing to an old black aircraft instrument displayed amid his memorabilia on a large display shelf.

'That's the clock out of a Stirling. You wound it and set your ETA. It still goes,' he says, his eyes sweeping over the other objects. 'Those are my goggles. Yep, they're all mine.' It was the most I could get out of him on the subject before he was buttonholed by the first of many locals for a ten-minute catch-up. Still, I'm in no hurry – there's a whole museum to get through, including his original dark blue battle dress tunic which, I note, bears a Saville Row label.

'Vivid' would be the word to describe the way Ralph talks about his flying. Even the stories from his training are imbued with a kind of first-person breathlessness that belies the fact that more than sixty years have passed since the events took place. When he speaks, I feel like I'm in the cockpit with him. Coming from the wide open spaces of Canada to the crammed landscape and unpredictable weather of England was a shock for all aircrew, and Ralph quickly decided that his instruments were his best friend. 'When you're in the air, you just have to stick to your instruments – don't leave them for a second, because you can go in – in no time!' he tells me passionately. 'Sometimes it feels like they're wrong, especially at night. You feel like the aircraft is standing on one wing, but you look at your instruments and they say, "No, everything's right." You have to trust them!' I nod my head, taking in what he says, as if there's a chance I might one day be able to take up the advice.

At his Operational Training Unit in Warwickshire he experienced having to land in fog, aided by 'FIDO', the Fog Investigation and Dispersal Operation. This was truly a triumph for the egg-heads of British wartime engineering. On certain aerodromes, pipes were laid beside the main runway, through which fuel was pumped. In heavy fog, burners were lit from which the rising heat not only dispersed the fog for a height of several hundred feet, but made the runway highly visible to returning bomber crews. It used vast amounts of petrol but saved many a wounded, inexperienced or simply blinded aircrew after its introduction in mid-1944.

Again in the dramatic first-person, Ralph describes what it was like coming in to land on FIDO at night. 'You come in on a normal approach. You're watching your instruments. You might be coming in on the blind navigation radio beam – move too far off it one way and you hear "dit-dah" in the headphones, or "dit-dit-dah" if it's too far the other. When it's a solid "da-ah", you know you're right in the middle. You reduce your rate of descent – six or seven hundred feet a minute – then all of a sudden you break through the fog and there's the runway right in front of you. You do a last-minute check: kick her over a bit maybe, or lift your left or right wing and come in for a landing.'

At the end of Ralph's training, he expected to be transferred to Bomber Command. But in late 1943, with the invasion of Europe rapidly taking shape, it was decided that whole armies would be moved entirely by air. Newly trained crews were selected from OTUs around the country and transformed into the brand new 38 Group. 'It was formed up especially to move an army from A to B by air,' says Ralph.

We've said goodbye to the museum and Ralph's legion of friends and admirers, and returned to his unit where I am strangely absorbed by an extraordinary collection of eggcups he has acquired over the years, taking up an entire bookcase. He makes me coffee and we share the remnants of an extremely good cake, leftover from a recent birthday, as it turns out, and I am genuinely astonished to learn that Ralph has just celebrated his ninetieth. You would never guess it by the man's energy. He's so active and keen to talk, I have trouble getting him even to sit down.

Training complete, Ralph went to Horn near Bournemouth to join No. 295 Squadron to learn, among other things, how to pull a glider full of soldiers through the air and drop it into the middle of a battle. His was a new crew in a new squadron. 'It was all strange for a while,' he recalls, 'but once we were given an idea of what it was we were supposed to be doing, well, you became used to it.'

Normandy would involve, for the first time in history, the deployment of thousands of paratroops and glider-borne soldiers, not as an adjunct but an integral part of the battle itself. It would be Ralph's job to get some of them there, at the right time and in one piece. First though, he would have to survive the Whitley.

The Whitley was a truly woeful aircraft that should really have been retired very soon after it started rolling off the Armstrong-Whitworth production line at Bagington in 1936. Instead, it was used operationally for a variety of wartime tasks, failing to distinguish itself in any of them. 'It was like driving a four-ton truck,' says Ralph. Although his experience of this heavy and unwieldy beast was limited to training, it added nothing to his confidence in it to be told that the Germans were occasionally conducting fighter sweeps along the south coast of England, and that it was forbidden to leave the ground without the rear gunner in place. 'Otherwise we were likely to get our tail shot off,' he says. Still, the paratroops Ralph was carrying had to learn to jump from something and the ageing Whitleys were available.

Ralph trained extensively, amassing 150 tows or 'lifts' in practice over twelve months. With characteristic drama, he conveys to me the feeling of what it was like pulling a Horsa glider into the air full of men and equipment. In another startling present-tense rendition, he tells me how speed and power were of the essence. 'Travelling down the runway, you *have* to reach a certain airspeed. You look back and see that your glider is flying twelve to fifteen feet above the ground. He takes off first. Then we bore along and use as much runway as we can and get up as much speed as we can. We have four strong motors and they're all going full bore. The cylinder head temp goes up to 330-plus and the needles are knocking on the top. They're hot. The moment we leave the deck, we can only leave the engines a short time on that full take-off speed. They're working flat to the boards. As soon as the air begins to cool the motors a little bit you throttle off, taking off some flap too. Not too much at the one time. See? Get your wheels up to reduce drag.' To an aeroplane tragic like myself, it's all terribly exciting.

With training complete, it was time for Ralph to begin operational flying. With the invasion still some months off, however, it was decided that the best way to use his skills was to drop not soldiers but supplies to the French resistance on special night trips for the clandestine Special Operations Executive.

I stop him here and draw his attention to his logbook entry (he has graciously allowed me to borrow it from the museum) for the night of 3 March 1944. It is extremely vague. 'We weren't allowed to put down where we went or what we were doing,' he says. One such entry bears only the cryptic entry, 'Ditcher', code for the agent they were supplying with some unknown cargo on a grid coordinate in the dead of night. 'We had to go in and find a tiny little field way down in the south of France and put that stuff down from 1000 feet,' he says. At the appointed rendezvous, Ralph's crew would look for the pre-arranged letter being flashed up from the ground. They would then circle and wait for the lighting of three fires in succession, which would indicate which direction to drop. Ammunition, food, clothes, weapons. All were vital to supply the French Marquis resistance in the months leading up to D-Day.

Then the day itself. He pauses, and shows me an old copy of *Flight* magazine dated 15 June 1944. In it, there's a photo of Montgomery and Eisenhower addressing a crowd of assembled aircrew. 'That's me with my navigator,' he says, and points to himself in his distinctive RAAF dark blue. 'They came in to brief us the night before we took off.' He's proud of that photo, and why not?

At 1.30 a.m. of the morning of 6 June, D-Day, Ralph took off carrying one of the first gliders into Normandy, filled with the men whose job it was to prepare the landing fields for the glider-borne Sixth Air Landing Brigade, scheduled to arrive late that afternoon to meet the expected German counterattack. The gliders themselves were piloted by specially trained soldiers – two in each in case one got a bullet in the back. Once down, they would resume their normal job as foot soldiers.

Ralph has such an exciting way of speaking that I feel I'm about to embark on the great crusade myself. 'The whole sky was lit up for miles and miles along the coast with fire and smoke and tracer,' he says. Not that he could do anything to avoid it: when towing, evasive action was impossible. 'How did they miss us?' he asks, still wondering. 'It was just a miracle.' At the appointed moment, he spoke to the glider pilot via the intercom running through the towrope. 'Pilot, can you see your landing strip?' 'Okay,' replied the voice, 'this will suit me fine.' With a 'good luck', the pilot pulled a lever to set himself free and was on his own, sailing down on the wind to land into the battle, with no chance to abort or come around again.

Later, he would befriend that same English pilot, who went on to have adventures of his own on the ground. He and Ralph shared a correspondence over many decades. 'Every letter I've got from him in the last sixty years says, "Thanks, Ralph, for keeping straight and level that night."'

After D-Day, Ralph's night drops to the resistance resumed. Shot at many times, he would occasionally come back with incendiaries still burning, lodged in the wings. 'We had to get the extinguisher onto it straightaway,' he tells me.

One night, he had a load to carry almost to the Swiss border: two big baskets and twelve steel cages loaded in the bomb bays. He was by now flying another of the lesser lights of World War II aviation, the Armstrong-Whitworth Albermarle. From the same stable as the hapless Whitley, the twin-engine Albermarle was also beset by problems. It was designed as a bomber that could be built from steel and plywood to save aluminium, but its lack of performance relegated it to the roles of transport and glider tug, a fact which may explain why only about 600 were built. The Albermarle has always looked a little forlorn to me, not really an aircraft unto itself but a composite from bits of others. No. 295 Squadron was the first to fly them.

To avoid the German defences around Paris, Ralph was told to bypass the city by at least fifteen miles. At this stage of the war, however, German units were on the move everywhere to join the battle in Normandy, and one night Ralph flew right over the top of one of them. 'Everything came up, everything.' In quick succession, he felt the concussion of five 88-millimetre shells from a mobile ground battery below. 'We got a line of them all along the fuselage. Bang, bang, bang . . .' But the shells were incorrectly fused, set to detonate at an altitude higher than the 5000 feet at which Ralph was flying and failed to explode. Ralph did a quick intercom check of the crew. One by one, they all called in, unharmed. 'None of them was touched,' says Ralph. 'The shells all went between them.' Their luck continued – the engines were intact and even the radio still worked. He got back on the intercom. 'Right, we're still all here, we've still got our engines going, so we'll continue on the course to drop the baskets. We might be carrying something these people want.'

At the designated rendezvous, Ralph spotted the correct signal and released the two parachute baskets which were manually pushed out of the aircraft by the crew. But when he went to put the flaps down to slow the aircraft and release the cages in the bomb bay, they failed to respond, as did the bomb doors. What he only then realised was that one of the shells had taken out the aircraft's hydraulics, cutting power to the bomb doors, wheels and flaps. With a sour taste in his mouth, Ralph had no choice but to turn around and take the load back to England. He could only imagine the looks of despair and bewilderment on the faces of the resistance fighters as the sounds of his engines faded away to the north. He also realised that without power to lower the wheels, he had a belly landing to look forward to.

Approaching his aerodrome several glum hours later, something else – something rather serious – also struck him. What was it exactly he was carrying? And was it something likely to explode on a rough landing? He radioed in to the control tower. 'I want to know what it is I'm carrying. I'm not going to land on something that's going to blow us up,' he explained in no uncertain terms. The alternative was to climb and let the crew bale out. 'Alright, Proctor, we'll have to ring through to Group,' came a response. So, while his Commanding Officer manoeuvred his way through the appropriate levels of British military bureaucracy to find someone who could get their hands on the appropriate form to indicate just what it was in Ralph's bomb bay, he and his crew hung on the line, 'on hold', circling the aerodrome with no hydraulics, the petrol gauges knocking on empty and hoping that they weren't going to be blown to kingdom come by their mystery cargo.

'Boys,' he said to his crew, 'you'd better get ready to jump.' He called up again. 'Yes, just hang on a minute,' came the reply. Ralph circled again. It was becoming farcical. One more circuit with them about to open the escape hatch, and the call came up. 'Okay. You can belly land. You're not carrying anything that's going to explode.' Ralph picked the softest piece of ground he could see between two runways and came in on the grass. After all that, it was surprisingly easy. 'All the props got bent up, but that was about it,' he says.

For the big aerial armada which was planned for Arnhem, Ralph converted to the Stirling, and did four trips into northern Holland in a week. He began on 17 October carrying a group of paratroopers in a glider, one of the first groups into Nijmagen – men doomed to be pinned down in the maelstrom that became the very rushed and very botched Operation Market Garden.

A couple of times he dropped supplies to the remnants of the

British First Airborne Division on the northern side of the Rhine River, where it had been caught on the wrong side of the infamous 'bridge too far'. I ask him what of the battle he could see from the air. 'All we could see was a heck of a mess,' he says. 'The Germans had opened the dykes and flooded the countryside and had dug poles into the ground for the gliders. A lot of them were smashed to pieces as they landed.'

Recalling his last Arnhem trip, he relives coming in at a thousand feet, a sitting target if ever there was one. Church steeples were smashed and bent over at right angles. Small-arms fire pelted the fuselage. A shell exploded in the port wheel undercarriage nacelle and also punctured the starboard tyre. On the way back, the crew went to their crash positions behind the bulkheads and the main wing spar. Landing as gently as he could at Harwell, Ralph put the port wheel down, but it was wrecked to the rim. With more weight, it collapsed and the whole undercarriage was wrenched at right angles up into the fuselage. The tearing, wrenching metallic sound was deafening, and Ralph grits his teeth remembering. He quickly switched off the electrics as the aircraft spun into a ground loop. 'Out, boys!' he ordered, and out they all tumbled again, amazingly without a scratch.

I can see that it's all coming back a little too fast for Ralph, and he simply sits quietly for a while with a wide-eyed look. 'Now you're making me shake,' he says. I've probably been pushing him a bit too far, but we press on.

On Ralph's last dramatic moment in the air, it wasn't enemy action that was nearly his undoing but the weather. On 2 November 1944, five aircraft from No. 295 Squadron, led by the station commander, Wing Commander Wilfred Surplice, were detailed to make a drop to the Norwegian resistance at a spot forty miles west of Oslo. When they arrived, it was a white-out. 'We reached the drop zone but you couldn't see a thing,' says Ralph. Once again, they were forced to turn around with their twenty-four steel containers still secure in the bomb bays. But when Ralph turned the control column, the Stirling's response was a dreaded soft, spongy feeling on the control surfaces that meant one thing: ice. In moist, subzero air, it could happen in just a couple of minutes, and it was a killer: water vapour condensing, then freezing onto the sub-zero metal surface of the wing, upsetting its ability to lift and instantly weighing it down with hundreds of pounds of ice. There were ways to get rid of it, but you had to be quick.

'Engineer, put on all the de-icing you can!' yelled Ralph to his engineer. 'I've got to put the nose down to lose height!' But could they? They were, after all, over the Norwegian mountains. 'Okay, Proc,' came the voice of the navigator. 'We're just clear of the rough country.' Ralph pushed the column forward to build up speed and descend to a thousand feet above the water. Here, the air was warmer and the fatal straightjacket of ice began to shed in clumps. Amazingly, even the spinning propellers had iced up and chunks began to fly off the blades, hitting the fuselage with a terrible noise, 'like someone throwing bricks', Ralph says. It also made a ghastly screaming noise, adding to the cacophony of wind and engines. 'We didn't lose all the ice until we were halfway back to Scotland,' says Ralph. 'The boys were frantic. So was I, but I didn't tell them that!' They made it back, but Wing Commander Surplice didn't. His crew baled out, but he went in with his aircraft as it crashed into the same Norwegian mountains they had so narrowly avoided.

It's been a tough couple of afternoons for Ralph, and at one point, the emotions get too much for him. He apologises, unnecessarily. It's been a privilege to meet him. At the end, both exhausted, we talk over another cuppa about his time before the war, mustering cattle in outback Queensland. It's a relief to wind down in this more gentle way, talking about his days on the big cattle and sheep stations out near Charleville and Longreach. He still manages to convey the colour and motion of his memories, but more gently, without the whiff of terror that I have managed to stir up in his mind from his time spent flying in the long dark night of wartime Europe.

STUART THOMPSON
Wireless/Air Gunner, RAAF

'So why do you want to join the air force, son?' asked the officer behind the desk when a young Stuart Thompson went to join up right at the beginning of the war.

'Well,' he said, 'I've always been keen on flying but I've never had the chance to take it up.'

'Well, aren't you lucky!' replied the man in the uniform. 'Now you can learn all about it and serve your country at the same time.' It was just what the lad from Moe wanted to hear, and the air force, in turn, were happy to have him. Unlike 99 per cent of new volunteers, Stuart wasn't even fussed about being a pilot. He just wanted to get into the air. So, with a background as a cinema projectionist and a dab hand at tinkering around radio sets, the job of 'WAG' – Wireless/Air Gunner – suited him to a tee.

A few months later, throwing up in the back of a clapped-out Fairey Battle at No. 1 Bombing and Gunnery School at Evans Head, New South Wales, the gloss had worn off somewhat.

'I came down that sick one time I was going to tell them what they could do with their air force!' he declares. But then an officer stepped up and handed him a glass of strange white liquid. 'Here. Drink this,' he was told. Stuart swallowed it down, felt better immediately and was never airsick again. He still has no idea what it was.

Soon after, Stuart was on a ship sailing through the Suez Canal to join No. 211 Squadron RAF in the Egyptian desert to fly reconnaissance missions against the Italians. It was at times a surreal war against a reluctant enemy. 'The Italian Air Force had some decent sort of blokes,' says Stuart. 'Instead of bombs, they'd drop thermos flasks and fountain pens. If you picked them up, they'd explode.' Once or twice an Italian bomb did land, but failed to go off. Investigating, the squadron armourers found the fuses hadn't even been attached, just the threaded hole where they were supposed to screw in. Inside the casing was a handwritten note: 'Sorry, this is the best we could do for you', it read! 'They just didn't want to fight, you see,' says Stuart. Later, when the squadron was making a speedy withdrawal to another airstrip, a group of Italian prisoners were released and told they could rejoin their own rapidly advancing army. Horrified, they instead stole some lorries and followed hot on the tails of their retreating captors!

The Western Desert campaign was a fluid one with armies advancing and retreating back and forth along the southern edge of the Mediterranean. Sometimes, Stuart would take off from one nameless desert airstrip, not sure if he would be landing at the same one. 'They'd post a man standing at a certain spot on the perimeter of the aerodrome. If he wasn't there when we came back, we'd have to go and land somewhere else,' he says.

For further training over jungle terrain in the newer and marginally better long-nose Blenheim bomber, Stuart was sent to an Operational Training Unit at a place called Wadi Gazouza in Eritrea. One night, his pilot, Alf Longmore, called up on the intercom, concerned. 'Scotty,' he said – for some reason they all called him Scotty – 'the mountains are playing up with our compass. As far as I can make out, we're twelve degrees off course.' Stuart radioed back to the aerodrome to report their problem. From this point, the aircraft's compass became completely disoriented and they were soon hopelessly lost. After a while, the pilot made an even more sobering announcement. 'We're getting low on fuel and we're going to crash. Do you want to bale out, Scotty?' Stuart looked out the window. All he could see was darkness and a vast, black mountainous jungle below.

'What are you two blokes going to do?' he asked. The pilot and navigator said they were going to stay put and take their chances in the crash-landing. Stuart decided to join them. 'I got out of the turret in case the trees took it off and decapitated me, and crawled into the bomb well.' In the dark, the Blenheim hit the ground and skidded. 'The noise was tremendous,' he says. 'Bushes and rocks and everything came hurtling through the aircraft.' But when it stopped it was so quiet, he could hear the ticking of the instruments. 'You alright, Scotty?' asked the pilot. All three had made it down without a scratch.

When the sun came up, however, they saw how close they had come to catastrophe: the aircraft had ground to a halt right between two enormous series of rocks – inches from either wingtip. 'If we'd have hit those we would have just burst into flame and that would have been the end of us.' If he could have taken out a lottery ticket, he would have. Two days later, thanks to Stuart's radio reports, they were picked up. From here, Stuart said good-bye to Africa, but not to the jungle, because No. 211 Squadron was on the move to the Far East to meet the rapacious Japanese.

The official language of the squadron history describes the squadron's next chapter. '211 Squadron then took its Blenheims to the Far East and, in the black days of early 1942, did good work in both Sumatra and Java before being overwhelmed by the Japanese invaders.' The reality wasn't nearly so tidy.

'Things were a shambles when we got out there,' remembers Stuart. The squadron had flown itself out, ahead of its own ground staff who never managed to arrive. Malaya and Singapore had already gone, so several RAF and RAAF squadrons were put into the hopeless position of repulsing the Japanese invasion from the island of Sumatra, home to the giant oil refinery at Palambang which the Japanese were desperate to capture.

There were two airstrips on Sumatra, P1 and P2. The first was a civilian aerodrome with concrete runways but no place to disperse the aircraft, while P2, the military base, was carved out of the jungle and so well hidden that several aircraft ran out of fuel and crashed trying to find it.

For a desperate few days in late January 1942, Stuart and his crew flew constant missions, often in the middle of violent monsoons, strafing and bombing the Japanese along beaches and landing grounds up and down the Malay Peninsula as best they could. Joining them was a thrown-together collection of Hudson bombers, Hurricanes and some utterly hopeless Brewster Buffalo fighters flown in near-suicide missions by the incalculably brave pilots of the Dutch Air Force.

In the rapidly disintegrating situation, the pace – never too far from panic – was relentless. 'We'd come in, refuel and rearm then immediately take off again,' says Stuart. With few spares or toolkits, servicing the aircraft was impossible and most of the ground crews were borrowed from the Buffalo squadrons. The attitude of some of the permanent RAF ground crews was astonishing. 'They'd been living out there so long on wine, women and song they just didn't give a damn,' he said. One afternoon, his Blenheim taxied in and Alf, the pilot, indicated he needed to be refuelled and rearmed immediately. 'This bloke on the ground just looked at his watch.

"I knock off at half past five," he said. Amazed and furious, Alf drew his service revolver and pointed it at him. "Refuel me immediately or you'll knock off right now!'"

Then there was the episode of the incorrectly laid flare path. The squadron's Blenheims were lined up at night, fully loaded and ready to take off at two-minute intervals along the row of lights. The first three took off into the darkness. Suddenly, red Very lights started to appear from everywhere. Something was terribly wrong. 'Everything stopped and we wondered what was happening,' remembers Stuart. The path had been laid too close to the trees. The first two aircraft had taken off and gone straight into them, the third hit the orderly room and killed the entire crew. The fourth aircraft in line stopped dead on the runway. Stuart was right behind him.

In early February the airfields started to come under direct attack from Japanese aircraft, with no radar to warn them of their approach. It went on like this for a couple of days.

'Then, one morning, we were having a cup of tea in the mess before taking off again,' remembers Stuart. 'I heard some noise, walked out and saw parachutes coming down.' Some on the airfield apparently thought the aircraft overhead were Hudsons, but when everyone saw they were being escorted by Zeroes, a terrible sickening feeling crept in. Two hundred and sixty crack Japanese paratroops were descending on the P1 aerodrome and another hundred at the nearby oil refinery.

Some of the defenders abandoned their weapons and fled, others fought bravely and hopelessly, firing over open sights of Bofors anti-aircraft guns at zero trajectory. Stuart remembers a few people firing pot shots with rifles to little avail. There was no time even to get all the aircraft away, and those that were still airborne were radioed not to attempt a landing and continue on to Java.

'Right,' announced Stuart's commanding officer, 'we're going to make our way through the jungle.'

In commandeered trucks, the remnants of the squadron headed east towards the coast along choked roads – breaking open the bowsers of abandoned petrol stations along the way. Arriving amid the chaos at the port of Oesthaven, they saw that the Dutch appeared to have left in something of a hurry. 'There were all these beautiful cars abandoned along the docks,' says Stuart. 'We had a great time pushing them over the edge into the sea to stop the Japs getting them.'

In Sumatra, Stuart and the remainder of his squadron found a ship to Java, mindful of being only one step ahead of the Japanese. They made it to the port of Chilachap, roughly halfway along the southern coast of the long island of Java. Here under the command of their CO, they commandeered a couple of powered lifeboats bobbing up and down in the harbour. 'They were beautiful boats that could carry a fair amount of people each,' he says. They raided the local warehouses to get supplies – primarily beer – and their small party of about twenty set off in a convoy of pairs out to sea, and hopefully, Australia. Sadly, they didn't get very far.

'We pulled into a nearby island to reorganise ourselves and our supplies. On the way in to shore, our boat hit the rocks and was smashed to smithereens.' Stuart swam, then scrambled to the shore. The squadron CO, in the other boat, ordered them to stay put until rescued while he continued the dash over to Australia.

With the meagre supplies they had managed to salvage from their wrecked boat, the small party stayed on the nameless island for about three weeks. 'Then the Japs found us,' says Stuart.

So began Stuart Thompson's three-and-a-half-year ordeal as a prisoner of war under the Imperial Japanese, enduring the horrors of the Thai–Burma Railway, a story which could easily fill a book on its own and can in no way be done justice here. Suffice to say, his character, to me, represents the archetypical Australian spirit of the time: open, self-effacing, relentlessly cheerful, seemingly without anger or bitterness – one which the Japanese, with their dismal, monolithic worldview, found so completely bewildering and so hard to break.

Stuart was beaten, starved and threatened with execution on a daily basis, yet chooses to speak not of the brutality but of the odd acts of kindness shown to him on a handful of occasions by his captors. The time when, bathing in a river after a day slaving on the railway, a guard came to the bank and ushered the men out of the water. He then threw in a hand grenade which stunned some fish and provided a rare meal that night. Later, on parade, the men were ordered by the camp commandant to point out this renegade who had shown kindness to the enemy. They feigned ignorance to a man. Later that night, a carton of cigarettes surreptitiously appeared in their hut.

Or of another who, after Stuart had bowed and scraped in the standard manner, indicated he take a seat on a bag of rice and spoke to him in perfect English. Before the war, it turned out, this man had been a schoolteacher and was fascinated by Australia. 'It sounds like a nice place. I wish I was there now,' said the young guard. 'Me too,' replied Stuart. At the end of their conversation, the guard indicated his own officers and said, 'Don't tell them I speak English.'

I also learn why Stuart cocks his head when listening. Once he was bashed so hard his eardrum perforated. It never healed and he's deaf as a post in it to this day.

We talk, Stuart and I, for a good while longer, not about flying but of his time in the jungle as one of Weary Dunlop's original 'thousand men from Java'; how he was put onto a ship and then walked through the jungle for a hundred miles and told to build his own accommodation; how he would often work from six in the morning until midnight on nothing but three pitiful meals of boiled rice; how he helped construct the Thai–Burma Railway out of hand-hewn logs of teak and bamboo; how he cut a pass through a mountain with a hammer and chisel, and how, when sick, his life was saved by the skill and almost messianic presence of Weary himself. And how, one day, they were all called to parade as usual and told by the Japanese that no one would work today because the war had ended. 'They told us the war had finished,' he says, 'but we didn't know who'd won.'

He shows me some pictures, taken postwar, of some of the construction works and the bridges built in captivity, and exudes an unmistakable pride in having played a part in their creation, despite its being done in the service of a brutal enemy amid an ocean of suffering. And why not? Who is to deny him, and others like him, this small but inextinguishable scrap of achievement to help make sense of it all? I am touched by this pride, this inviolable morsel snatched from all the cruelty that this kind and cheery man has endured, a pride his captors could never have understood.

JEFF McKAY
Navigator, RAAF

The pilot, regardless of rank, was always the boss of a bomber crew, but without the constant, meticulous assessment of speed, course and direction provided by the navigator, he was useless – able to do little more than fly in circles around the aerodrome. As has been said to me countless times, the navigator was the 'brains' of the plane. It was a point brought home to me within minutes of sitting down with Jeff McKay in his rural Victorian home. I had heard some extraordinary things over the many interviews I had conducted, but never had I been quoted poetry.

'Do you know "The Brook"?' Jeff asks me as a piece of fruit slice is handed across the table.

'Um, I . . .' My mind splutters back to schoolboy literature classes. 'Is that the one by, er . . .'

I come from haunts of coot and hern (he begins)
I make a sudden sally,
And sparkle out among the fern,
To bicker down a valley.

He recites it perfectly. Mind like a steel trap. I had noticed an elaborate game of patience still open on his computer, to which he no doubt intended to return after I had gone.

The little stream in Tennyson's poem, penned in the middle of the nineteenth century, ran its way to the sea along the bottom of a delightful Lincolnshire valley. It was still there a century later, as was the village named after it, Binbrook. By this time however, the tranquillity of the setting had been somewhat transformed because, in 1943, the long flat hill overlooking Tennyson's charming scene was home to No. 460 Heavy Bomber Squadron, Royal Australian Air Force, the most famous Australian bomber unit in the RAAF.

Jeff, I would discover, was full of such interesting pieces of information.

The air force couldn't believe its luck when Jeff McKay joined its ranks in 1942. Most potential young airmen were obsessed with becoming pilots, and would whine and pine if not chosen as such. Jeff on the other hand, upon being offered the coveted pilot's job, turned it down and asked instead to become a navigator. He immediately got his way. Why on earth would you shun the glamour of being a pilot? I ask. He tells me he'd worked briefly as a surveyor, and the job just suited his temperament. 'The idea of navigating by the stars appealed to me,' he says.

He learned the basics at Bradfield Park in Sydney, then sharpened his skills in the icy flat plains of Canada. It was on his way over in the ship, though, that Jeff had his closest encounter with the enemy, in the form of hundreds of German soldiers who had been captured in the North African desert. Like Jeff, they too were en route to Canada, but in their case to sit out the war in peace.

'They were all down in the hold,' he says, and there they would have remained, if not for the fact that Jeff happened at the time to be learning the steel guitar, which he had lugged with him for the trip across the Pacific.

The Germans, it seems, wanted to put on a concert to amuse themselves and their CO had asked if anyone on board would lend them an instrument or two. Jeff volunteered his, and a mate of his a banjo, and so both of them scored an invitation to be in the audience, guests of several hundred recently vanquished members of Hitler's Afrika Korps.

Standing on a table at the back of a vast, packed dining room to see the stage, they were both, says Jeff, 'a little apprehensive. We didn't know what they were going to do.' I ask how the Germans responded to him. 'They weren't unfriendly, but there was no conversation,' he says. A couple even smiled, perhaps realising just how lucky they were. 'Lilli Marlene' is one of the numbers Jeff remembers from the show. I tell him it's one concert I would love to have had a ticket to. He thinks for a moment. 'Yes. And it was a pretty good one, too.'

Twice a day the Germans were allowed up on deck for some fresh air. Some hardliners would take the opportunity to jump overboard rather than face living with the shame of captivity. Jeff remembers watching their heads bobbing in the ship's wake for a while till they disappeared beneath the water. 'Rather sad, really. They looked like fine young fellas,' he says.

In fact, he came close to knocking off one or two of these 'fine young fellas' then and there. Their British guards would occasionally tire of the job and give it to others for a while. One day, Jeff was asked to watch the Germans while they ate in the main dining room. So, with his Sten submachine gun, he took his place at the side of the hall while they tucked in. He hadn't actually had any training on the Sten, and started fiddling around with it. 'I was trying to uncock it but the spring was that strong when I pulled the bolt back it flew out of my hand and it started firing!' he says.

Thinking a massacre was in progress, the Germans coming

into the hall doubled back in the doorway; chips flew off the walls and general panic ensued. Eventually, the magazine emptied and Jeff was immediately frog-marched off to the CO. 'The Germans thought there was going to be a bloodbath!' he says. He was reprimanded for his foolishness and confined to his cabin for a couple of days. Further requests for guard duty were not forthcoming.

In Canada, he saw snow for the first time in his life and learned to deliver an Avro Anson from one frozen pinpoint on the tundra to another, as well as to read the wind direction by watching the cows – when it started to blow hard, they turned their backs into it and faced the other way.

At his Operational Training Unit in Staffordshire, a man with pilot's wings whom he'd never met approached him. 'You're McKay, are you?' he said. 'Well I wouldn't mind you joining me, if you're interested.' The man indicated a couple of other figures milling around in uniform. 'I've got a bomb aimer. Oh, and that redheaded bastard over there is our wireless operator. I've got a couple of gunners lined up too. I think they'll be alright. One of them's a Sydney taxi driver.' Thus, Jeff's crew was formed.

The composition of the seven men in a bomber crew gave it its own individual personality. Some were cool and efficient, sticking strictly to protocol both in the air and on the ground. There was usually always camaraderie, but in a far more class-conscious age – even among Australians – distinctions between officers and NCOs set the atmosphere. Then there were the crews like Jeff's – a little more on the larrikin side.

There was Jock Buchanan, the Scottish bomb aimer who took a while to adjust to the vernacular of his Australian crew. 'One night,' says Jeff, 'he stood up on the bed and threatened to beat up the next person who called him an "old Scots bastard".' This naturally led to an immediate barrage of the offending remark.

'He started frothing at the mouth,' says Jeff. 'But then he saw the funny side of it. In the end he was one of the most unifying personalities in the crew.' (Eventually, he became so enamoured of the Aussies, he migrated to Sydney and married one. It lasted just one day!)

Then there was Paddy Dowling, the wireless operator, who told everyone he was a third-year medical student studying gynaecology, a line he used when taking out girls. 'Turns out he worked as a clerk in the Sydney Gas Company,' says Jeff.

On their first evening together, they headed to the local to celebrate, but not before the taxi driver gunner, 'a square, tough-looking bloke of twenty-nine', felt he needed to check the young Jeff over.

'Do you drink?' he asked.

'Er, no,' Jeff replied.

'Do you smoke?' Jeff said that he didn't care for that either. The man looked alarmed. 'How do you feel about women?'

'Oh, I like women!' said Jeff enthusiastically.

Relieved, the man turned to the others. 'Thank God for that,' he said. 'They say only the good die young, so we don't want to be flying with any saints!'

And saints they were not, with the possible exception of Jeff who, with his quiet, slightly scholarly demeanour, was less attuned to the ways of wine and women. 'They were a fun crew. All wags and liked chasing women and drinking. I was a bit of a wowser in comparison but I enjoyed their company. Our pilot gave us all the impression we were all at the top of our craft. We weren't, of course, but he made us feel like we were. He was a good leader like that.'

While still in training, a Lancaster, probably running low on fuel after a raid, landed at his relatively quiet aerodrome. It was the first time Jeff had seen one. He remembers thinking the aircraft in which he would soon be flying to attack Germany was enormous. A few weeks later, at Lindholme in Yorkshire, he underwent his conversion course, and was reassured. 'The Lancaster just felt safe,' he says. 'You thought that if you had to fly in anything, this was it.'

The navigator's escape route from the Lancaster was, however, an awkward one. From his position behind the pilot, he had to make his way over the main wing spar to a door at the rear of the fuselage. In flying gear with a parachute, this was never an easy task, even in level flight. In an aircraft diving and in trouble, it was virtually impossible. Literally thousands must have been the numbers of uninjured men who were simply unable to reach the doors to exit their doomed aircraft.

Training complete, the crew were told to have their kit packed and be ready to go by 1530 the next day. 'We're going to 460 Squadron at Binbrook,' announced the pilot. 'Where the hell's that?' asked the crew (Jeff had yet to discover the poem).

The next day, the truck arrived. 'It was a trip I'll never forget,' says Jeff. After hours of driving across England up and down little country lanes, someone eventually called out, 'There it is!' He looked up and saw at the top of a hill 'three black shapes outlined against the sky' – the Lancasters of his new squadron. 'Well, this is it,' he thought sombrely to himself.

No. 460 Squadron was the most famous Australian squadron in Bomber Command, possibly the entire RAAF. It was also the most dangerous. Among its many proud achievements – highest number of operations, highest tonnage of bombs dropped – one statistic stands out: 1018 aircrew killed in action. With a flying contingent numbering 200, No. 460 Squadron in its brief four-year lifetime was effectively wiped out five times. This one unit made up just two per cent of the RAAF's wartime strength, but accounted for an astonishing twenty-three per cent of its casualties. This was the reality facing Jeff McKay as he trundled up the hill in the truck towards Binbrook's main gate.

Two weeks after their arrival, the crew filed into the mess for breakfast. Pinned to the wall was the 'battle order', the ominous sheet of foolscap upon which were typed the names of the crews detailed to fly that night. 'We're on!' Jeff remembers someone announcing.

Rumour went around that the target was Nuremberg, the same city that barely a year before had claimed ninety-six aircraft shot down in the most disastrous single night in the RAF's history. Vague thoughts about trying to postpone their debut crossed their minds, but 'No, this is what we do now' was the thought that settled them as they made their way to the briefing.

Jeff's tour was a short one, but his evocation of the day-to-day life on a bomber station is like a window into another time. 'Have you seen those old movies?' he asks, referring to the ubiquitous briefing-room scenes in black-and-white war epics like *The Dam Busters*, where smoking, fidgeting airmen – gathered as if in the assemblies they had so recently attended as schoolboys – prepare themselves to be told the 'target for tonight'. 'That's just what it was like,' says Jeff.

On a stage at the front of the long briefing room, a curtain was drawn back to reveal a map of Western Europe with coloured tape showing the routes to the target and home again. Often, an audible gasp from the men would release some of the tension. The Commanding Officer would perform a role: part host, part lecturer and headmaster. 'Well, gentlemen, tonight we're off to . . .' and the briefing would begin. But at this school, everyone listened with an intensity that was almost unbearable. From this point on, the airfield was in lockdown. Telephones were disconnected, and no one could come or go. The whole community of the aerodrome was essentially cut off from the outside world. For some, it would be forever.

After the main briefing, the various crew members would break off to receive their particular, specialised instructions. Jeff's began first, in the 'nav room' sometimes as early as two p.m. Here, he and his fellow navigators worked side by side, digesting the myriad details of weather, wind direction, bombing altitudes and courses, plotting the zigzagging route to the target on maps with coloured lines.

At around 5 p.m., the trucks would arrive to take the crews, kitted out in flying gear, to the aircraft. Standing under the big black planes, Jeff remembers hearing the low distant roar of hundreds of other aircraft running-up their engines from the dozens of other airfields for miles around. It was a sensation both comforting and frightening.

At the appointed time, they would climb into the aircraft, settle into their positions, recheck their equipment and wait for the order of take off.

'I wasn't particularly nervous,' says Jeff of his first trip, which indeed turned out to be Nuremberg. He even recalls some bravado, announcing with gusto over the intercom, 'Righto, everyone, Nuremberg and back!'

The navigator often saw almost nothing of the fiery world into which he was flying. He sat behind the pilot in a small, curtained-off area that hid the glow of his map-reading light. If he wanted to, he could poke his head up into the perspex astrodome at the rear of the canopy, but he usually chose not to. 'The job was quite absorbing,' he says. 'Anyway, I didn't want to see too much.' But he could hear everything.

When the bomb doors opened underneath him, he could feel the draught coming up through the floor, then the 'pings' as the spring-loaded releases let go of the bombs. Then the aircraft surged upwards, and he would need to hold his pens and pencils to his small metal desk to stop them flying around.

His job kept him busy. At the start of every leg of the route, he would wait for the sweep hand of his watch to touch '12' then give the pilot an instruction: 'Turn 040 . . . now.' Every six minutes, he would plot their position on the chart, which was checked meticulously by the Navigation Officer back at the squadron.

He was plugged into the intercom, an audience to the dramas unfolding around him. He could hear the two gunners in particular. 'Is that a fighter out there on the port beam?' and the pilot cutting in, 'Don't talk unless you have to!'

Once, hearing a description of a nearby aircraft on fire, he remembers his hand shaking as he filled in his log. 'If anyone asked how much my life was worth now,' he thought, 'I'd say about thruppence.'

Only occasionally did Jeff peer out into the battle. Once, he immediately saw an aircraft explode on the starboard side. On another, a daylight to Heligoland to attack U-boat pens, he saw a huge chunk of cliff hit by bombs and detach, crashing into the sea and throwing up an enormous wave. On that trip, a Halifax, in trouble and signalling that it was losing height, gradually went down into the water. Jeff radioed its position somewhere over the North Sea but later heard the rescue launch failed to locate it or the crew.

'After a couple of trips, though, you got used to it,' he says.

It was an old Staffordshire farm worker back in training who gave Jeff's crew their own piece of folklore in the form of 'Jasper's Hat'. Jock, the bomb aimer, was apparently a fine singer and would nightly entertain the locals in the pub. One of them, old Jasper, wore a distinctive bowler and would lend it to the singing Scot to get him going. On the night before they left to commence operations, Jasper presented his hat to the crew in a brown paper bag as a keepsake. It immediately became their talisman, accompanying them on every trip into Germany. Only when the lights of the target could be seen would the ceremony begin. The two gunners, Snowy and Jack, would start it off. 'Have you got the hat on, Titch?'

'Yes, rear gunner,' the pilot would reply. 'The hat is now on.' It must have looked ludicrous: a pilot in flying gear and helmet, atop which sat a battered bowler hat while flak and searchlights erupted around him. But it gave them all just a little something extra to cling to. 'He looked rather ridiculous,' says Jeff, 'but we all felt a little bit safer.'

In newspaper articles over the years, the story of 'Jasper's Hat' has been retold, and the surviving members of the crew have been asked many times to bring out the tale. Today, the hat itself resides somewhere deep within the bowels of the Australian War Memorial in Canberra. One day, perhaps it will be on show, a testament to the dangers and eccentricities of the bomber war over Europe.

One trip to Hanau was spent in a particular state of tension. Petrol from one of the wing tanks leaked and the entire aircraft reeked of fuel. One spark in the wrong place could have turned the aircraft into an inferno. It was too risky even to drop the bombs and the aircraft had no choice but to risk landing with a full load.

Only once, on a trip to Hamburg, was Jeff's aircraft attacked by a German fighter. 'I had an upset stomach and had gone back to sit on the Elsan toilet at the rear of the aircraft just as a jet fighter attacked,' he says. At 25 000 feet, while his trousers were down, the aircraft went into a corkscrew, throwing Jeff, his bare bottom and most of the contents of the pan into the air. As the Lancaster manoeuvred, he was thrown hard back onto the bare metal seat, sticking to it like the inside of a freezer. 'If I ever get out of this I'll never be scared of anything again,' he said to himself, leaving a fair amount of skin behind on the seat. 'I laughed about it, but only later,' he says. It was very nearly a most ignominious end.

One trip he remembers particularly well is the Anzac Day visit to Hitler's home at Berchtesgarten in the Bavarian Alps – 25 April 1945. 'I looked out and could see all these aircraft – black spots all flying in one direction against the solid white clouds,' he says. Amazingly, just as the force of over 300 bombers reached the difficult mountain target of Hitler's chalet and the local SS barracks, the clouds parted. 'I looked down at the barracks and could see tiny ant-like figures running everywhere before the bombs started hitting.'

At war's end, he was flying still, this time dropping not bombs but supplies to the starving populations of Europe on 'Manna' raids, as well as bringing home some of the many thousands of prisoners of war, some of whom – emaciated and exhausted – had been in captivity for four years. 'They cried as we came over the white cliffs of Dover,' remembers Jeff.

One of the most memorable stories Jeff told me occurred on the Berchtesgarten raid not to himself but to his good friend, 'Lofty' Payne, whose Lancaster had taken several direct flak hits approaching the target and was the last to bomb. Despite the plane's severely damaged wing, fuselage, engine and bomb doors, he continued the run to the target. The outer engines then caught fire and the aircraft began to lose height. Payne ordered the crew to bale out, as he intended to do himself.

For the rear gunner however, it was not so easy. His parachute was stowed back inside the fuselage and he needed to access it, clip it on and exit via the rear door. On this occasion, in his excitement, he grabbed it not by the handle but the ripcord, and the whole thing burst open inside the aircraft. Gathering it up as best he could, he made his way forward through the riddled fuselage. 'This is all I've got,' he said to the pilot who was himself preparing to bale out. Payne looked at the forlorn young man clutching his pathetic bundle of white silk. 'Okay. Well, take a seat and we'll see if we can bring her down'. And he did. The rear gunner resumed his seat and the pilot brought the aircraft down for a miraculous crash-landing on the shores of Lake Constance.

'Worth a medal I think. But he didn't get one.' I think they all deserved one, at the very least.

ALISTAIR SMITH
Flight Engineer, RAF

'Right, now dig in. They're wholemeal, and the funny ones there are ryebread.' Thus I was welcomed into the home of Jean and Alistair Smith – a groaning plate of cakes and sandwiches set in front of me and a teapot the size of my head that was never allowed to run dry. I had come to talk to Alistair, because he was the only bloke I had met who had filled the very specialised and rather tricky role of Flight Engineer, perhaps the greatest unsung heroes of Bomber Command. Hardly any Australians were trained as flight engineers, so I had to rely on the goodwill of an immigrant from the British Isles. But in reality, I could have interviewed both him and his remarkable wife, for she also had served in the wartime RAF as a WAAF. They were quite the double act.

Alistair, in his eighties, though you'd never know it to look at him, speaks with one of those wonderful, ancient-sounding accents, so soft as to be almost undetectable yet redolent of faraway places. Alistair comes from the Isle of Lewis, in the Outer Hebrides of Scotland, and his is no typical brogue, but gentle, an accent probably unchanged in 500 years. I half expected him to break into Gaelic at any moment. His wife Jean, on the other hand, grew up twenty miles from London and her voice boomed in comparison. Strangely they complemented each other perfectly.

'He took me up there before we were married to be vetted by the family,' says Jean. 'They were all so softly spoken. I felt like a bull in a china shop!' Lucky for Alistair, she got the nod and they've been together ever since. Having seen the horror of the trenches, Jean's parents, as well as her aunt, swore off having children to be 'cannon-fodder for the government'.

'Me and my cousin were mistakes!' she laughs. And when the time came, Jean was as keen as any male to don a uniform. 'I would have loved to have been somewhere where I could have had a rifle and a bayonet!' she says, but had to content herself with being secretary to the chief instructor at No. 27 Operational Training Unit at Lichfield in Staffordshire. Not that this closeted her from the awfulness of war.

'There was a form called Category E,' she says: paperwork that needed to be completed after an aircraft crashed with no survivors. One night she listened to a Wellington circling the airfield, obviously in trouble. 'They were still under training and we watched from the flying control tower. Eventually it came in and bounced, crashed, started burning then skidded towards us.' Frozen with their faces to the window, Jean and some other WAAFs watched helplessly. 'We were just mesmerised by this flaming, smoking thing. Then we heard the screaming, and then the smell. Later I saw them taking the bodies out. It was just horrible.' Training accidents in the wartime RAF were common. 'After a few weeks I got hardened to it,' she says.

One of her jobs was handing out the maps and sweets and other comforts to the airmen as they prepared to depart, primarily on training flights, but occasionally on raids, such as the first '1000 bomber' attack on Cologne, at the end of May 1942.

The crews in their flight gear filed past Jean seated at a table. 'There was a young navigator we knew – a lovely boy with blond hair. As I handed him his map, he leaned over the desk and gave me a hug and a kiss. "This is just to say goodbye," he said. "I won't see you again."' 'What do you mean?' Jean asked. 'I know I won't be coming back.' 'He said it so casually,' says Jean – and he didn't. 'He'd had a premonition, you see.'

From beside the runway at take-off, Jean and the other WAAFs would see the big black bombers off, and she can still recall the pale young faces of the pilots who were waving from the cockpits as they lifted into the failing light. Soon, she would be married to one of them.

With no recruiting depot on his remote Scottish island, Alistair joined up in Inverness, agreeing to his father's plea to avoid any of the actual flying himself. 'Your mother would be terribly worried, you know,' Dad had said. Dutifully, Alistair became a mechanic, but quietly harboured ambitions to re-muster later as a pilot.

Happy enough as an engine fitter, Alistair never missed an opportunity to scrounge a trip in the air. One of them he will always remember. On a chilly day, a flight lieutenant he knew was preparing to take a Wellington up for an air test, and Alistair asked to go along. 'He was a nice chap,' he remembers, but he couldn't help noticing the small dog under the pilot's arm, who likewise seemed to be coming along for the ride. It didn't get off to a good start. As the Wellington thundered down the slushy, slippery runway in winter, a man on a bicycle suddenly appeared in front of them. 'The pilot swore like anything and we only just missed him,' says Alistair.

Once aloft, a hatch in the floor of the nose which had been left open began flapping in the wind. 'Go down and close it for me, will you?' asked the pilot. Alistair crawled down past the cockpit. Just as he put his hand on the hatch, the dog – 'a little fat thing' – appeared from nowhere and dashed straight through the open hole! Alistair just managed to get a hand on it, but for a while the mutt – not to mention a significant part of Alistair – dangled outside the aircraft. 'There wasn't much of him to grab hold of,' he says. 'I managed to get him in in the end but I nearly lost the little fellow.' The dog, one presumes, was not wearing a parachute.

At his OTU, Alistair befriended Norman Jackson, another mechanic who, among other things, introduced him to a particularly perky girl in a WAAF uniform one night at a dance. Jean fills in the rest.

'All us girls had parked ourselves on a table near the bar. Norman wandered over and introduced us to all these boys.'

'No, there was only *me* with him,' protests Alistair.

'*No*, there was somebody else,' says Jean.

'We were the only two that worked together.'

'Well there was somebody hanging around, then.'

'No, I think I was the only one there.'

I quietly reach for another cake and scoff some more tea, while they wrangle over the details of their courting days. Eventually they arrive at a compromise, the details of which escape me.

One day in early 1942 as Alistair and Norman worked on a Beaufighter engine, someone wandered over from the orderly room. 'There's a new trade out, and you people are eligible for it.'

Alistair remembers it well. 'Norman and I went straight in and put our names down,' he says.

The advent of the four-engine bomber meant an almost quadrupling of the aircraft's fuel and electrical systems, which needed to be monitored full time when in flight by a specialist, and so the highly technical position of Flight Engineer was created. They were mainly drawn from the ranks of ground crew, retrained for the job, and had to know the aircraft inside out. The flight engineer sat behind and to the right of the pilot, who he would assist in take-off by securing his hand on the throttles, and with some very basic straight-and-level flying training, he could sometimes assist in an emergency. His 'office' was a seat in front of a panel of dials and switches, all of which he would have to read like a book: oil temperature, oil pressure, coolant, ammeters, boost and so on, more than twenty gauges vital to the internal running of the aircraft. He also had to monitor the complicated fuel system. The Stirling had no fewer than fourteen separate fuel tanks which needed to be balanced and monitored for consumption. The engineer was always the last to join the crew at a Heavy Conversion Unit but, paradoxically, was often its oldest member. It was a job Alistair enjoyed. 'I liked to be always in front of the gauges because if we were hit, I wanted to be on top of things. And we were hit quite a bit,' he says.

For Alistair, the transition from ground crew to aircrew was a quick one: Birmingham to front a selection board, further training at St Athen in Wales, joining a crew at Stradishall Heavy Conversion Unit and, finally, posting to No. 90 Squadron, 3 Group, Bomber Command at Wratting Common, Cambridgeshire, flying Short Stirling heavy bombers.

His skipper was Colin Hodges – like Alistair, a sergeant. He was brilliant, says Alistair, but already with a chequered career after a court martial for what Alistair euphemistically describes as 'a low-flying incident'. With a little prodding, he elaborates. As an instructor in Tiger Moths, Hodges had apparently amused himself with a spot of pheasant-shooting from the back of the aeroplane with a shotgun! Unfortunately, the pheasants in question belonged to the estate of some influential toff or other, and the full wrath of military justice descended upon him. Despite this, Alistair freely acknowledges owing his life to Colin on more than one occasion.

The Stirling had the essence of a great aircraft, but was compromised from the start. It was in fact the RAF's first four-engine bomber and Short Brothers won the contract to produce it in the mid-1930s. They had already made a name for themselves for the manufacture of flying boats and initially proposed using the wings of their Sunderland on the new bomber. This, however, would bring the Stirling's wingspan to 110 feet, ever-so-slightly too wide for the doors of the standard RAF hangar. Eleven feet were therefore 'chopped off' the wingtips, upsetting its aerodynamics and condemning it to a lifetime of problems. It was wretched to handle when on the ground, difficult to get off it, and when it did, showed a reluctance to get up very high – 16500 feet was the Stirling's woefully inadequate ceiling, a full 7000 feet closer to the ground, in fact, than its contemporary, the Lancaster.

On take-off, the Stirling took so long to get itself into the air that they decided to jack up the undercarriage to increase the angle of incidence and improve the airflow over the wings. It worked, but made the nose sit a ludicrously high twenty-two feet off the ground, and its complicated, extended undercarriage was prone to collapse. It was also extremely difficult to steer with the rudder. 'We'd start on the right-hand side of the runway and invariably take off across the grass,' remembers Alistair. Accidents were frequent.

Once fully airborne, however, the Stirling was a lovely aeroplane: highly engineered and very manoeuvrable. 'We could even out-turn some of the fighters,' Alistair says. It was extremely robust and could absorb significant punishment, and its four sleeve-valve Bristol Hercules engines were also relatively quiet.

After just a couple of days orientation, the new crews were placed on the battle order and given some 'easy' mine-laying or 'gardening' trips. Designed to break the newcomers in gradually, laying sea mines was nevertheless highly dangerous work. The mines themselves were extremely sensitive – a jolt of more than 6G would automatically detonate them, so emergency landings with them still in the bomb bay were out of the question. When deployed in busy harbours and sea lanes, they had to be dropped at low speed and at no more than a frightening 1500 feet. 'One time we went all the way down the Bay of Biscay, and could see the lights of San Sebastian in Spain,' says Alistair. Other trips were not so benign. One night, Alistair's Stirling was one of three sent to mine Flushing Harbour in Holland. A mobile flak platform shot the other two into the sea. His aircraft returned alone.

Although he participated in a number of conventional bombing raids ('We hit some railway yards. You'd see whole carriages coming up in the air in the glare of the bomb bursts like toys,' he remembers), high losses led to the Stirling's eventual withdrawal from main-force attacks. But its strength and excellent low-level handling made it just the thing for night-time cloak-and-dagger business, supplying resistance organisations across occupied Europe.

Alistair and his skipper Colin liked flying low. Six hundred feet was the recommended height, but even this was sometimes too high to be safe. 'At six hundred, they could see you coming, but lower down you were on top of them before they realised,' he says. This is when the Stirling's robustness came into its own.

'They threw everything up at us,' he says. 'The bomb aimer even got hit with a rifle bullet.' He recalls it clearly. It had been a quiet night, and they were on their way back from Strasbourg. Approaching a hill, the pilot called upon the bomb aimer to assist with the rev controls. Alistair remembers them passing over some great Chateau in the moonlight. As the bomb aimer leaned over – bang – a lucky round, probably a lone pot shot from the ground, passed through the aircraft nose into the middle of the bomb aimer's seat and right through the bone in his arm. 'I bunged it up as best I could,' says Alistair. 'If he'd been sitting back he would have been killed.'

Even over-flying supposedly safe areas of open country could be dangerous, as the Germans employed mobile flak batteries, mounted on trucks that could hide and wait undetected. One night, on the way out to a rendezvous point on a map, Alistair watched as the ploughed fields and houses passed beneath him in the moonlight. 'I liked these low-levels,' he says. 'You felt you had a personal connection with the people you saw.' In a memory that borders on the surreal, he recalls seeing the door of a house opening and a woman 'in a long black dress' illuminated for an instant in the light of oil lamps before the image vanished into the darkness a moment later. It's stayed with him for more than sixty years.

Sometimes the only way to find the target was to pinpoint your way there in stages, and much of Alistair's time was spent looking out with a map in his hand, finding his way to a field in the corner of a wood at the foothills of the Alps. 'Fly up a road here, over a bridge there. It was often the only way to do it,' he recalls. He rarely knew what it was they were carrying, but at the appointed spot, he would watch for a signal from the ground and release the cargo from the bomb bay. Figures would then dash out into the moonlight below to collect the booty, the fuel with which they carried on their difficult and dangerous war. Once they were about to drop when all hell suddenly broke loose below. Gun flashes indicated the resistance had been surprised by the

Germans. 'We would have used our own guns on them, but in the dark we couldn't tell who was who,' he says. Helpless, the Stirling turned around and took its cargo back to England, a glumness pervading the trip home. 'That was a wasted drop,' he says, still a little bitter.

Sometimes, they would be required to drop high up in the Alps. Looking out the clear astrodome behind the cockpit, Alistair would watch as shining black walls of wet rock rose out of the darkness and passed by alarmingly close. In an aircraft with a poor ceiling, this was risky indeed, and needed all the skill of an excellent pilot. In that, Alistair was lucky. 'We had several Stirlings lost in those Alps,' he says.

Standing under the astrodome one night, he watched a long, white road with poplars on either side pass beneath him, as he listened to the sound of his skipper's breathing in the intercom. 'The pilot was the only one always on the intercom. If you could hear him breathing, you knew you were alright,' he says.

Suddenly, the blinding glare of a searchlight hit him, then up came the flak. The rear gunner began firing away with his four machine guns, and the pilot, to put the Germans off their aim, dropped even lower. 'We were actually beneath the tops of the trees,' says Alistair. 'I looked back and could see the road dust coming up from our slipstream.' On the tape, I can hear myself release an audible gasp.

Sparks began shooting off the wings and he knew the aircraft was taking hits from small-arms fire. He returned to the fuel gauges to monitor any leaks in the tanks when, as he puts it suddenly, and in the loudest voice I've heard him use, '*Wham!*'

'Something hit me on the chest and knocked me out. I didn't know where I was.' He found himself on the other side of the fuselage upside down between the radio racks. Looking back to where he had just been, something struck him as odd – the sight of the aircraft's spinning propellers. His mind clearing, he realised that in place of the panel of gauges he had just been reading was a vast hole in the side of the fuselage. From me, another gasp.

His knee hurt, and the buckle on his parachute harness was mangled, but otherwise he thought he was pretty much unhurt. Breathing, though, was very difficult, and this worried him. The radio operator was out cold, slumped over his wireless and covered in light shrapnel wounds – tiny jagged holes in his tunic, and his hand bleeding. Then the rear gunner called up, 'Fuel's pouring all over me!' Alistair looked out towards the wing. The flak had ripped through the leading edge and shattered one of the fuel tanks, and the contents were being sucked into the rear gunner's compartment.

The electrical instruments had gone, as had the compass and the gauges indicating how much fuel remained. In this state, they carried on to the target and dropped successfully, then returned home. It was the kind of thing that would often earn a pilot and his crew a decoration for bravery. They got nothing. Court-martialled pilots, it seems, whatever their courage, were ignored. Alistair couldn't care less. The plain old campaign medals, he says, mean far more to him anyway.

'Tell him about crashing with a full bomb load and petrol when three engines failed,' Jean calls out from the kitchen, no doubt preparing another feast. I blink a bit and look at him expectantly.

Their own aircraft had been borrowed one night by their flight commander who was promptly shot down, leaving them with the squadron spare – a kite with the appropriate designation of D-Dog. It was not a popular aeroplane. 'We'd flown to Kiel in this thing and had to feather the engines coming back. It was a horrible rogue of an aircraft; nobody wanted it,' says Alistair. Reps from the Bristol company even came down to look the engines over and sort them out, to no avail.

D-Dog, however, was what was available, and D-Dog was what they flew for several uneasy trips. Having just left the runway en route to a target on one of them, Alistair hit the switch to bring the electrically powered undercarriage up and . . . nothing. Probably just a fuse, he thought, and changed it over. It blew immediately. Feeling distinctly uneasy about all this, he checked the current: 'positive earth'. Somewhere in this lame duck of an aircraft was a short. He informed the skipper.

'What shall we do, engineer?' was the reply. 'Do we carry on or turn back?' The mission was in his hands. It was a moment, Alistair says, in which he felt himself grow up very quickly. Turning back would mean having to dump much of the fuel, as well as the valuable cargo of high explosives for the resistance. Alistair considered his reply. 'Well, if we can get the two gunners to wind up the wheels manually, Skip, we might be able to carry on.' The decision was made. They flew on into the night.

It took no fewer than 774 turns on each side to wind the wheels up. As Alistair watched the gunners sweat away on a long handle, he heard the pilot's urgent voice in his ears. 'Engineer, starboard outer's cut. Come up to the cockpit!' The evening was rapidly deteriorating. There was no question of carrying on to the target now. The pilot turned the aircraft around back towards the airfield for an emergency landing. Then, 'Starboard inner's cut – crash stations everyone!' He looked forward through the canopy. 'The nose was tilted straight down towards the ground. I remember seeing the aerodrome controller's caravan door wide open,' says Alistair. 'He must have heard us coming and run for cover!'

The faulty engines now decided to catch fire as 73 000 pounds of aircraft, explosives and 100-octane fuel crash-landed near a wood off the side of the runway and skidded along the ground. 'I remember earth coming up the stairs from the bomb aimer's compartment,' says Alistair. The burning wing sheared off as they scraped along, expecting oblivion at any moment. 'The sound was horrible – a twisting scraping noise,' he says, likening it to a recording of Cyclone Tracy he once heard in Darwin Museum – I've heard the same thing – a demented, shrieking whine. Incredibly, it remained in one piece – testament to this aeroplane's construction. Unhurt but slightly shocked, Alistair became aware of the rest of the crew filing past him through the escape door. 'Come on, Smithy!' shouted the rear gunner. They huddled in the trees and watched the aircraft smoulder a bit but there was no explosion.

Nor was there any subsequent enquiry as to why they had been made to fly an aircraft they had already reported as faulty. 'They gave us a check-up, a bottle of rum and seven days' leave,' says Alistair. At least they would never again have to fly D-Dog. It was written off, mourned by no one.

On one of the last trips of his tour, Alistair dropped dummy parachutists behind the German lines near Rouen on D-Day. Upon hitting the ground, a spike would detonate very noisy flashes and explosions to kid the Germans that these painted wooden midget soldiers were the real thing. As the cool, grey dawn broke on that momentous day, he skimmed low over endless lines of numbered ships, agog at the power spread out below. 'Are they all ours?' he said to himself. 'They can't be all ours.' But of course they were. As the momentous battles in Normandy and beyond got underway, Alistair's war drew to a close.

Late in the afternoon, I take my leave, thanking the quietly spoken Alistair and his vivacious wife for their time and hospitality. I drive away, no doubt leaving many newly dredged emotions to be dealt with in my wake. Heading home, my mind returns to a comment made by Jean on the doorstep, a comment that oddly seems to put some kind of perspective on those few brief but tumultuous years spent over the course of a long, shared life. 'Yes, they were exciting days,' she said, turning to her husband of more than six decades, 'weren't they, love?'

HEINZ (HENRY) HAMPEL
Pilot, Luftwaffe

It was a long, long time before Henry could talk about the war, even to his own family. Oddly enough, it took another ex-air force bloke to get him to open up, and then only by way of a sleight of hand. A couple of years ago, a mate of his persuaded Henry to come along to a local air force association meeting in the country town where he lived. It wasn't the thing he usually did, and he felt awkward among all these chummy ex-RAAF blokes who all seemed to know each other so well.

A guest speaker was a regular feature of these half-yearly get-togethers – usually a local retelling the same well-worn anecdotes most had heard many times before. More often than not it was the cue to duck out and get another beer or catch up with a mate by the bar. But tonight would be different. 'Tonight we have in our midst a very special person,' Henry's friend announced to the gathering. 'Someone who can tell it from the other side. I'd like to welcome as our guest this evening, pilot and former Leutnant of the German Luftwaffe, Mister Henry Hampel.' Stunned, but with no escape route in sight, Henry had no alternative but to walk awkwardly to the lectern, every eye in the room upon him. 'I . . . don't know if I have much to say,' he began hesitantly. Forty minutes later however, he found he indeed did have much to say, and to people who very much wanted to hear it. Throughout his impromptu talk about his five years in the Luftwaffe, the room stood still and the bar remained empty. Not bad for a bloke who had once been 'the enemy'.

His first instinct was to be angry at the host who'd thrown him so cruelly into the deep end, but, to his surprise, he'd so enjoyed the experience that all he could say was why hadn't he simply asked him?

'If I'd asked you, you would have said no,' replied the man with a grin. Henry couldn't argue with the logic of that one. He is German after all.

For Henry, it was the start of a minor flood of requests for talks and engagements from groups and clubs and individuals, all of whom wanted to hear first hand what it was like to fly and fight in Hitler's air force during World War II. For a while, it turned him into something of a local celebrity before health troubles, and the death of his beloved wife of fifty years, made him retire from the speakers' circuit for good. I, he was at pains to point out, would be his last audience.

'You're lucky to talk to me, I can tell you that,' said Henry, wagging a finger as we sat down in his lounge room.

'Oh, I know that, Henry,' I replied. 'I know that very well.' I thought I'd been lucky enough to find just one old German in Peter Mehrtens. Henry was a bonus I could hardly believe. Thanks to his twilight career as a speaker, though, word had gradually trickled out and found its way circuitously to me. When I spoke to him on the phone, he was a little more dubious at the idea than had been Peter, but my powers of persuasion must have been on form that day. Besides, there was no way I would take 'no' for an answer.

Henry sat across the room from me in a comfortable chair,

a walking stick laid across his knees, his left leg jigging a little, sizing up this stranger who had come into his home and was now setting up a tape recorder on a coffee table in front of him. 'What on earth is he going to ask me?' I could almost hear him thinking. I start off, as I do with all the men I speak to, by asking where he came from. I repeat some of the names back to him and try to show off a passable schoolboy German accent.

Henry is a little on the short side, which surprised me for a pilot, but even in old age he is healthy looking with a zest for life and an impressive head of thick white hair. His voice is loud and enthusiastic, his strong accent, like Peter's, corrupted by decades of exposure to the Australian vernacular. He doesn't mind swearing, laughs frequently and, in keeping with his beloved, adopted *Heimat*, particularly enjoys using the word 'mate', savouring the mish-mash of European and Australian vowels: 'Have another cup of tea, *ma-aiyyt.*'

'I spent five years in that bloody war,' he tells me. 'I had ten days off in the whole time – *ten days!*'

The town in which Henry was born – or Heinz, as he was known back then – doesn't exist anymore, or at least not as the same place. On 5 August 1945, courtesy of the Potsdam Conference – as well as the desire of Stalin to compound the misery of the German people by carving off a few hundred square kilometres of their country – the German city of Breslau became, overnight, the Polish city of Wroclaw. Not that Henry had any desire to return to it anyway – by 1945, the once elegant Silesian capital had been wrecked – flattened by the Red Army in a ghastly fourteen-week siege in one of the final battles of the war.

'My father was a member of the Party. I learned to fly gliders in the Hitler Youth,' he tells me upfront, a fact of which he is neither proud nor ashamed. 'It was what everyone was doing at the time,' he says. Henry says that he himself never joined the Nazi Party, despite his early sympathies. 'I had a stepmother who didn't like Hitler. Long before the war – I forget exactly when – she said to me, "That man will start a war." I was disgusted. I hated her for that. Later I came to know she was right.'

A few months before *that man's* war started, Henry was required to complete a form, nominating the service in which he would most prefer to serve the Fatherland. 'I just wrote underneath, "I would like to fly aeroplanes,"' he says. When required to elaborate he added, 'Because I already have a glider pilot's licence.'

Henry could almost taste the glamorous air force career stretching before him, and confidently awaited the arrival of the telegram congratulating him on his selection for pilot training. A telegram came alright, but instead of flying school, it ordered him to report to an anti-aircraft battery in Essen. Luftwaffe pilots, it seemed, were expected to conform to the Nazi image of the master race, and Henry fell short of the mark – a full two inches short. 'I thought, "Shit – that's finished it for me."'

Small in stature he may have been, but Henry was smart, and decided the quickest way upwards was to make himself indispensable to his seniors. Thus, he volunteered to be the battery's telephone exchange operator. This kept him out of the weather a bit, and was slightly more interesting than feeding shells into the muzzles of 88-millimetre guns. Still, it was hardly the way he'd envisaged spending the war.

Late one night, a single phone conversation changed everything. In December 1939, an important call came through from the Air Ministry in Berlin. 'Write this down,' said the official-sounding voice at the other end. As Henry wrote, he could barely keep hold of the pencil. 'Kannonier Heinz Hampel is immediately transferred to pilot training school in Bavaria . . .'

'Shit!' Henry blurted down the line.

There was an astonished silence at the other end. 'What did you say?' Henry spluttered an apology. 'Look,' the voice demanded, 'do you have a *Heinz Hampel* in your battery or not?'

'Yes, and you're talking to him,' replied Henry, and the ice was broken.

'You lucky bastard!' the man said.

Unknown to Henry, a rule had come in stating that all prospective pilots must first complete a glider course as part of their training. Someone had come across Henry's form, was prepared to overlook his modest stature and shove him to the head of the queue.

The Luftwaffe was nothing if not thorough. It was six months in the classroom before Henry even got his hands on an aircraft, a sturdy Jungmeister biplane, but once he did, he excelled. After lights out at ten, Henry would continue studying with a torch under the blankets in his barracks. Nine months later, it paid off as he stood to attention alongside a batch of similarly fresh-faced young airmen to receive the distinctive badge of the Luftwaffe pilot – a flying eagle clutching a swastika. 'I knew I was good,' he tells me. 'I passed all my exams well and I was a nut behind the stick!'

The sobering words from their instructor, however, tempered their enthusiasm. 'No matter what you've learned here,' he told the raw airmen on their departure, 'it's all going to be completely different when you get to the front. So don't get too pleased with yourselves!'

Henry begins the lengthy and at times rambling tale of his long war. Without a logbook, and given the fact that so much has remained locked up in his memory for so many years, the chronology is a little all over the place, a fact for which he apologises.

'I can tell you what happened, but it's like a big soup,' he explains. No problem, I say, tell it any way you want.

Initially trained up on fighters, Henry was sent to a Kampf-geschwader – a bomber squadron – near Honfleur on the newly conquered French Channel coast, flying the Junkers 88 twin-engine medium bomber, an aeroplane of which he remains particularly fond. 'I could do anything with that aircraft,' he tells me. The first thing he did do with it was fly to London and drop bombs on oil refineries along the Thames. 'That was the first time we had shit in our pants!' he says, laughing, although somewhat nervously.

He still talks affectionately of the Junkers 88, reminiscing about it as one would an old lover. Indeed, the speed and per-formance of this aeroplane made it one of the most versatile – and feared – in the Luftwaffe, and Henry flew it in several of its many incarnations. Despite being attacked during the Battle of Britain, he seems not to have been too concerned. 'We flew in Staffels of nine aircraft, each one protecting the other. I had quite a few holes in my aircraft, mainly from the Hurricanes. They weren't as good as the Spitfires, though,' he says.

Having been the victim of a life-long obsession with the Battle of Britain, I find this rare encounter with one its participants – particularly one from the other side – has me groggy with the pictures he is putting in my head. The various arms of the Luft-waffe were considerably more integrated than those of the RAF, and in a way that would have been impossible for a British pilot, Henry alternated between both bombers and fighters as the tactics of the campaign developed. But I begin to notice a certain cagi-ness creeping in when I ask him to elaborate on his time flying the twin-engine Messerschmitt 110 heavy fighter.

Successful over Poland and France, these 'destroyer' Messer-schmitts were themselves destroyed in spades by the more agile

Spitfires and Hurricanes in the sunny August skies above Kent. 'Like a bloody big truck in the air!' he says. 'You couldn't dance round with the 110 like you could with the 109!' But apart from that, I can't get Henry to give too much away.

'No comment,' he says abruptly when I try to push him. No matter. I decide to bide my time. He does, however, provide one particularly interesting anecdote. 'The RAF would talk to us on the radio,' he tells me. For some reason, I have always found the notion of combatants communicating with each other fascinating. There are indeed one or two accounts of pilots exchanging insults over the same radio frequency, and Henry tells me how the British would try to sap their morale by reading out the names and squadrons of those German airmen already shot down. They hardly needed to do so. The Luftwaffe's own lengthening list of losses was enervating enough.

One day over London, Henry's own luck ran out. Peppered by shrapnel from anti-aircraft guns near the coast, one motor in his Junkers 'just collapsed', as he puts it, and the other soon began spluttering. He trimmed the aircraft as best he could and headed out over the Channel, hoping to maintain height long enough to reach the French coast. 'I told the crew to check their life jackets and prepare to go in,' he says. He ditched as gently as he could. 'I was lucky,' he says. 'The shrapnel made only small holes.' The aircraft stayed afloat long enough for the crew to scramble out and into the water. Unbelievably, they weren't issued with a life raft, in contrast with the RAF who obsessed about such things and drilled their crews endlessly. Henry just shrugs his shoulders. 'Some of us were issued with them, some of us were not.' I suggest this might be a part of the Nazi doctrine of 'no surrender'. Henry thinks about that one for a moment, then laughs out loud once more.

Bobbing around in the English Channel, then picked up by a

German rescue launch, Henry was hauled aboard and given some whisky. 'As soon as I drank it, I felt fire going right through my body,' he says. He then became violently ill, found he couldn't move his right arm, and blacked out. Two of his crew of five didn't make it onto the boat and were never seen again. He tells me he feels responsible for their deaths to this day.

In hospital in Le Havre, a doctor told him that he was a lucky young man. 'Lucky?' said Henry indignantly, 'I can't move my arm.'

'You're lucky to *have* an arm,' said the doctor. Evidently, Henry's toughly constructed life jacket had softened the blow from a large chunk of English shrapnel which would otherwise have sliced through his bone below the shoulder. He was stitched up and allowed to recuperate for all of ten days. As he healed, his legs began to itch. 'I scratched and scratched, and started to pull out bits of metal,' he says. 'Some are still in there today.'

Although very much the weapon of a totalitarian state, with ruthless consequences meted out for cowardice and disobedience, the Luftwaffe – indeed the German armed forces in general – incorporated some curiously democratic aspects which contrasted with those of the British, and even the Americans. There was, for instance, far less class distinction between officers and men, who would often eat together in the same mess – a practice abhorred in the British Army. In some ways, too, the common soldier was accorded comparative respect, such as by not being required to ask for 'permission to speak' before expressing a cautious opinion in the field. Most German officers also went without batmen – still standard among their counterparts in the western Allied armies.

They had not, however, dispensed with all their arcane notions. As late as mid-1943, young German officer cadets were being instructed on such niceties as the correct way to drink a glass of champagne or how to hand a bouquet of flowers to a young lady. This, while their comrades endured the catastrophe of Stalingrad, perishing in their hundreds of thousands.

The German crews were, however, made to fly – virtually continuously in fact – until either wounded, captured or killed. The Luftwaffe even issued their pilots with a special brooch to commemorate the completion of two hundred missions. Such a figure was almost unthinkable in the RAF where, in Bomber Command, completing the obligatory thirty was hard enough. But in the short-range engagements of the Battle of Britain, where pilots would perform two or three sorties in a day, men such as Henry were proudly wearing their '200' brooches on the left breast of their blue-grey tunic in just a few months.

Once or twice a convoy of shiny black Mercedes-Benzes would arrive at the airfield and out would step Hermann Goering to hand out medals. 'What was he like?' I ask Henry. Peter Mehrtens likewise had had a close encounter with the Reichmarschall, and was less than flattering. Henry offers a contrasting, if slightly disturbing, assessment. 'Terrific,' he says, 'like a *ma-aiyte*,' and then, 'He was a big bloke, too.'

By successfully completing a great many air operations over Britain – including, again like Peter, the infamous night attack on Coventry; he still shudders to think of the intensity of the fires he saw that night – Henry soon gained for himself a reputation, a promotion to Leutnant and a telegram from his chum, Goering. He and his entire crew were duly summoned to the Reichministerie in Berlin. It could only be good news – a decoration. As he already wore the Iron Cross both First and Second Class, it had to be for one thing – the coveted Knight's Cross.

Standing to attention in an anteroom beside his crew as the obese, drug-addled Goering muttered platitudes about the

Fatherland, Henry watched proudly as each of his men was handed a small black box containing the Iron Cross. Then it was his turn. The big Nazi greeted Henry warmly, gripping his hand in one fat paw and handing him a box with the other. He could feel the Knight's Cross already hanging around his neck.

At last he lifted the lid to reveal – not the Knight's Cross at all – but possibly the gaudiest, least popular bauble in the obsessive pantheon of Nazi regalia, the *Deutsches Kreuz* – often referred to by its underwhelmed recipients as 'The Order of the Fried Egg'. The *Deutsches Kreuz* wasn't really a cross at all, and was steeped with none of the old Prussian pedigree so imbued into the traditions of the German army. It was a showy, blatantly political decoration, a splodge of metal – in gold or silver – surrounding a large ugly swastika. Some recipients not particularly enamoured of the Nazis hated wearing it and even found ways to lose it. Henry, despite being the first Luftwaffe pilot ever to receive it in gold, felt a rise of disappointment that he dared not show. The Knight's Cross would forever elude him.

Henry moved around a great deal throughout the war, flying about a dozen types of aircraft over England, Russia, the Mediterranean and even having a stint on convoy patrol flying Germany's only operational four-engine aircraft, the long-range Focke-Wulf 200 Condor. Flying deep out over the Atlantic, the throbbing drone of his engines came to be dreaded by the men in the ships far below, who, their location revealed, could expect a subsequent U-boat attack.

In late 1942, Henry did something he would forever tell other pilots never to do under any circumstances: he volunteered. Coming up to Christmas that year, word got out that an entire army had been cut off and surrounded in a pocket on a bend of the River Volga in southern Russia, and pilots with multi-engine experience were being asked to put their hands up to make supply flights. Although he didn't know it, Henry was about to fly into the infamous 'Kessel' of Stalingrad. Taking off from an aerodrome in Poland in a heavily laden Junkers 52 tri-motor transport, Henry swung the nose around to the southeast for the long flight into hell on earth.

Defeated, starving, and slowly freezing to death in the subzero temperatures, the Germans at Stalingrad already knew they had been left for dead, or would be taken prisoner by the Russians, which amounted to much the same thing. The last attempt to relieve them by land, 'Winter Sturm', had been blasted into the ice by the Russian armour weeks before. The only hope of succour for the 200 000-odd trapped men was by air.

'They were mad, the soldiers in Stalingrad, mad,' Henry tells me. 'They knew they were going to die in Russia.' The aerodrome, such as it was, was a patch of frozen steppe, constantly under fire from the Russian guns just a few hundred metres away. The first aircraft Henry flew in had its undercarriage shot out as soon as he had landed. He only managed to get out again by hitching a ride in another aircraft taking off. At least he was able to do so. For the soldiers in their ragged uniforms, hysterical with starvation and fear, it wasn't so easy. I ask him to tell me what he saw around him.

I suspect he hadn't intended to tell me about his time at Stalingrad, but having stumbled into it, he has no intention of sugar-coating the pill.

Henry looks far away for a while. 'I get very . . . sentimental about this,' he says, and the jolliness in his demeanour has vanished. In their desperation, he tells me, the men attempted to grab the freezing wings of the aircraft with their gloveless hands as Military Police shot them to keep them from swamping the planes.

'You see, we were already overloaded with wounded,' Henry says, perhaps feeling a need to atone. He took off, dodging fire both large and small. 'Later, when I landed, I could see pieces of their skin left behind on the metal,' he says. I look up, and he is in tears and apologising – I'm not sure why.

Volunteering on each occasion, Henry flew into the Stalingrad Kessel five times before the surrender, each one of the missions like a nightmare.

A welcome change in the dynamic comes from Lil, Henry's younger and elegant companion of the last few years, who comes and sits with us for a while. It gives Henry a chance to regroup as we sip tea. It's likely Lil just came to say hello but she stays longer, listening, I suspect, to the story of Henry's war in detail for the first time.

In contrast to his time in the snows of Russia, Henry continued his operational tour of the Third Reich with a short stint in support of the Italians in the Mediterranean. 'The bloody Italians were bloody useless!' he says loudly, perhaps having held it back for years. Coming over to the south of Italy with a squadron of Messerschmitt 110s, the crews were told of the dangers – not from the enemy, but from the local women! 'We were warned not to go near them,' he says. 'The mafia were very jealous about their sheilas, you see. We were told there was a knife behind every one of them!'

Henry bombed British and American airfields on Sicily and Malta. 'They had airfields in the mountains. They covered them with netting so we couldn't see, but we knew they were there. We dropped bombs right in front of the doors where they had the aircraft so they couldn't get them out!' He's quite proud of that one.

A call comes in from his district nurse, just checking up. Sitting listening to him, his animation rising again, his natural preoccupation with health contrasts with the frenetic descriptions of his youth.

Some things Henry talks about easily, while other information is harder to extract. I gradually glean that as well as being decorated for his work with bombers, he was an outstanding fighter pilot, particularly in Russia. Here, he again flew the 110 against the legendary Russian Sturmovik ground attack aircraft, of which a staggering 36000 were built – the Soviet factory workers rolling them out the factory doors often in bare, unpainted metal. These virtual flying tanks were heavy, powerful and full of armour plate – even on the undersurface of the wings. 'You had to know how to attack one,' says Henry. 'They were by no means easy to shoot down. From the wrong angle you just watched your bullets and cannon bounce off the sides. I attacked them from the top.' Here again, he becomes a little cagey.

Did he consider himself a good fighter pilot. 'Well, yes,' he says. 'I think so. I had bloody good eyes back then, you know.' 'So how many did you shoot down?' I'm in touchy territory here. He has already told me how much he hates being asked this question. 'The core of my fighting – well, that's my business and nobody else's,' he says. Then, almost inaudibly he mutters, 'Around sixty.'

I have met fighter pilots who have been credited with three or four kills, but sixty is astounding. Doing my best to conceal my amazement, I politely tell him it sounds like an extraordinary total. Upon reflection, however, I decide that it's really quite conceivable. There is, after all, no reason I can think of for Henry to make it up – he's already let me know a few things that wouldn't necessarily reflect well on him and which he could quite easily have concealed – and besides, the numbers of Soviet aircraft destroyed by the Luftwaffe against the often barely trained pilots of the Red

Air Force are incredible, running into the tens of thousands.

For the German fighter pilots, Russia was at times a shooting spree. Nearly eighty aces have been recorded with 100 kills or more: Wilhelm Lemke is accredited with 125; Rudolf Trenkel 138 – with ten kills in twelve days. Walter Nowotny was at 252 when his Messerschmitt jet fighter ploughed nose-first into the ground, and then there was the master of them all, the slightly built, almost girlish-looking Erich 'Bubi' Hartmann, the highest-scoring ace of any war and any nationality. This remarkable young man accounted for an astonishing 352 enemy aircraft, every one of them in Russia, and survived postwar imprisonment to eventually become part of the West German Air Force.

Next to these giants, Henry's sixty looks relatively modest.

It was always his wish to fly single-engine fighters. Goodness knows what his total would have been had they let him.

'The Russian pilots weren't trained like we were, you see,' he assures me. Henry met and spoke to a Russian fighter pilot after the war. 'He had thirty-three kills and was wearing the Hero of the Soviet Union. I didn't tell him what I'd been doing, or how many I had.'

I thought this might be an opportune time to try and get him to open up a little about his earlier exploits over England – how many Spitfire and Hurricane pilots similarly fell victim to his guns? But he is not to be fooled by my clunky efforts, and appeals to me instead.

'You know, I just can't tell you that. My son has asked me and I didn't tell him either. I'm in a different boat, you see. Those people are my friends now.' Feeling about the size of a matchbox, I promise myself not to push him again. 'And you know what,' he adds, 'no Australian has ever called me a Nazi.' One day, though, some Russians weren't so sure, and it nearly cost him his life.

At the end of a long war Henry found himself in Yugoslavia, scuttling his remaining Messerschmitts on an airfield far from home. It broke his heart to do so, but those were his orders. Despite the years of continual flying and combat, it was here, on the ground amid the chaos of a collapsing Europe that Henry Hampel had his closest brush with death.

He doesn't remember how long the war had been over but it can only have been a matter of days. Victorious, rampaging Russian soldiers were everywhere, taking what they liked, doing what they liked to whomever they chose.

In a small village, his war lost, his aircraft gone, an exhausted Henry lay under a farmer's cart. 'I must have fallen asleep,' he says, because he was startled by a swift kick to his leg. Peering out, he saw three sets of Russian army boots. 'Shit. Moscow here I come,' he thought. They were two young soldiers and an officer, all holding machine-pistols and staring at him in chilly silence. They dragged him to his feet and looked him up and down. They spoke to him in Russian. Acting as docile as he could, he nodded and smiled, barely understanding a word. Then he remembered the Luger pistol he had concealed in his trouser pocket. Henry knew that if the Russians searched him and found it, they would shoot him on the spot. 'It was the worst moment in my life,' he says today. 'After five fucking years fighting in this war, I was going to be shot right here or be put on a train and die in snow and ice in Russia,' he says.

For some reason, they did not search him. Instead Henry was led into a paddock, watched closely all the while by the Russians, who appeared to pay particular attention to his trousers. This triggered something in Henry. The trousers! A little earlier, fearing just such a reprisal against officers, he had changed into a pair of ordinary soldier's pants he found in an abandoned truck. He couldn't, though, find a tunic to match. So, instead of an airman disguising himself as a soldier, the Russians believed they had in their hands a soldier disguising himself as an airman. That he was disguising himself at all could mean only one thing: he was SS and therefore deserving of an instant death sentence. Sure enough, Henry picked out 'SS' in their conversation and knew he had to think fast.

'Kamerad, Kamerad!' he protested, gesticulating in pidgin Russian as they seemed to clutch their machine-pistols a little tighter. 'No SS! Pilota! Neminsky pilota!' He then undid his trousers to show them not the printed flash of the SS on the lining, but the standard German Army eagle. The Russians took it in, talked a bit more, then, says Henry, 'just turned around and walked off'.

Henry is now looking quite tired. He says quietly, 'I stood there in the paddock for a long time, just wondering what to do.'

Eventually, he wandered off, at one stage approaching another group of defeated Germans in uniform. Something, though, made him stop. He turned around and decided to make his own way back to Germany.

After an ordeal of many weeks spent dodging internment, scrounging food and grabbing lifts on anything moving westwards – as well as countless miles on foot – Henry found his way back through the turmoil of defeat to his home in Breslau. Like much of the rest of Europe, it had been flattened. Listlessly, he gravitated to a small village where, after a long time, he settled and met his wife, formed a small musical band and eventually rebuilt his life.

'When I came back from the war I was a different person,' he tells me. 'I didn't give a fuck about Russians or Americans or anyone and I let them know it. My wife said, "You'll finish up in Siberia if you carry on like that."' Instead, eight years later, they both ended up in a Victorian country town and never looked back.

Henry's war was a long one, told to me in an amazing series of anecdotes that weave in and out in fits and starts. In talking to me, he has shown bravery and much honesty and I indeed feel privileged to have been his last audience.

As I prepare to leave after many hours, Henry seems relieved of some of the burden of his memories and is again in good spirits. He tells me he has enjoyed himself and invites me to come back to talk some more. I promise to do so.

We emerge into a clear, cooling sky in his quiet street and a flight of yellow-tailed black cockatoos pass lazily overhead, squeaking like rusty door hinges.

For men like Henry, as well as Peter, there were, of course, no parades, nor should there have been. But neither have they had the sympathy and support of a grateful nation, or even that little comfort given to those other men whose experiences can be shared on days of reunion in pubs and clubs amid laughter and memory and tears. Like them, their youth was hurled into a cauldron of loss and destruction, but this legacy has been one dealt with entirely alone.

'You know, Michael,' Henry says, turning to me at his gate, 'some people tell funny stories about the war. I have no funny stories to tell. I've seen people falling out of planes when their parachute didn't work – desperately twisting and turning in the sky to try to make it open. Other things, too, that I can't tell you about – can't tell anyone about. I had ulcers from all the flying – vomiting all the time from the stress of it. I'm a soft bloke now, but I was a bastard in the war. Some people have said I should write a book about it all, but what I have seen and what I did, and saw others do, well, it would just make me cry.'

I can see the old blokes of the RAAF listening to him, mesmerised, and thinking how similar it had all been for them, and for all the young men caught up in the terrible storm.

MAX DURHAM
Pilot, RAAF

Some people age in both body and spirit, some in mind only, while others seem to escape the process altogether. Despite some lucid encounters with a wide variety of men of the World War II generation, there was always the inevitable gulf of years that yawned between us. But when I sat down and started speaking to Max Durham, I felt like I was in the company of a contemporary, and a pretty sharp one at that.

Max even remembers what they asked him on the form when he signed up, just to make sure he wasn't a complete dill: 'Captain Cook made three voyages of the Pacific. On which one was he killed?'

To join the air force, Max had made the trip into Melbourne from his home in Bacchus Marsh. He still lives there, in a house he built himself after the war. It's a lovely home, with some interesting works of art, and we sit looking out over his immaculate garden drinking tea and devouring (well, I devoured them) a packet of Mint Slices. 'That's where my crew and I used to have our reunions,' he says, indicating the lawn through the large window.

Initially, though, he was a little wary of me, and whatever it was I was up to. When I phoned him, we chatted cautiously for a while before he asked me one particularly pointed question: 'Tell me, where do you stand on the whole Dresden business?' I considered my answer carefully. 'Well, Max,' I began, 'I think the reasons for attacking Dresden are still murky at best' – at this point I heard a disapproving grunt – 'but blaming the airmen who took part – who were ordered to take part – I've always thought unfair, and even absurd.' That was good enough for him, and he agreed to my request for an interview.

I've often felt that many former Bomber Command men knew just what those young men returning from Vietnam in the early 1970s went through. Like them, they had felt bitterness and confusion when, having answered their country's call and headed overseas to war, they had returned to face often open hostility from their own community.

Even before the firebombing of Dresden, the tide of opinion regarding the area bombing of German cities had begun to turn, with many British politicians – particularly those from the incoming Atlee Labour government – keen to promote the idea that the nurturing of Bomber Command from its virtual incompetence at the start of the war to the terrible weapon of mass destruction into which it had evolved six years later was akin to the creation of a Frankenstein.

Numbers of deaths quoted from Dresden have been revised up and down over the decades. Depending on who you believe, between 60 000 and 160 000 people were killed in the raid and debate still rages fiercely as to why this relatively unindustrialised city, swollen with refugees, was chosen for a major attack twelve weeks before the end of the war. Was it really that important a communications centre? Was the Zeiss optical works a 'significant' military target? Was it all done simply to terrorise the German people, or to impress the Russians? These and other matters will no doubt be speculated on for another sixty years at least, but the facts are that it took just fifteen hours for over a thousand heavy bombers to wipe out Dresden's magnificent Baroque centre in a massive, manmade firestorm, along with countless treasures of Western art.

When news of the devastation started to filter out, a sourness began to pervade the upper echelons of Britain's fragile wartime coalition government. A planned Bomber Command campaign medal was cancelled, and a disgusted Air Chief Marshal Harris turned down a peerage in protest. Winston Churchill, one of area bombing's earliest and most slavering enthusiasts, began to turn against the whole idea, and in hushed tones, an unfamiliar term began to be uttered in the corridors of Whitehall: 'war crime'.

The airmen of Bomber Command themselves began to sense the turning of the worm. Having lost 55 000 of their number executing a policy once deemed vital to the defeat of Germany, it is understandable that some survivors might have felt a little bitter. 'Harris was virtually in disgrace,' says Max, 'and so were we.'

Whether Max was even on the Dresden raid remains to be seen. What is certain is that the young Max wanted to be a pilot. That, after all, was the reason he, along with 90 per cent of the 400 other inductees of 34 Course, Number 1 Initial Training School, had joined the air force in the first place. In late 1942, Max stood on the parade ground waiting for his name to be called out. 'The following will fall out to be trained as navigators,' announced the booming voice of the flight sergeant. He survived the first cut. 'The following will fall out to be trained as wireless operators.' He waited with bated breath for the Ds to go by, then with a quiet exhalation, knew at that moment he was to become a pilot. 'There were a lot of happy faces, and a lot of blokes just about crying,' he says.

Then it was down to Western Junction in Tasmania for Elementary Flying Training, where he went solo in seven hours and was assessed 'sound average'. Much of it depended on what kind of trainer you had. 'Some of them were brutal bastards who just abused you,' he says. 'I was lucky. I had a real gentleman.'

The thoroughness of Max's recollections extends to his logbook, in which he has preserved such intriguing memorabilia as a diagram of the fuel system of the Airspeed Oxford trainer, which he had to learn by heart.

'You were always frightened you were going to be scrubbed. Even though you were going to a war. Sounds silly, doesn't it?' he says. In fact, Max was very lucky not to have been scrubbed – for an indiscretion entirely of his own making.

'I came over and shot this place up,' he tells me, glancing out the window towards some fruit trees. Based just a few minutes flying time away at Point Cook, Max decided on a quick low-level home visit after a training flight one afternoon in his twin-engine Oxford. 'We lived up on the side of a hill back then. I came in and flew level with my own back door!' he tells me.

The fun stopped, however, when he caught sight of the air observer's post in the corner of the local reserve and a figure clearly looking up at him through a pair of binoculars. 'God help me, I'm caught,' thought Max. He needed to come up with something fast. Hightailing it back to Point Cook, he immediately put in a leave pass and quickly made his way home by road. There, he approached the same observation post he had seen from the air a few hours earlier, its occupant now nowhere to be seen. Inside, he found what he was looking for: the report slip, filled in with all the details of his afternoon's indiscretion – aircraft type, number, time etc., and tore it out of the book. 'I've still got it,' he says, laughing. 'I didn't hear anything more about it.' With the authorities none the wiser, Max received his wings on a rainy afternoon in July 1942.

To Sydney he went, then San Francisco, and across America to New York by train en route to Europe. 'The Americans were fascinated by us,' he says. 'They huddled in little groups and listened to us talking, saying, "They even talk American."' (I tell him I had a similar experience there five years ago.) Then on to Britain via the *Queen Mary* at thirty knots to avoid the U-boats and start his war in earnest.

Arthur Miller once said that you never really forget anything. Think hard, and you'll recall a piece of orange peel you once glanced at on the footpath twenty years ago. Talking to Max, I well believe it. I feel I could ask Max to tell me exactly what he was doing at any given hour of his wartime career. Sometimes he'll skip over seemingly uninteresting parts (though to me none of it is uninteresting) but I pull him up and ask him to elaborate further, even down to the meal he ate on the train travelling down the Clyde towards the south. Looking out the window, he and his pals saw bombed buildings for the first time, and there was silence among them. 'Suddenly we realised we weren't playing anymore,' he says.

At his Advanced Flying Unit, Max learned to fly in the completely alien conditions of the very crowded and often foggy British Isles. In the open spaces of Australia, one could pick up a feature sixty miles away on the horizon and simply head towards it. But here, amid the mist and rain, you sometimes couldn't even find the horizon, and every close-packed little village looked just like the next one.

Advancing to their Operational Training Unit, the men were told to sort themselves into crews. A redheaded wireless operator and a navigator approached Max and started chatting. The three men looked each other up and down. This fella might be a terrific bloke, but it was something else you looked for, something that made you think he'd be good to fly with, something you could rely on in a crisis. The wireless operator mentioned that a friend of his topped the gunnery course. At this, Max abandoned his reserve. 'Well, go and get him then!' His crew was born.

Max was posted to 115 Squadron, 3 Group, RAF, at Witchford, a mile and a half from the lovely cathedral town of Ely.

'Been to Ely?' he asks me, and I'm able to impress him with my recollections of a visit years ago, and the strenuous climb I made up to its unique Byzantine square tower. 'Yes. That was our homing beacon,' he says. The flat Cambridgeshire fen country was perfectly suited to flying, but in winter the wind cut like a knife. Witchford was a temporary wartime base, spread out with a mile between the accommodation, the mess and the ablution block. 'You didn't take too many showers there,' says Max, 'especially in winter.'

Max arrived as a newly commissioned Pilot Officer on 1 December 1944, assigned to B Flight, but was straightaway pulled out of it by an oddly rattled Flight Commander, who mumbled something about an administrative mistake. Later Max discovered the real reason: there had been Australians in B Flight previously, and not one of them had survived.

With only thirteen hours on Lancasters, Max had been told to expect a further few weeks' training. But just three days later, his name appeared on the battle order for his first, compulsory 'second dickie' trip, where a new pilot went along for the ride with a more experienced crew to get the taste of a real operation. 'I was wide-eyed,' he remembers. 'I didn't know what to expect.' The target was Mersberg. It was a daylight, and an eye-opener. In the run-up to the target, Max remembers just noise and chaos. 'We had a Canadian skipper. Over the target, the bomb aimer started screaming like a maniac, then someone else started to screech and

I thought, 'Oh my God, is *this* what operational flying is like?' All of a sudden in front of them appeared a huge yellow flash of flame and a ball of black smoke. 'That's an aircraft blowing up,' said the skipper over the intercom, dryly. It was quite an introduction. When he got back to Witchford, the rest of his crew were bursting with questions. 'What's it like?' they asked their skipper, who did his best to hide his shaken nerves. 'I just couldn't tell them,' he says.

Many of the men I speak to, particularly from the bomber crews, seem to feel a need to talk about the fear of operational flying, of quietly, day after day, facing the statistical probability of one's own violent death. The balance sheet was indeed formidable. Averaged over the six years of the war, out of every 100 Bomber Command aircrew, fifty-one were killed on operations, with just twenty-four surviving their tour without capture or injury. At various stages, these figures rose substantially.

For a pilot in charge of an aircraft, fear was a constant, dangerous and unstable element, like an extra, rogue member of the crew or a virus that had to be contained. What was it like for Max? 'Oh, you were scared, but you controlled it. You had to. I still can't explain the feeling,' he says. 'As skipper you just couldn't show fear or anxiety, otherwise it would spread.' Only once did he have to exert himself to calm a panicking crewmember. 'I just had to shut him up,' he says bluntly. He is still reluctant to tell me who it was, but his authority was obviously effective and nothing was mentioned later. 'I decided to keep strict procedure over the intercom. No first names, no idle chatter. I figured that if the crew weren't talking, the panic couldn't spread.'

Max and his crew operated mainly in daylight, their trips marked with distinctive green ink in the pages of his logbook. The German air force had been significantly diminished by the time Max began operations, with flak a greater menace than fighters. 'My mid-upper reckons he could see the 88-millimetre shells coming up at us,' he says. There were, however, exceptions, and one of them occurred on 12 December 1944 when 140 Lancasters of 3 Group attacked the Ruhrstahl Steelworks at Witten in the Ruhr Valley.

Max winds himself up slowly to tell the story.

'Yep, that was our fifth one,' he says, exhaling, as I pore over his logbook, picking out names and places. It was a daylight attack utilising an early form of airborne radar known as 'G-H'. This electronic 'blind bombing' device was used exclusively by 3 Group, and allowed a target to be hit through cloud. Those aircraft fitted with the device, G-H leaders, provided a visual cue for the others to bomb simultaneously, similar to the American practice. When the leader bombed, so did you.

On this day, a fighter escort of Spitfires and Mustangs picked up the bombers as they crossed into Germany, and scouted out twenty to thirty miles ahead. 'Generally, we wouldn't see much of them,' says Max. This time however, approaching the target, Max could make out a swarm of moving black specks through the windshield ahead of him. 'They just looked just like flies,' he says. 'Then I woke up to what it was – dogfights.' The German air force had decided to make a rare appearance.

'I was in formation on the port side of my G-H leader. The fighters were attacking the outside of the stream and so no one wanted to be there. Lancs were dodging around all over the place trying to move out of the way,' he says. He still doesn't quite know what happened, but looking out, he saw another Lancaster coming at him on his port side. 'I knew we were going to hit,' he says. 'I wanted to get away so I went down at the same time as he pulled up.' There was a terrible bang, a ghastly noise and vibration, and in an instant, the propeller of the other aircraft's outer starboard motor had sheared seven feet off the end of Max's wingtip. 'It was a bit close,' he says. I let out an expletive, and he chuckles a bit.

Max had no idea how much damage had been done but immediately ordered the bombs to be dropped. He then found he did not have full control over the aircraft. 'It took the wingtip off just short of the aileron, which was slightly jammed and restricted in its movement.' He had now to execute an extraordinary balancing act: being caught in the turbulent slipstreams of the aircraft ahead could throw his fragile Lancaster into an irretrievable spin, but dropping out of the formation to avoid them exposed him as a lame duck to the German fighters. He thought carefully, and reckoned that from side-on it would be hard to tell his aircraft was damaged. He elected to duck slightly below the stream, and move back into it if there was any sign of fighters. He just hoped that they didn't spot him from either above or below. The ruse worked, and he made it home.

Occasionally, dirty yellow trails of smoke zigzagged their way across the sky and Max witnessed the precursor to a new and terrible age of warfare as Germany's V2 rockets made their way to southern England to cause death and mayhem.

As 1944 closed, ushering in the last year of the war, Max and his crew were due for some leave. It was the custom for crews about to be rested not to be posted on operations the night before, so Max was surprised to see himself on the battle order to attack the railway yards at Vohwinkel in the industrial Ruhr, a tough target if ever there was one. His Flight Commander, Squadron Leader Mills, was apologetic. 'Look,' he said. 'I'm very sorry but we're short of crews and I have to put you on.' He offered to buy him a drink when they got back to make amends. It was a short, five-hour trip to Vohwinkel, but turned out to be anything but uneventful. Max was holed by flak – the only time, he says, he actually heard it above the roar of his four motors – collecting thirty shrapnel holes in his aircraft. A German night fighter, also the only one he encountered for the entire war, passed directly in front of him, and over the target he became coned in searchlights which he couldn't escape until, for some reason, they simply switched off. Then, with ten days' leave awaiting them on their return, they flew home.

The return was a melancholy one. 'We got back and looked up at the board. Squadron Leader Mills wasn't there,' says Max. Mills was the only casualty of the night. 'The Yanks shot him down,' says Max, and I can still hear the hurt in his voice. Friendly fire events were a frequent occurrence in the Allied forces between trigger-happy and confused armies, but I decide to reserve my judgement on this one until I can investigate further. Later, I find it confirmed in the squadron history. *'It is believed that Squadron Leader Anthony Mills (118465 RAFVR) and his aircraft (NG332 IL-D) was mistakenly shot down by gunfire, possibly from the US 184th AAA Gun Battalion who had been transferred to Namur and the Meuse river 10 days before. On 1st Jan. 1945 whilst returning from a raid on Vohwinkel, his aircraft crashed in Belgium, killing all on board,'* etc.

As he became experienced, it would be Max's turn to become a G-H leader himself, and on one of his later trips, he found himself leading a large attack on Münster in northern Germany. 'I had the Wing Commander formatting on *me*,' he remembers. It was, however, as he puts it, 'an abortion of a raid'. With his navigator watching the cathode ray tube of the G-H box, Max bombed on the given coordinates and returned to base, then turned in. The next morning he encountered his navigator in 'an extremely distressed state'. The target had apparently been missed and an enquiry had been going on all night. As the navigator in the lead aircraft, the finger was being pointed at him. After an exhausting investigation where calculations were reconstructed, and wind directions averaged and compensated for, it was discovered that Max's crew had been given the incorrect coordinates, and no amount of compensation would have brought the formation correctly onto the target. One squadron, however, the New Zealand No. 75, had seen the mistake visually, made an orbit, then bombed on their own. Suddenly exposed, and on their own, three of their Lancasters were shot down in the process.

Even though he was in no way to blame, I can see that this is something that's worried Max ever since. 'Three out of the one squadron. That's a big loss,' he says quietly. Perhaps, he says, if his bomb aimer had been in the nose rather than helping the navigator with the equipment, he may have seen the New Zealanders turn and alerted Max to follow them. But Max will never know, and puts it down to one of those imponderables of life and war.

Having completed his thirty, Max was awarded the DFC. Not that you'll ever see it adorn his chest. Out of respect for the many deserving airmen who remained unrewarded, he refuses to wear it. One of those is his friend Pat Kerrins, who I have already met.

It turns out Max was never on the Dresden raid, but he still feels for those who have had to bear the brunt of some of the ghastly decisions made in war. When it was all over, he returned to Bacchus Marsh where, ironically, he was confronted with the first dead person he had ever seen, his grandfather, lying peacefully in his coffin at home. He had also saved £1500, which built the house in which we are now sitting, watching the autumn sun set on his well-kept garden.

In 1977, Max went back to the peaceful Cambridgeshire countryside to see what was left of the old aerodrome at Witchford. There wasn't much to look at. The massive 2000-yard east-west main runway had long been pulled up, leaving only a ten-foot wide strip. Cattle now occupied the hangars. Just like any other curious tourist, Max hired a car.

'I drove along what was left of the runway until I hit a haystack. Felt a bit funny that, driving a hire car along the runway, after you used to fly off it.' I can but agree.

BARNEY BARNETT

Pilot, RAAF

For a boy from the west of Queensland whose father had been badly wounded on the Somme, who'd lost his mother and been brought up by an aunt, whose family Soldier Settlement block had succumbed to depression and drought, the idea of being paid to come down to the coast, carry a rifle and learn how to be a soldier sounded something akin to paradise. So, for the first year of the war, Barney Barnett was a soldier in the militia, and could well have ended up slogging through the mud of New Guinea. It wasn't until an air force recruiting train chuffed its way into his home town of Richmond in late 1940 that young Barney got the first, exhilarating sense of his future. He stepped aboard, put his name on the line and began a new life that would see him become a fighter pilot, and lead him to one of the most astonishing adventures of survival I have ever heard.

My meeting with Barney had been a long and very pleasant time coming. Driving down his street looking for his house just behind Eagle Farm Racecourse in Brisbane, I was hoping I would soon be ushered inside one of these wonderful timber 'Queenslander' homes that I, from southern climes, find so exotic.

I forget how many scraps of paper, phone calls and messages

from interested parties measured out the stepping-stones of separation between us, but when I called up Barney out of the blue one afternoon from Melbourne to talk about his past, it hardly mattered. Barney is the truest of gentlemen, a kind of Australian version of an Old Southern Gent (minus the awkward overtones of slavery), and said he would be delighted to meet me, whenever I could find the time.

Half a continent away as I was, I pledged to visit him soon, but for something to go on with, he sent me down a small library of interesting material. Weeks later, as I drove down his street on a sweltering day, it formed a pile on the back seat of my car, and I felt a strange sense of completion in the knowledge that I would soon be returning it to its source.

First though, I had to find his house. It was one of those streets where the numbers bore no correlation from one side to the other, and seemed to start again halfway down. I called him on my mobile and became even more confused. Perhaps he could just come outside and wave me in?

I waited a couple of minutes with the engine running. A group of kids began to eye me dirtily. Then . . . yes, way down the other end, the strange sight of a tall and stately elderly figure, standing right in the middle of the road, quite still. He saw me but didn't wave – I guess he figured I'd work it out for myself.

I smiled at a small child who immediately bolted off, and coasted a few hundred metres down the street. Barney's house was as much like a Queenslander as I was. No big rustic tree-trunk timbers here, but a large postwar blond-brick and curved glass wedding-cake – the predominant style in fact, in the suburb where I reside, 1700 kilometres away.

With typical southern – well, northern – hospitality, I am ushered in to the cool interior where lunch has been prepared, at which I am the guest of honour. I almost expect a mint julep to be placed in my hand, but the glass of crisp white is welcome – if dangerous – enough.

Barney and his wife Peg are a testament to the noble institution of marriage, and they speak to each other with a delightful affection that has endured for well over half a century. She has prepared for me a wonderful lunch – a rich tuna and rice concoction. I make no effort to resists seconds, then thirds, then to my horror another bottle appears, the first having been already demolished, seemingly in minutes.

The conversation is warm and engaging, and soon I am so relaxed I am talking about all sorts of things, and start to think about heading over to the couch for a snooze. I'm sure they wouldn't have minded if I had done so, but no, Barney and I have work to do, and I need to get a grip.

'I still remember one of my instructors,' Barney tells me, after some very hot tea has been drunk, and some very cold water applied to my face. We are seated on an old lounge suite at one end of a large rectangular room overlooking a garden. It is filled with all manner of things – desks and shelves piled with projects and memorabilia (one object in particular has caught my eye) – and lined floor to ceiling on all sides with books. 'His name was Campbell,' he continues. 'He's still a horror to me.' Campbell was a screamer – the worst kind of instructor a raw pilot could have. They usually formed two types: superannuated civilian instructors hauled out of retirement and collapsing under the stress, or frustrated combat pilots seething with rage and venting on their hapless pupils. Either way, Barney can still hear his tormentor's near-hysterical voice as he practised landings on the little grass runway at Sydney's Mascot aerodrome. 'There's the ground, you fool! You'll never make it! Jeez, give me the bloody stick!' etc.

'I had a terrible time,' says Barney.

Still, he made it – first to selection for single-engine pilot training and then all the way to Canada. Here in their bright yellow Harvard trainers, the young pilots delighted in sallying over the border to Buffalo, New Jersey, and buzzing the P-39 Airacobras as they rolled out of the Bell factory.

'They must have absolutely hated us,' Barney says. 'But gee it was fun.'

In a large convoy, the threat of U-boats ever present, Barney headed off across the Atlantic, experiencing a storm so fierce that ships close by disappeared from view between grey walls of water.

Disembarking at Liverpool, he trained it down to Bournemouth on the south coast, experiencing a sense of disbelief at just where he was, and why. 'I'd spent years in western Queensland, then in suburban Sydney. Now here I was on a train in England. It was quiet unreal,' he says.

Barney was sent to Annan, on the banks of the Solway Firth in the rugged southwest of Scotland, to learn to fly the Hurricane fighter. 'I'm still nostalgic about Hurricanes,' he tells me, as is everyone who had the pleasure of flying this wonderful machine. 'Kindly' is the word he uses, a true pilot's aeroplane – responsive, fast and forgiving. Here he experienced several idyllic months in training, flying low over the ancient face of Britain, discovering the castles and ancient monuments he had read about in his boyhood. 'All historic places were in italics on the flying map,' he says. 'I picked out castles with moats and flew along Hadrian's Wall – still so clear stretching out across the countryside.'

At last, trained up and ready to enter the European air war, Barney received his posting – to South-East Asia. His anguished diary entry – 'How stupid can they be?' – captures his impotent railing at the vagaries of military logic.

A few weeks later, he was once again aboard ship, heading back almost to where he had started his long journey. Instead of fighting the Germans in the cool climates of France and Britain where he had trained, Barney would face the Japanese in the sweltering heat of India and Burma.

No. 136 Squadron was formed in England early in the war, but was quickly sent out to help protect the Empire's far-flung Indian jewel from the Japanese attacking from Burma. At first they went to Rangoon, then had to hightail it back to Calcutta when the Japanese overran the Burmese capital in early 1942.

By the time Barney caught up with them in November, No. 136 Squadron was operating from what was then, and remains today, Calcutta's main airport, Dum Dum. 'Heard of Dum Dum bullets?' he asks me. 'That's where they come from.' Barney, I am discovering, loves a digression, and our tangential conversation takes us on all sorts of fascinating if unrelated journeys: paintings, shooting buffalo from a moving jeep, and parking his Hurricane in the protective bays of the local HMV factory, from where he purchased a portable gramophone player and some seventy-eight records, one of which – 'a lovely Glenn Miller 10-inch' – he can't wait to play me. But I'm a hard taskmaster, and with one eye on the clock, I corral him back to the task at hand.

The Burma campaign was a bloody, murky affair, full of heroism and brutality, now all but forgotten. It has been dubbed the Longest War, Lost War or even Forgotten War, and began with a catastrophic thousand-mile rout – the longest retreat in the long history of the British Army – a disaster, however, later forged into stunning victory by a publicity-shy travelling salesman's son who had once worked as a schoolteacher to pay his way through military college. Though barely remembered today, William Slim arguably ranks as the finest Allied general of the war.

It was fought in sickening heat and blinding monsoons over an ocean of jungle criss-crossed with rivers, deep gorges and dustbowls – the kind of war to throw up bizarre figures, such as the bearded, religiously deranged General Orde Wingate, who led his 'Chindit' guerrillas behind the Japanese lines with the messianic zeal of a crusade.

Disease and starvation took a higher toll of men than the fighting, which was always savage and usually at close quarters. At one outpost on the India–Burma border, Kohima, the fighting was so close that bodies from both sides lay in piles at either end of the District Commissioner's neatly manicured tennis court.

By year's end, No. 136 Squadron had been moved closer to the fighting, to the port city of Chittagong, in present-day Bangladesh, launching their Hurricanes off rough strips flattened out between rice paddies. 'The dust was so thick we couldn't see,' says Barney. 'Formation take-offs had to be abandoned.'

Almost as soon as he arrived, Barney encountered the Japanese air force, in the form of one of its finest aircraft, the nimble, amazingly manoeuvrable and aptly named Nakajimi-43 'Peregrine Falcon' Hayabusa – but to the Allies simply 'Oscar'.

'We were scrambled against 18 Betty bombers attacking the docks,' says Barney of his first engagement. In squadron strength, the Hurricanes took off and were 'vectored' by the ground controller away from the battle area to gain height. 'Buster! Buster!' was the coded call that rang in the pilots' ears – *get high, and fast*. Then, hopefully with the sun behind them, they steered back towards the fray until, 'Tally-ho!', the Flight Commander sighted the enemy and took over.

'I was flying number two to a Welshman,' says Barney. 'The first thing I was aware of were fighters coming in very fast behind me.' Calling out that they were under attack, Barney took evasive action and put the Hurricane down into a spin. 'They didn't follow me, but when I recovered, I could see the Jap bombers heading south.' Endeavouring to catch up with them, Barney was attacked again. 'I was pushing the aircraft too hard and my radiator temperature had gone off the clock. This chap ran absolute rings around me,' he says of the experienced Japanese pilot who performed virtual aerobatics around Barney's comparatively heavy Hurricane. Tough and robust, it was nonetheless no match for the lightweight Oscar in a dogfight, and the pilots had agreed not to be so foolish as to try and take one on. 'I woke up to the fact that I wasn't winning,' says Barney drolly. In such cases, the prescribed method of breaking off was the 'everything in one corner' technique – 'stick, rudder, the lot.' Over and down went Barney and the lightweight Oscar was unable to follow. 'It was all pretty sproggish,' he says of his first, rather scrappy engagement. 'None of us had done any of this before.'

Parked back in the blast-pen at Chittagong, Barney walked around his Hurricane and counted 75 bullet holes. It was quite a debut.

From their base on the outskirts of the large port city, Barney flew at low level down the Arakan Peninsula to the battle area, and back again. A landmark close to home was a rusting Bren carrier that was slowly sinking into the sand – the site of an earlier VC-winning skirmish. Passing it one day as usual over a white ribbon of beach, Barney noticed his rear-view mirror was slightly askew. Reaching up to adjust it, he was confronted with the image of a prop spinner and a large radial engine immediately behind him – an Oscar had snuck up unnoticed. Barney put the aircraft down, almost to the water level, hitting his rudder bar left and right to give the pursuing pilot the impression he was yawing sideways rather than moving forward. The ruse worked. 'I flew as I'd never flown before. We had recently lost two fellows in that area that we thought were safe back over our lines,' he says. 'And I was nearly another one. The only reason I even saw him was because I was adjusting the mirror.'

One hot tropical summer morning in February 1943, Barney was flying top cover to a group of Blenheim bombers attacking Akyab Island, the Japanese main coastal base above Rangoon. The effectiveness of the Blenheim's jungle camouflage was such that to see them, Barney had to fly uncomfortably close, at a low 8000 feet. 'That's terribly dangerous. You really wanted to be at eighteen,' he says.

In the long list of virtues ascribed to the Hawker Hurricane, its radio set is notably absent. Pilots had been cursing the notoriously unreliable monoband TR9D ever since the Battle of Britain, when it was said to be good for little more than picking up dance music on the BBC. Barney's set was always intermittent, but this day it wasn't working at all. Had it been, he would have heard his fellow pilots call out the warnings of the Japanese 'bandits' they had just sighted closing from above.

As it was, the first thing he knew about them was a 'stench of explosives' and the inside of his cockpit disintegrating around him. 'My panel smashed and disappeared,' he says, 'the cockpit became filled with smoke, a gaping hole appeared in the emergency panel on my right, and the aircraft went into a violent spin.' In a daze, the thought occurred to him, 'This is the end of Barnett and his war.'

But it was also a moment of clarity, and his brain calmly reminded him of the pilot's maxim never to exit an aircraft on the outside of a spin. He unstrapped, and pushed himself out of the Hurricane.

'People have often asked me what it's like to bale out,' he says. 'I tell them it's like the drowning man and the straw. You're just so happy to have something to grab on to.' But his happiness faded somewhat as he floated down in the thick tropical sky, contemplating his Hurricane, now a burning wreck a few hundred yards offshore, and hearing the fading sounds of engines as his fellow pilots headed away to the north. 'People talk about being lonely, well, at that moment, I was lonely,' he says.

Barney came down in the mouth of the Mayu River, in sticky, swampy mangrove country. One of General Wingate's men, a Major Bernard Ferguson, describes the area as, 'nobody's country. Perhaps the Almighty never made up his mind whether his creatures should regard it as land or sea . . . the whole place buzzes with mosquitoes, crawls with crocodiles and stinks.' It was also in the hands of the Japanese.

'I'm not a dedicated Christian, but I do believe there is some supreme entity in charge of us,' Barney tells me earnestly. As the swampy water rushed up to meet him, he thought about how visible his parachute must be, as well as the very real prospect of being machine-gunned right there in his harness, and the unspeakable stories of brutality he had heard about Japanese treatment of prisoners. 'My chances were remote,' he says, always a master of the understatement.

He hit the water and nearly wrenched in half the little CO_2 bottle that inflated his Mae West life jacket and dinghy before remembering the pin that held it in place. Instantly it appeared around him, bright and conspicuous yellow. The shore a few hundred yards to his right, he knew, was occupied. What was less certain was what side the locals were on. Barney's own CO, Squadron Leader Ridler, had recently come down in these waters and been assisted back to safety by the inhabitants of the tiny Oyster Island. When the story got out, the Japanese beheaded all seventeen of them as punishment. Barney knew he could expect few favours, but he did have something of a plan.

If by some miracle he was not captured immediately and tortured to death, and if he could somehow evade capture long enough to make his way slowly upstream and cross the mile-wide river, there was a chance he could make contact with British or Indian forces he knew to be currently fighting their way down the Mayu Peninsula. Nor did Barney find the idea of the mangroves too intimidating. He was, after all, a Queenslander, and knew how much cover they could afford. He did, however, wish he'd put on his sturdy flying boots that morning. The thin, crepe-soled shoes he was wearing were useless, sucked off by the mud in two steps, and he was forced to face the agony of millions of tough mangrove shoots in bare feet.

He managed to hail down some 'diffident' natives in a canoe and, scuttling his dinghy, made it to shore. The natives soon left him and, climbing a tree to get his bearings, he consulted his almost useless 1:1 000 000 scale map and waited till nightfall. His route, he decided, would be north through the mangroves.

Barney has previously written his own fine account of his ordeal. '*I was reduced to moving in the mass of tidal waterways criss-crossing the mangrove-covered mud flats,*' he recorded. The black tropical night moved in quickly, black and incredibly still, his steps stirring up an eerie phosphorescence in the water that glowed as he moved through it, startling large fish which he could follow as they darted away. Above him, he gleaned some companionship from Orion's three-star belt, the same one he'd gazed on so many times as a kid at his farm in Queensland. It now seemed a world away. At one stage, as he rested under some mangroves, he was startled by a man's cough close by in the darkness, and the sounds of oars moving in rowlocks. 'About as far away as you're sitting from me right now,' he says, a boat glided past in the still water. It didn't sound like a native craft, he says. 'I'm quite sure they were

Japanese.' With only the light of the stars, they swished past him into the blackness.

He continued on into the next day, facing a strong current with waves sloshing over his head, was pushed back by the tide beyond where he'd started, and had to begin again.

I ask him if there was a moment he considered giving up. He shakes his head curiously, as if he's asked himself the same question countless times, but is still amazed by the answer. 'You know,' he says, 'I had this surge of confidence that I would survive. I prayed to cope. Not to get back to our lines – that seemed impossible – but just to cope.'

Another night came on, and again he came close to being discovered by natives hauling boatloads of supplies for the Japanese in the dark. He slept for a while in his buoyant, neck-supporting Mae West, and pushed on through the maze of creeks and mangroves in chest-high water, one clump to another. He was becoming exhausted, hungry and incredibly thirsty, and knew his energy was draining away.

At a point where the river seemed a little narrower, he made a dash for the far bank. The sun came up behind him, and he clambered ashore. Staggering on, he found not the paddy fields he had expected, but, in front of him, another expanse of water. The 'bank' had merely been a small unmarked island with another massive stretch of river beyond it. After recovering what strength he could, Barney pressed on.

This time he was spotted by some copper-skinned natives, foraging in what was left of rice paddies near the shore. 'They came out and carried me from the water,' he says. Risking cholera, he drank deeply from one of their water vessels and indicated he was 'British'. To his amazement, their sign language signalled that they regarded themselves likewise, and that there were more of them inland. Through the haze of exhaustion, Barney vaguely remembers being bathed, stripped and wrapped in a sarong before being carried by the entire tribe of forty across the Laungchu-ung River to the other side of the peninsula and into the arms of a forward unit of the 14th Indian Infantry Division. Grateful beyond words, he began distributing some damp 10-rupee notes to his saviours from the wallet he'd somehow managed to keep with him, and was too far gone to remonstrate with the suspicious Punjabi guard who began snatching them back and shooing the natives away.

'He didn't like the look of me either,' says Barney. Resembling God knows what in his sarong, he was blindfolded with his hands tied behind his back, put into a small boat and taken across another river, where, at the end of his incredible odyssey, he distinctly remembers the sound of a very English voice saying, 'That will be alright now, Subadar.' He was, as he says, 'back amongst my own'.

I have no idea how many times Barney has told the incredible story of his survival, but I suspect the wonderment at just how he managed it has barely faded over the years, and has perhaps even grown a little. There was certainly no hint of tedium or weariness in the telling of this momentous event in his life.

'It's beyond my understanding,' he tells me bravely. 'I'm not a brave fellow, or even a particularly adventurous one, but I believe I experienced my own personal miracle.' Barney later discovered that he met his saviours, a Punjabi regiment, at the southernmost extremity of their advance, and in a Japanese counterattack that crept over some seemingly impassable rivers, they were all but wiped out barely a week later.

Hospitalised for a few days, then a 20-mile walk and a trip by steamer later, Barney found his way back to the squadron at

Chittagong and began retrieving his possessions, which had already been distributed among his colleagues. Quite naturally, they had assumed he would no longer be needing them.

As he found out, he was just one of four casualties the afternoon he was shot down. It had not been a good day for the squadron. When he returned, he found morale at rock bottom.

In June, No. 136 Squadron was rested, and late in the year returned with Spitfire Vs. Barney flew again, was given a commission, and exacted a little revenge.

Scrambled one day, he flew number two to his squadron commander, 'a man unbelievable at playing jive on the piano, but not the most courageous of fighter pilots,' he says. It was not customary to break off from your number one, but Barney's CO quite clearly wanted nothing to do with the large formation of Japanese aircraft whirling around the target area, and hung back. Barney felt no such inhibitions. He went in and caught an Oscar from behind. 'From a smoke point of view, I got a good strike,' he says.

The CO played his part, though, and for the record confirmed Barney's kill. Still, he knows it was a lucky one. Even the Spitfire was outclassed by the manoeuvrability of the Japanese fighters. 'The traditional First World War dogfighting didn't enter our war at all,' he says. 'All we could do was just dive and shoot and climb – never stop. They could turn inside a Spitfire, easily.'

I glance up at the object suspended from a bookcase that has intrigued me since I sat down. It is the spade-shaped ring grip from the steering column of a Spitfire. I have seen one countless times in books but never handled the real thing. Barney indicates for me to reach up and grab it. It feels solid and heavy in my hands, still with the safety switch and brass gun button attached. I press it and it gives a solid, slightly exhilarating 'click'.

Barney seems to be cut from a different cloth to most of the former fighter pilots I have met and is far more thoughtful and reflective. Even in his late eighties, he's in terrific shape. Still tall, he uses neither stick, glasses nor hearing aid and is resolutely cheery.

He watches me playing with the relic with amusement. I ask him to show me how he held it when throwing his aircraft around the sultry skies of India and Burma, but he politely declines.

Perhaps, though, it sparks something in him, because in his final words to me, I see a glimpse of the young pilot, the kid from the sticks who had overcome a difficult start in life to become a fighter pilot and, then, flying the world's most magnificent aeroplanes, unable to believe his luck.

'There are two lovely things I remember in my war,' he tells me as we part. 'One of them was taking off. Especially in the Spitfire. The feeling of being pressed in the back and the world rushing by, gaining speed and imperceptibly lifting off the ground. Then playing among the big isolated clouds 25 000 feet up. It's a feeling out of this world,' he says.

I'm sure I'm getting just a fraction of this feeling gripping the control of his old Spitfire, the hairs on the back of my neck standing on end, but for me, it's enough.

IAN ROBINSON
Air Gunner, RAAF

I soon cottoned on to the fact that Ian Robinson is a funny bloke. Not in the joke-telling, thigh-slapping sense, but with that particular Australian dryness that has all but disappeared. I think I would have enjoyed hearing Ian talk about almost anything, but I was lucky enough to be treated to his amazing account of being a mid-upper gunner on heavy bombers in Europe during one of Bomber Command's grimmest periods.

This was very much an interview of two halves. I knew little more than the basics when I approached Ian, and the first part of our talk was laced with entertaining stories of bureaucratic foibles, bad luck and a healthy Australian disrespect for authority. But when I sat down with him in his living room, reading the titles of the books about organic gardening that lined the shelf, I had no inkling of the jaw-dropping tale of survival that he would deliver in the same matter-of-fact tone. That made it all the more poignant.

Ian, from Kew in Melbourne, wanted to be a pilot, wouldn't have minded being a navigator, was willing to consider a career as an air gunner, but there was absolutely no way he was going to be a wireless operator. Yet, that's the job the air force in their wisdom had in store for him. They were in for a fight.

In actual fact, Ian reckons he would have made a pretty good wireless op. His morse code was up to twenty-one words a minute, and he had a reasonable handle on the theory too. It's just that working a radio didn't happen to fit in with his plans. In 1942, with the Japanese in the war, wireless operators were in short supply everywhere, and were being sent to sit behind desks at ground stations all over Australia. Patriotic young nineteen-year-old though he was, Ian wanted to fly.

At Wireless Air Gunners School in Ballarat, the battle lines were drawn. 'There was another bloke there, Sonny Thomas. He was old – twenty-eight,' remembers Ian. Although too old to be a pilot, Sonny was as determined as Ian not to spend the war on the ground. Over a couple of beers, they concocted a plan.

After four months, they were both required to sit a three-hour radio theory exam. They both failed. 'We were brought before the Chief Ground Instructor. He gave us a burst on "England in her hour of need" and "bludgers like you" etc.' They were ordered to re-sit, and told in no uncertain terms that they were expected to pass. They nodded deferentially and left the room. 'I bet I can get less marks than you,' said Sonny to Ian a little later. 'You're on,' he replied, and waged ten bob on the result.

An hour into the exam, Ian got up and left. 'I handed in two sheets of foolscap with a bit of writing,' he says. Sonny stayed for the whole three hours and submitted no fewer than fifteen sheets, double-sided with writing and diagrams. 'I got 8 per cent, he got 4.' Sonny was ten shillings richer.

The two miscreants were again hauled before the furious instructor. 'You deliberately failed!' he thundered. 'What have you got to say for yourselves?'

'You're getting the message, aren't you, sir?' was Ian's laconic reply.

Their recalcitrance, it seems, eventually paid off. Both of them got their wish and were sent to the air gunnery school at Sale, although their victory was not as sweet as they had hoped. 'The whole thing was a complete disgrace,' says Ian. As he fired coloured rounds at a drogue from a Battle bomber, the instructors would assess the accuracy of Ian's shooting and mark it in his logbook. Some entries are indeed alarming: '200 rounds fired. Accuracy: nil.' 'Actually, nil wasn't bad,' he says. His logbook attests his unpreparedness for battle. After just three hours and ten minutes in the air, feeling he knew very little indeed, he was marked, 'qualified'.

Ian's relationship with the air force on the whole seems to have been a fractious one. Bad luck played its part, too. 'I'm a lucky sort of a bastard. If anything's going to happen, it will happen to me,' he says.

He'd lost both his paybook and his hat on the voyage over to Europe, and coming down the ramp of the liner *Queen Elizabeth* when disembarking in Scotland, the sling on his kitbag broke sending all his worldly belongings to the bottom of the Atlantic.

His 'complete bloody idiot' of a CO was less than cooperative. 'I asked him for a chit to be re-kitted out. He told me to get out of his sight. Useless bastard!' he mutters, still with a touch of vitriol. At least at his Operational Training Unit, he found sympathy with a more experienced officer. Inspecting Ian's logbook, he too was aghast at his lack of training. 'This is bloody disgraceful!' he remarked. Ian concurred. 'Is there anything I can do for you?' the officer asked sympathetically. 'Well, I'd like a hat,' he replied.

Ian's not the sort of bloke you want to get on the wrong side of.

The task of getting into the mid-upper turret of a four-engine bomber was a tricky one and, still in good health, Ian stands to give me a remarkable re-enactment of the procedure. Inside the aircraft, the gunner had to stand on the roof of the bomb bay underneath him, then put his left foot into the bottom of a small retractable step-ladder. A lunge was then required to grab the base of the turret and pull yourself into it from below. It was not an easy operation. His seat was a small padded board which clipped underneath his backside – after an eight-hour flight, it was extremely uncomfortable.

As likewise for the rear gunner, there was no room for a parachute inside the turret, and the mid-upper's was stowed on a rack on the fuselage. One night over Berlin, a seemingly innocuous decision would save his life.

Ian became the sole Australian in a Lancaster with No. 207 Squadron RAF based at Spilsby in Lincolnshire. His crew sound like a perfect cross-section of the English class system. Gordon Milton-Barrett, his skipper ('a superb pilot and a wonderful bloke'), was quite posh and somehow related to the Barretts of Wimpole Street. Once in training, Ian witnessed him standing up to a Wing Commander over a Wellington he thought unsafe to fly. 'Well, if you think it's so safe, sir, take the bloody thing up yourself,' he said. Looking on, Ian thought to himself, 'This bloke'll do me.'

He clashed initially with his bomb aimer who was 'a bit up himself' and to whom Ian was just a 'bloody colonial'. His rear gunner, whose heart never seemed to be in the job, came from a family who worked the estate of some aristocrat or other and who, as Ian puts it, was something of 'a shingle short'. Then there was the dour wireless operator from London who wore oversize footwear and who everyone referred to simply as 'boots'. It sounds like the cast of a typical British sit-com.

Ian's tour began right at the start of Bomber Command's bloodiest campaign, the so-called Battle of Berlin. Over the winter of 1943–44, bomber chief Arthur Harris was given a free hand to attack the 'big city' as he saw fit, famously declaring, 'It will cost us between four and five hundred aircraft. It will cost Germany the war.' He was wrong on both counts. After losing 1000 aircraft and having 7000 airmen killed, he failed to deliver the promised knock-out against Germany. It was a grim time. 'Your chances of getting back to Australia were not high,' says Ian. 'About one in fifty.'

And it was cold. Ian runs through what he had to wear to keep warm in his turret high in the dark winter sky: knee-length woollen underwear and woollen long johns worn under the standard battle-dress trousers, singlet, shirt, heavy woollen jumper, battledress, and covering this an electrically heated suit. Over all this was another canvas suit packed with buoyant kapok as there was no room for the standard Mae West life jacket. On his hands he wore four types of gloves: silk, chamois, electrically heated wool and leather. And still it didn't keep out the cold. Ian remembers experiencing an incredible minus 47 degrees, the sort of temperatures experienced by Antarctic explorers. At this point you can barely blink your eyes.

'How did you pee?' I ask. He laughs grimly and explains that once he had to urinate in his suit, which promptly short-circuited the whole thing. Just one glove on one hand remained warm. 'When we got back I couldn't move. Three blokes had to pull me out of the turret. They just put me down on the runway to thaw out. I had a few aches and pains after that, I can tell you.'

The mid-upper gunner's field of view required that he constantly patrol the sky rearwards from the trailing edge of the aircraft, wingtip to wingtip, looking down as far as he could see. He also needed to keep an eye on the front quarters as well. In my travels, I have spoken to a number of gunners, many of whom had experienced close encounters with flak but only the odd sighting of an enemy fighter. Ian came as close to them as you could get.

He saw fighters on his very first op, a trip across the Alps to Genoa where the Italians came up to have a look but (as was their wont) chose to leave it at that. Further encounters would not be so benign.

Most of Ian's flying was done at night where visibility was sometimes limited to a few dozen yards. 'At night, you wouldn't actually see a fighter until it was about halfway across the road from here,' he says, looking out into his quiet street. 'So you developed a sixth sense. You'd get a feeling about one spot, a feeling that something was out there, then look back, and sure enough, that's where something would be.'

On the way to Berlin one night, Ian watched one Lancaster flying past the other way with all four engines on fire. Three Junkers 88s were lined up behind him. 'I could see them firing into the rear of the fuselage and watched the cannon shells coming out the front,' he says.

One night a German followed him for forty minutes, sometimes so close that Ian could clearly see the pilot. 'The tracer of his cannon went whizzing just past my turret. One shell burst the hydraulics,' he says. 'I don't ever want to see fireworks again.'

Sometimes Ian would get hits on the attacking fighters but would try to aim for the vulnerable canopy. 'I'd see the bullets just bounce off,' he says. And fighters weren't his only worry.

Over the target on one particularly dark night, Ian's sixth sense made him look upwards, and into the gaping bomb bay of another Lancaster directly above, about to drop its bombs. 'Turn port!' he yelled down the intercom to the skipper. Nothing happened. Despite wiring made to endure constant extremes of temperature, intercom failure was common. He hit the failsafe – a button that illuminated a 'turn port/starboard' light on the pilot's dashboard. The aircraft skewed left, just as two incendiaries crashed into the starboard wing from above. Ian had seen the power of these fire-bombs demonstrated on the ground, burning through three-inch armour plate in seconds. 'They were just like a bloody great oxy torch,' he says. He waited for the phosphorous ignition, which would cut through the wing like butter, but incredibly, their fusing pins were held in by the very wing into which they had been embedded, and the bombs remained safe. Back on the ground, they were found to be wedged right between the petrol tanks. It would have been an inferno, but Ian was lucky. Luck, though, has a habit of running out.

Trip number sixteen – one of several he made to Berlin, Christmas Eve, 1943. Ian didn't have a good feeling about it from the start. They were in a replacement aircraft which they'd not had time to test properly. Take-off, set for 8 p.m., was delayed continually due to bad weather. By the time they were in the queue, it was nearly midnight. 'The crew,' says Ian, 'were in a state of acute nervous tension.' In the dark, the pilot, Milton-Barrett, misjudged a turn and put one of the Lancaster's wheels into the soft turf, bogging the aircraft and requiring it to be pulled out by a tanker, putting them further behind. 'I remember a distinct feeling of not wanting to go,' he says.

The ill omens continued. Breaking through cloud into the moonlight at around two thousand feet, Ian watched another Lancaster emerge close by on the port side. 'He was just hovering above the cloud when another aircraft came up through it directly underneath and hit him dead centre,' he says. The two aircraft, two full bomb loads and fourteen airmen were instantly obliterated in a huge mushroom cloud. 'It looked like an atom bomb.'

And then Berlin. 'We were never sure if they were Junkers 88s or Messerschmitt 410s,' says Ian. Whatever they were, there were three of them and they came at him line astern, just before they reached the target city. 'I could tell they were old hands. Two got either side of us, and the other right behind,' says Ian. 'Corkscrew starboard, go!' he said to the pilot. The Lancaster turned violently, evaded them, then straightened up and bombed. 'Just as we were beginning to think, "We've bloody well made it again", we got hit.' As Ian was facing forward, a burst of cannon shell ripped into his turret, exploding next to him, blowing the left-hand gun clean out of the aircraft and taking away half the perspex canopy as well. A piece of flak hit his arm. He shows me a scarred middle finger, the result of a phosphorous burn from the explosive round. 'This took four months to heal,' he says.

Shells then struck the starboard wing, taking off several feet of the tip and peeling back the metal skin like a sardine tin. The petrol tank then ignited, throwing out a river of burning fuel which trailed past the tail. Then a confusion of voices and sensations. 'Feather starboard inner!' Ian heard the skipper yell. 'It's not the motor, it's the bloody tank!' responded the engineer. 'The wing's going!' someone shouted. 'Righto. Abracadabra – jump, jump!' The code to abandon the aircraft. Ian sits telling me this like it happened yesterday.

Climbing down to the fuselage floor from his turret, he instinctively went to the rack to retrieve his parachute. It was gone. There was no chute, no rack, just a 'bloody great hole' where the fuselage had been – torn open by the German cannon burst. It was here that a simple, inexplicable act took on extraordinary dimensions. Before take-off, for this night, and this night only, Ian had for some reason chosen not to stow his parachute on the rack as normal, but to hang it on the lower rung of the small retractable stepladder under the turret, and here it still swung. He still doesn't know what made him do it.

Without time to ponder his good fortune, Ian was standing with the rear gunner, attaching his parachute, when they were attacked again by the night fighters. The forward fuselage was aflame. Shells tore through the tubes protecting the aircraft control cables, and like a lame bird, the big aircraft began to flop around uselessly in the sky. It lurched upwards, stalled, then dived, repeating the action and throwing everything inside about. 'We stalled and dived, stalled and dived,' says Ian.

The rear gunner was thrown into the fire. 'I never saw him again.' As the aircraft lurched downwards again, Ian climbed up the fuselage and hung onto the toilet with his legs swinging in the air. He somehow managed to reach the back door but it was jammed up with ice. He reached for the axe in the rack above the door, but it was missing, legacy of them not having had time to check their replacement aircraft. 'You've had it now, Robbie,' he thought to himself.

Then, the aircraft exploded.

He doesn't know how long he was out, but coming to, he realised he was no longer in the air, but lying on the ground. 'I could see the lines from my parachute stretched out, all burned up. My suit was smouldering,' he says. It was 4.30 in the morning. For a moment, the thought struck him that he had come down in England. His knee hurt and his boots were missing. Looking around, he saw he was on the edge of a pine forest. He went into it, hid what he could of his pack then fell unconscious again, 'I think for about two hours,' he says. At first light, he could hear voices, and the note of an unfamiliar aircraft engine passing low overhead. Then he became aware of the pain, and could raise himself only with the help of a stick. 'The voices were speaking German, and the aircraft was a Junkers 88 coming in to land at an aerodrome on the edge of the forest.'

I pause here, just to take in what he has just told me. I ask him to explain what he thinks happened, and he tells me in a quiet tone, as if in the third person. 'The aircraft blew up and I got blown out. Somehow my chute opened and I came down. You know as much about it as I do,' he says, with a sense of bewilderment that has endured sixty years.

At first light, and in bare feet, Ian followed a track around the perimeter of the aerodrome to the edge of a village. As he tried to read a sign, a policeman passed by on a bicycle and stopped. 'He didn't think it right that people should be wandering around in bare feet, so he picked me up.'

This moment marked the start of Ian's sixteen months in captivity. At this point he asks me a question, which I sense he has been wanting to ask me since we sat down. 'Your name,' he says cautiously. 'Is it German?' There's a slight coldness in the way he asks it, and when I tell him it derives from Scotland with origins in France, he seems relieved.

'I have certain . . . misgivings about Germans. I've overcome it to a certain degree, but I used to be quite neurotic about it,' he says, and proceeds to explain why.

The German policeman took him to a cafe in the village where a local crowd gathered, some clutching old shotguns. 'They all had coffee. I didn't get any.' A phone call was made, ending with a 'Heil Hitler!' Ian began to think that he was very much in the wrong place. A pistol was placed on a table next to him by someone hoping he would make a run for it, providing the excuse for the locals to use their shotguns. 'I declined the invitation,' he says.

Robbed of their satisfaction, they took Ian to a downstairs room at the local police station and made him sit on a small kitchen chair. Here, for what he remembers as a long period, 'a huge bastard belted the piss out of me'. He was a big man in a soldier's uniform and he bashed Ian continually until he passed out, breaking two of his teeth. Then he waited for him to revive, and bashed him again. And on it went.

Next morning, Boxing Day 1943, Ian was taken away by some Luftwaffe men in a small VW to Templehof aerodrome through the battered streets of Berlin. Ian remembers the road cleared through the mountains of rubble, just wide enough for a car. 'Seeing that pleased me at the time,' he says.

He was given a 'quite passable' stew with potatoes that he was in too much pain to eat and, to his amazement, reunited with his wireless operator, bomb aimer and flight engineer. With the exception of the rear gunner, all had managed safely to bale out of the aircraft before it exploded. Gordon, the pilot, was still on the run, but would not be for long. The emotion in the reunion must have been overwhelming. 'I just hung around their shoulders and they carried me everywhere,' he says.

As they sat on a train in Berlin's old Anhalter railway station on their way to prison camp, German guards protected them from civilians, who glared at them murderously. On the other side of the platform, Ian watched blinded and wounded civilians – some of them children – boarding a hospital train. Later, Ian heard that six aircrew who had baled out the same night as him were lynched on streetlamps. 'You can't really blame them, though,' he says with unexpected magnanimity. 'The Brits did the same to their blokes in London.'

An immaculately uniformed army officer managed to reach the carriage, and in true Teutonic style, slapped Ian about the face with his gloves while he hurled abuse. His navigator understood a little German and explained in subdued tones. The man's wife and daughter, it seemed, had been killed on their raid of a few days before. In addition, two of his sons had just become prisoners of the Russians – a virtual death sentence. 'You could see he wasn't too pleased with us,' says Ian.

The men were taken to the famous Dulag Luft transit camp for POW aircrew near Frankfurt, where Ian was interrogated for six days. He refused to divulge anything but the standard 'name, rank and serial number', was beaten again, had a cigarette butted out in his face and was hurled down a flight of stairs. Eventually, he was taken by cattle truck to Stalag 4B near Muhlberg. Here, he sat out the war until one day in 1945, a Russian tank showed up and ran over the perimeter fence, flattening it from one end to the other.

In his sixteen months in captivity, Ian experienced nearly being bombed by American Flying Fortresses by day and by his own RAF by night, observed a tank battle take place outside the camp, pilfered a Luger from a dead German soldier, went from thirteen stone to six and developed a life-long disdain for those of German extraction.

Except perhaps one. I ask him if there was any fraternisation at all between the prisoners and the guards in the camp, or whether all his jailers were as bad as each other. Only one man he remembers with any affection, and I am amazed when he tells me his name. 'Max Schmeling. Have you heard of him?'

Eight years before meeting Ian, the great German boxing star, Max Schmeling, beat Joe Louis for the international heavyweight boxing title and was touted a hero of the Nazi regime. Schmeling, however, refused to play along, resisting pressure to join the party and even insisting on keeping his Jewish coach. Decades later, it was revealed Schmeling had protected two Jewish children in his hotel room on Kristallnacht in 1938, later spiriting them away to America, a gesture which, hero or not, would have sent him to a concentration camp.

Hitler eventually soured on his hero, and sent him into the army where he became a paratrooper and was wounded on Crete in 1941. His later stint as a guard, a final ignominy, brought him into contact with Ian, who saw in him another side to the Germans.

'There was a Russian prisoner in the camp who was an Olympic weightlifter. I know that Schmeling used to smuggle extra rations in for him. He was the only one I'd pay as being decent,' he tells me.

I'm glad that we finish on this vaguely positive note. By the end of our long talk, Ian has regained some of his earlier, drier self. He tells me it took him quite a while to recover, especially from the beating he received on his first morning. 'Up until five years after the war, if I'd seen that bloke I think I would have killed him,' he says. It's good to know that time mellows some of the passions, if not the memories.

DAVID ROBERTS

Wireless Operator/Air Gunner, RAAF

'On the edge of the granite country' is where David Roberts hails from, courtesy of a soldier settlement block earned by his father who, as a trooper in Palestine in the 4th Australian Light Horse in 1917, was one of those gallant young Victorians who leaped over the heads of the astonished Turks cowering in their trenches, taking nearly a thousand prisoners as well as the town of Beersheba in the last successful cavalry charge in history. 'He didn't talk about it much,' says David. For my sake, I'm hoping it's a family tradition he has chosen not to uphold.

I know the 'granite country' of southwest Victoria. It's an odd place, lush and fertile but buffeted by winds from the Southern Ocean and dotted with volcanic lakes of a murky, opaque hue. For some reason my father insisted on taking us there on damp and miserable holidays. As a kid I'd go for long solitary walks among the boulders, spewed up aeons ago like marbles, thinking that this was a place where bad things had happened.

For far cheerier places, try Byron Bay in northern New South Wales, which is where I met David in his modern retirement unit on a warm, blustery afternoon. As a young man, he was dead keen to join the RAAF, but before flying aeroplanes, he had to be released from his job helping design them on the drawing boards at the Commonwealth Aircraft Corporation. As a seventeen-year-old junior draughtsman, David helped draw up the blueprints for the Wirraway and the Boomerang (a type he later had the satisfaction of witnessing in action), but made it clear to all and sundry that his intention was not to draw them but fly them. And come his eighteenth birthday, he was off to enlist. This is where his problems began.

'One day the boss came up to me. "I've heard you're intending to join up. Forget it. You're in a protected industry, son, there's no way you'll be released."

'Just watch me,' replied David. But it wasn't as easy as he had thought. 'I made noises, but it didn't do me any good,' he says. He began to think the only contribution he'd be making towards his family's military heritage was flying a desk. But as they say, it's not what you know but who. One day David spilt his woes to a visiting RAF liaison officer. 'I can always just disappear if they won't release me,' he said. The officer was sceptical. 'People have tried that,' he said. 'They just get dragged back. Why don't we go upstairs and have a chat to the boss?'

The 'boss' happened to be none other than Lawrence James Wackett – aviator, industrialist, swashbuckling hero of the Australian Flying Corps and now head of the CAC – just the kind of chap to help a keen youngster through the red tape to find his way to the action. 'Ah yes,' he said looking at David with a misty eye. 'That's just what I was like when I was your age. So, we'd better put a story together, hadn't we?' he added, no doubt with a great deal of winking.

It all worked brilliantly. Wackett oiled the wheels of bureaucracy and David joined the RAAF just after his eighteenth birthday, and was given the service number 431422. Things now moved quickly, and within a fortnight, he was on his way to basic training at Somers. After all, these were urgent times. The Japanese were in the war and aircrews were sorely needed.

He didn't make his dream of becoming a pilot and was selected instead to become the ears and eyes of the aircraft, the wireless operator/air gunner. At OTU at East Sale, the assembled mob of trainee pilots, navigators and 'WAGs' were told that they would be trained to fly the Bristol Beaufort, and by tomorrow, they were to have sorted themselves into fifty-six individual crews.

It was always a haphazard experience, as David says, 'trying to assess each others' capabilities purely on appearance and mannerisms', but his became a close crew. There was fellow gunner Fred Lewis from South Australia, and Lloyd Preece, another Victorian, who had trained as a pilot until his poor eyesight saw him scrubbed to navigator. At this task, however, he excelled and without him, says David, none of them would have survived. All they now needed was a pilot. 'Sorry, all the pilots have been taken,' said their instructor. 'Better come and see the CO to see what we can do.'

'Yes, they've all gone,' confirmed the CO. What were they to do? A crew isn't much use without a pilot, and it looked like David and the boys had missed the boat. It was an odd situation. 'Hang on,' said one of the instructors. 'What about Alan Tutt?'

Alan was himself an instructor at Sale but had already seen action on Wirraways in 1942 in Darwin and later as a test pilot for some of the more dubious American aircraft which were then arriving on our shores, including the highly ridiculous Bell P-39 'Airacobra'. This single-seat oddity was constructed around an enormous 37-millimetre cannon which could fire no more than thirty rounds through the propeller hub. It was set so far back in the fuselage the pilot had to sit *on top* of the engine with a drive shaft to the prop running between his legs. It also lacked a super-charger and was such a lemon the Royal Air Force actually sent theirs back to America and tried to cancel the remainder of the contract. Alan, says David, was constantly having to bale out of them on test flights.

He then also had a stint on the American 'Vengeance' dive-bombers, fitted with engines that spontaneously burst into flame and whose pilots could barely get them off the ground fully loaded. If you can fly aeroplanes like these, you can fly anything.

'He was champing at the bit to get back into operational fly-ing,' says David. 'We were very lucky to get him.'

David's respect for his former pilot is demonstrated by the small blue volume he passes over to me to peruse. *An Early Bird and His Beaufort Crew. Recollections of flying with Alan Tutt – RAAF pilot, WWII.* It is a modest, self-published history that David decided to write some years ago after Alan's death. On the cover is a photo of four handsome young men all sporting the parted hairstyles of the 1940s, sitting easily on the ground in air force summer khaki, their affection for one another evident.

Four specialists, four individuals who would bond into a team and galvanise into a crew. 'We lived together, trained together, knew each others' idiosyncrasies – even knew the smell of each others' sweat,' says David.

A quick conversion course at Adelaide, then a flight to Darwin to join No. 1 Squadron RAAF, the same unit which, a quarter of a century earlier, had flown over the heads of David's father in Egypt and Palestine, earning Australia's only World War I VC in the air. Its recent history, however, had been far grimmer. Sent to Malaya, No. 1 Squadron had been the first Australian unit to engage the Japanese when its Hudson bombers began attacking landing positions in Sumatra in December 1941. Weeks later, it was all but wiped out when 161 of its personnel were captured on their airstrip by the advancing Japanese. Less than half would survive more than three hellish years in captivity. The squadron effectively ceased to exist and re-formed almost from scratch two years later in December 1943. David became its youngest member.

An hour or so from Darwin by road, the aerodrome at Batchelor still exists today, a neat little strip of black tarmac used by Cessnas to treat tourists to the rugged delights of the Litchfield National Park. Back in 1944, however, it thundered to the roar of American B-17 and B-24 bombers. The Australians were relegated to the much more modest strip right next door at Gould.

David remembers the flight up from Adelaide in a DC-3, stopping at Oodnadatta on the way for corned beef sandwiches, and unloading his kit in the 30-degree heat of an early Darwin morning. Then, the 150-mile journey south by truck, and a timbered archway marking the entrance to the place from where he would commence his operational flying – an airstrip carved out of the bush.

For the first couple of weeks, David was lectured on anti-submarine techniques and attacking troop concentrations, and got a chance to meet the other crews who had been in action before. Then, it was his turn, and a baptism of fire it proved to be.

Tanimbar Island lies roughly 400 miles due north of Darwin in the Arafura Sea. Like many of the islands between New Guinea and the northern coast of Australia, it had been used by the Japanese to establish radar and radio transmitting stations which were regularly visited by their navy. At Saumlaki, its southern tip, they had recently begun construction of a transmitter more powerful than any in the neighbouring islands. Alan and his crew were asked how they felt about popping up and grabbing a few pictures as well as dropping one or two bombs. They were all eager to have a go.

David gives a fine, atmospheric description of the evening before a mission, each member of the crew preparing in their particular areas of expertise to ensure its success. Lloyd the navigator with his maps spread out – working on the details of the route; David coordinating the radio and frequency charts; and Fred the gunner polishing the perspex turret, testing the rotations and checking the ammunition bins. *'We went to bed early after laying out our gear,'* writes David: emergency rations, a .45 Smith and Wesson revolver, water bottles and even the big cane-cutter's knives they would need to strap to their legs in case of having to bale out over the jungle.

The next morning, pilot Alan Tutt conducted the external inspection of the aircraft and signed the EE77 aircraft work report form as the crew climbed aboard. Alan signalled the ground chief and the two big Pratt and Whitney engines fired up, powering the hydraulics and the controls. David radioed the control tower, 'Ready for take-off.' A green light appeared and the time was recorded in the logbook.

'I told Mum that I would say a little prayer whenever I felt like it, so I did then, and on every other mission,' says David. He also offers a brief description in his book:

Take-off was a sensational experience: our speed was awe-inspiring and we felt the tail wheel lifting. Below there were glimpses of aircraft parked near trees and buildings. Then a bit of a bounce or two and with Alan steering we left Mother Earth disappearing beneath us.

On the way, Alan told the crew of the importance of the job, and that the defences were likely to include anti-aircraft and two Zero float planes moored near the transmitter. With any luck, they would have the element of surprise, and Fred was to hold his fire from the turret to avoid disturbing the residents unnecessarily.

At first light, they made their first run. David, holding the wide-angle hand-held aerial camera, stood in the open hatch of the aircraft with his knees up against the fuselage to prevent him falling out. The towers passed underneath him, and he took the photo. So far so good, no one was seen on the ground. 'Okay, that was great,' called in Alan over the intercom. 'I think they're all asleep. We'll make another run and get a picture of those float planes.' This time, however, they weren't just shooting film.

Firing at anything they could see from the guns in the turret and nose, Alan dropped four bombs and shot low over a ridge, twisting and turning to put the now-alerted Japanese gunners off their aim. A nearby cloudbank provided cover. His manoeuvrings, though, were not quite enough. At 1600 feet, 'a terrific bang' was heard and the Beaufort fell on its starboard wing and into a spin. 'Shit! Hang on, it's OK,' yelled Alan and managed to right the plane to straight and level. Then another bang and flame began to flicker in the nacelle of the engine.

Alan's skill and experience on single-engine flying enabled him to quickly use the extinguisher and shut the motor down. 'Right, we've had an engine failure. Lloyd, give me the speed, height and position report. David, call Air Sea Rescue at the Catalina base and tell them the story.'

They were still three hours away from Australia, flying on one engine over a very big sea dotted with Japanese-held islands. The Beaufort could fly for some time on one engine but by no means indefinitely. After checking food supplies for the dinghy in case they needed to ditch, and hurling everything of any weight out the hatch, the 'tremendous sight' of a big black Catalina flying boat came up alongside. David could see the Cat's crew crowding at the windows and, amazingly enough, the two captains were able to conduct a conversation across the divide. 'How are you going, mate?' shouted the flying boat pilot. 'The sea looks pretty rough. We'd better go down and see what we can do if you get stuck. Don't worry, we'll stay up here with you for days if we have to.'

It was too rough for the Catalina, so Alan could either ditch and wait in the dinghy, or try to make it to an emergency aerodrome. The nearest was Gove on the Gulf of Carpenteria. 'Alan loved chatting to anyone on the radio,' says David, and he advised them they would soon be 'dropping in'.

The sea spared them, but twenty minutes later circling Gove they discovered that they could add undercarriage malfunction to their list of woes. The starboard wheel would lower but not lock. A belly landing was a far safer proposition, but when Alan hit the switch, the wheel now refused to go up.

Speaking to the tower at Gove, he advised them to have a crash truck and ambulance waiting at the end of the strip when they landed, and be ready to 'pull their finger out', as it was going to be a rough one.

Braced into their emergency positions with backs against the main wing spar, Alan's crew awaited the big bang. 'I'll do the best I can but hang on for the spin and the turn-over,' was his sobering assessment of their chances. 'Good luck, mate,' came the message from the control tower.

'*An almighty noise and a severe banging as we hit the ground, then everything came to rest and was silent,*' writes David. After coming to a stop, the only noise he remembers hearing was the ringing of the fire bell and the ambulance siren. The skill required to bring down an aircraft with one engine on one wheel, without it spinning out of control or flipping over is hard to comprehend. But, says David, 'Alan was one in a million.'

With the Japanese being pushed further north, No. 1 Squadron was finding its targets increasingly beyond its range, and a move north was deemed necessary. They converted to Mosquitoes, but Alan and his crew were regarded as valuable and so joined No. 7 Squadron who had just moved into Aitape – a recently recaptured dot on the northern coast of New Guinea. 'Spiders, insects, thunderstorms and snakes' remembers David of his first impressions. 'I even shot a snake one night,' he says. For a boy from the cool climes of Colac it must have seemed a strange place to find himself indeed.

I knew of Aitape, and so decided to look it up on the web, where I experienced one of those aspects of the modern world that make me feel like I've just spent twenty years in a coma. The satellite image, clearly showing the blue line of the sea meeting the green of the jungle, descends at the click of a button further and further until I am looking down upon the streets of a tiny little settlement scratched out of the forest. Not a dissimilar view, I reckon, to the one David must have seen many times from his Beaufort. I play with the little arrows that direct the rolling landscape right, left or up and down at my command and there, on the edge of a clearing, I can make out the remnants of the old wartime airstrip – Tadji – a slightly discoloured rectangle of green against green, jutting defiantly into the sago and the pandanus plantations.

'Rainstorms so heavy you couldn't see your hand in front of your face,' David continues. 'It was one thing living in it, but quite another trying to fly in it.'

But fly in it he and his crew did, every day having to negotiate the treacherous, cloud-concealed mountains, which rose cathedral-like around them as they set out to attack targets along the northern coast and Sepik River. These were in support of the often-controversial Aitape-Wewak operations, a campaign which has remained the subject of historical argument for over half a century.

By early 1945, the front-end of the Pacific War had long since passed on to the Philippines and the terrible 'island-hopping' campaigns of Okinawa and Iwo Jima way to the north. The war was really now an all-American show. But further to the south, where it had all started three years before, it was left to the Australians – who had first showed the world that the juggernaut of Imperial Japan could be defeated on land – to 'mop up' in a series of long and bloody campaigns against an essentially defeated and isolated enemy. But whether or not this was a wise, or even proper use of resources was not a question on which men like David were given the luxury to ponder. They had a job to do.

'At the beginning of '45 things were really hotting up there for the army,' he says. In shocking conditions, the men on the ground dragged themselves through steaming, fetid jungles, flushing out position after desperate position in gullies and clearings or up razorbacks and mountains.

'Sometimes we were called in several times each day to go out and help dislodge the Japanese,' remembers David. 'We demolished stores and strongpoints or whatever it was that the army was confronting.'

I look at his logbook. I'm getting used to reading them by now, and can glean the meaning in the different coloured inks and various abbreviations. I can see immediately that March 1945 was a very busy time for David and his crew. Running my eye down the page, I note he operated on the 20th, 22nd, 24th, 25th, 26th, 28th and 30th of that month, often carrying out several missions in a day. They were usually short durations of just over an hour, with another two or three hours added for briefing, debriefing and discussions with army liaison officers who were essentially directing the strikes.

'We operated right on the treetops locating the commandos,' says David. 'They would give us a location. Lloyd and Alan would work it out between them.' A smoke marker would be dropped. David was usually in radio communication with the soldiers on the ground.

'They'd say for instance, "Drop them on that little knoll to the right of the marker," and we'd have to know exactly where they meant,' he says. 'It was all jungle fighting and the distances between our blokes and the enemy were very small. We had to be extremely accurate.'

This was a pioneering method of warfare born out of the unconventional nature of the conflict. The army, aware of the advantage of working closely with the air force, approached No. 7 Squadron with the idea of forming a specialised low-level liaison unit for a pure army cooperation role. The CO immediately suggested Alan Tutt form and lead a Beaufort Tactical Reconnaissance Unit.

'We even took army blokes up with us sometimes to guide us close onto a pinpoint.' Occasionally they'd drop their bombs too close and David would receive an earful of abuse from some justifiably nervous men on the ground.

Later, they would use their skills in the amphibious attack on the Japanese strongpoint of Wewak. Alan commanded fifteen Beauforts which circled the invasion beaches, waiting for the word from the ground to strike. The target was a difficult one, a large Japanese 75-millimetre howitzer whose commander had earned the nickname 'Dead-eye Dick' for his previous disposal of several Beauforts and a DC-3 transport. It was difficult to locate, and even harder to hit. Lloyd was the first to spot it. 'Down by that big tree down there!' David remembers him saying over the intercom. Attacking an anti-aircraft gun was an inherently hazardous exercise, and Alan was urged to be careful. 'Leave him to me,' he said. 'I want to dive-bomb this bastard.'

As the throttles were rammed open, David felt the Beaufort keel over. It wasn't generally known for its dive-bombing characteristics but in the hands of a capable pilot could sometimes pass for one that was. 'Cabin crew, equipment, rubbish and dust flew everywhere,' says David. 'We all blacked out from the lack of oxygen. I thought this was going to be our Valhalla.' It would have been a sight to see, but from his position in the fuselage, David was unable to observe the destruction of the gun and its crew of eight, a prospect with which the thankful men on the ground no longer had to deal.

I have rarely met a former aircrew member who lets pass an opportunity to have a go at their other great universal adversary, the Americans, and David is no exception.

A new American squadron flying Bostons had arrived in Lae, full of bravado, and declaring to the Australians, 'Don't worry, *mate*, we'll clear those Japs out for you,' etc. No sooner had they been sent into action than the army began expressing grave concerns about the Americans above their heads dropping bombs at close range. 'They couldn't read signals and they couldn't drop smoke markers. They asked us to come in and guide them,' he says.

David still has a photo of the big green Bostons flying alongside the comparatively diminutive Beaufort on their way to lead an attack on the headquarters of the Japanese General Misaki. 'Lloyd was to drop several smoke markers so the Yank "greenhorns" wouldn't miss!' says David.

It must have gone well because the next day, the US commander flew in to thank them personally. After the formalities, the Australians asked him to stay for lunch, and treated him to their meagre provisions of a rather tough steak and some runny ice-cream. Apologising, they explained they didn't really have a refrigerator. At this the American perked up.

'Don't have a refrigerator?' he said, appalled. 'Don't worry, bud, we'll send you one. Anything else you want?' There was a pause until someone mumbled, 'Well, we could do with a jeep,' and the American headed off to win the war. A little later, a DC-3 touched down at Aitape and, true to his word, disgorged a brand-new Kelvinator fridge still in its crate, and a slightly older but perfectly workable Wily's Jeep. The local padre suggested they christen it, and 'Kelvin' was painted on the fender in recognition of their new beer cooler, largesse courtesy of Uncle Sam.

Occasionally, they would fly convoy escort duties. Once, they were submarine-scouting for three cargo vessels and two corvettes, one of which David knew to be the *Bundaberg*. He also knew that somewhere on that ship was his cousin John, the ship's radio officer. He radioed the *Bundaberg*'s Officer-of-the-Watch and asked permission to call him up. So, somewhere way out in the Arafura Sea, the two cousins chatted and caught up with family news, one on a ship, the other circling overhead in a Beaufort bomber.

Then in August 1945, with the squadron actually involved in an attack on one of the last remaining entrenched positions manned by starving and fanatical Japanese defenders, an urgent signal came through from base: 'Cancel all operations against enemy forthwith, including missions now airborne.' Thousands of miles away, the atomic bombs had been dropped and surrender announced. The crews flew back, strangely quiet, 'as the realisation dawned on us we could ponder a future beyond the war', says David.

David is rightly proud of his book, and the efforts he has made to keep alive the memory of his pilot Alan Tutt, and hundreds of others like him. Strangely enough, they lost contact after the war and only too late did David learn Alan had passed away in 1982. Perhaps the book is a way to atone for time lost.

He shows me through his wartime photo album and allows me to reproduce some of the images. As I place each one through my small scanner, I can't help but notice that each has been, at one stage, torn quite deliberately in half, then stuck back together with tape. It's a delicate area to pry into and I simply remark that they look like they met with an accident. 'Yes. Yes they did,' is all David says, and I press him no further.

Outside, the heavy, semi-tropical sky is low and it wants to rain. I walk back into the town, lugging a computer bag, as around me oversized drops begin plopping onto the footpath. I think about David's torn and re-patched photos and a sour mood comes over me. What would I know of the demons that still haunt the memories of men like David? In an hour or so, my mind will have moved on from him and his lucky, nail-biting escape over the sea, as well as the dozens of other missions they undertook. I suspect it will not be so easy for him.

As the rain really starts, I sit down in a small cafe as tourists scuttle inside. I pull out the little blue book David handed me when we said our goodbyes, and begin to read.

HARVEY BAWDEN

Air Gunner, RAAF

As a kid up around the very flat Victorian country of Pyramid Hill, Harvey rode to school on a horse. A very short time after that – still a kid, really – he was operating the mid-upper turret of a Lancaster on bombing missions into Germany. You could probably argue that he was still a kid upon his return to Australia after the war, but a faster or more terrible growing-up is hard to imagine.

One of the best things about having written one book about the flyers of World War II is the friends I have made along the way. Dick Levy, erudite, seemingly ageless and endlessly enthusiastic, had been one of my first interviewees, sharing with me his memories of piloting B-25 Mitchells with the 2nd Tactical Air Force in late 1944–45. 'It's extraordinary,' said his wife Barb bustling into her living room in a tracksuit one afternoon, having just returned from her regular session at the gym. 'He wouldn't talk about it for years!' But perhaps the passage of time, and a newly interested public, has released something in Dick and, perhaps, even some of the demons.

Dick told me about a recent phone call he had received from a man he did not know. 'Are you the Dick Levy in that book?' the man asked bluntly. A little uncertain, Dick said he was. 'I'm making you a model,' was the reply. A few weeks later, a beautifully put-together 1:48 scale plastic model of a B-25 – especially modified to match the mark and colour scheme of the very one flown by Dick – was dangling from the ceiling of his study. No payment of any kind was accepted.

I was not, however, sitting in Dick's living room devouring another bowl of his excellent Italian soup to talk about him. For quite some time now, he had been on at me to meet his old friend Harvey, who lived close by and who had a story to tell.

A little while later, having followed Dick's complicated meanderings through the back streets of a large country town, I was standing in a strange living room, shaking hands with Harvey Bawden. Dick, the wheels of introduction sufficiently oiled, headed home.

Harvey's dad was also a World War I Light Horseman, and, like David Roberts' dad, he didn't much like to talk about it. Sometimes, though, a member of his old troupe would show up and stay for a while. The men would sit and tell the stories of their old campaigns – the good times and the bad – and the young Harvey listened, enthralled. 'They'd talk for hours, mostly about their mates. They were so close. It was marvellous to hear them,' he tells me.

Like the young Harvey, I too get to hear stories from men who have been to war. Some are told with a sense of amazement, as if read from an adventure book in which they themselves are the central subject; others are delivered wryly, peppered with humour and talking up the lighter side. Almost all of them, however, contain an element of sadness that lingers with me for hours, often days. For the men telling them, however, this sadness has endured for sixty years. Harvey Bawden's was one of the saddest stories I had ever heard.

Unlike the homes of many former aircrew, there were few visible references to his air force days that I could see. No colourful aviation prints, no emblems or squadron badges, just a proudly arrayed set of family photos of children and grandchildren. A trio of attractive young women in mortarboards and gowns grabbed my eye. 'My daughters!' he beamed. By the looks of the hairstyles, the girls graduated a couple of decades ago. One of them had a familiar look about her. 'Here she is more recently,' he says, drawing me to another photo in which I recognise the face of a recently serving Federal Government Minister. Quite the family of high achievers.

Harvey begins his story by telling me the end of it. A few weeks after the finish of the European war in 1945, he walked out of the government-requisitioned Melford Motors building in Melbourne, having just been discharged. Pale, and terribly thin, he limped along Russell Street with the aid of a stick. A street photographer came up and snapped him. Harvey smiled weakly for the camera, but inside he felt lonely and isolated. A figure in air force drab came the other way. The two men stopped, recognising each other instantly. Two years earlier, Mack Holtern had been Harvey's flight instructor at Somers. The air force thought him such a fine instructor that that's what they confined him to for the entire war. He grabbed his hobbling former pupil's hand and swung him around, noticing the row of service ribbons attached to his well-worn battle dress. 'You lucky bastard!' he exclaimed warmly. At that moment, though, Harvey thought himself anything but lucky.

Twice selected for his dream job as a fighter pilot, he arrived at No. 5 Service Flying Training School at Uranquinty, only to be scrubbed. 'I was devastated,' he says.

The Commanding Officer was sympathetic, and suggested he

consider a new nav/bomber course. That, however, would require him going back to school for another seven months, and Harvey wanted to get into the war. So he made a decision. 'I'll be a gunner,' he said.

Harvey completed the short gunnery course at Sale, the standard couple of weeks firing paint-dipped rounds at a drogue towed behind a dilapidated Fairey Battle. Arriving in England, he was told to forget everything he had learned and start over again. This time he honed his skills properly, defending himself in a power-operated turret from 'attacks' by a real live Spitfire on 'fighter affiliation' exercises.

At his Operational Training Unit in Lichfield, Harvey crewed up, not by the usual method of mingling in a hangar but in true Australian style, around a bar. Here, he met six men who in one way or another would stay with him for the rest of his life: a young Londoner who was pleased as punch to be part of an Australian crew and who talked of emigrating there after the war; a wireless operator from Tumut in the New South Wales alps; a part-Chinese navigator from Melbourne; a fellow gunner from Brisbane with whom Harvey tossed a coin to decide positions; a young bomb aimer from Sydney just out of school; and the pilot. 'Fine fellows,' he says, showing me a framed photograph.

There is a certain magic about this picture. Seven young men in flying gear lined up in front of a large aeroplane. Seven young faces – each so different, but bonded nonetheless by something quiet and unspoken.

'And that's our skipper, Phil Morris,' Harvey says, pointing to the man with pilot's wings. 'He'd flown three types of heavy bombers but couldn't drive a car!' In late 1944, the two of them pitched in and bought a nice little open-top Riley 9. On their afternoons off, Harvey would give his skipper driving lessons. 'He was shocking! He'd grind the gears and slip the clutch, but he loved it.' He looks again at the photo.

After some toing-and-froing, Harvey and his crew began operating with No. 150 Squadron at Helmswell, a temporary RAF base in the Lincolnshire Wolds. 'It was pretty rough, but it grew on us. It was a bit more relaxed than the more established bases,' he remembers. 'Less red tape.'

With country gentility, Harvey asks how I'd like to proceed with the afternoon's discussion. Actually, this for me is a tricky one, and touches on the nature of my process, or rather lack thereof. I had started it all off with a distinct formula. An aspect of the male psyche, I believe, is our ability to be soothed by facts lined up correctly and in order, such as in the steady rhythm of an unfolding timeline. Hence, I would always try to adhere the interview to a strict chronological order, requesting the men start their story at the very beginning. This way I figured – if only from a reluctance to leave something incomplete – nothing would be left out.

Terrific in theory. Old memories, however, are sometimes patchy, and my attempts to pin down a rambling narrative could, I found, become self-defeating. If I curtailed a story being told out of sequence, I would often find it did not arise again, or else not with the same spontaneity. By the time I came to interview Harvey, therefore, I had reached the decision simply to shut up, listen, and see how things unfold.

But when he said, 'I thought we might just go through the trips in the logbook, one by one. Is that alright?' it was music to my ears.

He had also kept a series of little diaries, around ten in all – quite contrary to wartime service regulations – filled with his small, spidery handwriting, written at the time as a sort of appendix to the cursory information in his logbook. Starting at the beginning of his operational tour of thirty trips, he reads me the name of his first target – Düsseldorf – carried out on the night of Thursday, 2 November 1944.

'I can't remember any great trepidation about the first trip,' he tells me. 'No great drama. Just a feeling of satisfaction. The system was so good, you see. We were eased up to the point where we could be thrown into the fire.'

As mid-upper gunner, Harvey sat astride the spine of the aircraft in a rotating turret armed with twin Browning .303 machine guns. His 360-degree view was by far the best in the aircraft, but his only protection from the red-hot shards of flak or bullets was a thin screen of soft, clear perspex.

Over the target, an aircraft could be 'coned' in multiple coordinated searchlights, and a pilot had just seconds to slip their grip before radar-synchronised guns below commenced tearing them to pieces. 'I was his eyes,' says Harvey. 'I would watch them and shout to the skipper to dive to port or starboard.' Frequently, he would witness an aircraft not so nimble as themselves. 'They just fried up there,' he says. 'The concentration of fire they threw up at them was terrific.'

Harvey also needed to be aware of that other inherent danger of night flying: collisions. One dark night, he had a sense of something even darker looming towards him from the side. 'Then I saw the dull red glow of an aircraft's exhaust stubs.' He shouted to his pilot Phil to dive. 'He would have just about shaved my turret,' he says. 'That was the sort of thing that happened.'

Düsseldorf . . . Bochum . . . Gelsinkirchen . . . Harvey's logbook catalogues the placenames of Germany's industry as it was ground down by the terrible weight of nightly aerial bombardment. On their third trip, a sizeable chunk of flak, its force thankfully almost spent, crashed through the windscreen and severely bruised the skipper's arm. 'We were broken in fairly early,' he says. Aschaffenburg . . . Karlsruhe . . . Mersberg . . .

I pick up one of the smooth, leather-covered volumes, barely the size of a couple of matchboxes. The ink has faded a little after sixty years, but I can still sense the amazement in his nightly entries, written just hours after the events themselves. '*On battle order,*' he reads aloud from one of them. '*Took off 5 p.m. Target, Essen in the Ruhr. There was heavy flak. Our starboard outer engine was hit. Came home on three.*' He pauses for a bit. 'Yes, I remember that one,' he says. 'The flak had wrecked the motor's cooling system.' From his vantage point, he could see it throwing sparks and glowing red hot in the darkness.

One night their hydraulics failed and the pilot was unable to fully extend the flaps for landing, so they diverted to the long emergency runway at Carnaby. There, a bulldozer stood in readiness to push you off the tarmac should you 'go in', and broken bits of aeroplane lay strewn just off the runway. 'It wasn't very encouraging,' he says.

'*February 1945, Cleves.*' I enjoy the sound of Harvey reading the diaries, and sense he has not done so in a long time. 'They got us out of bed in the middle of the night for that one,' he recalls. It was an extremely low-level tactical attack in support of the First Canadian Army, held up outside the town. 'We bombed from 4000 feet through cloud. We were so low that we were tossed about by our own explosions,' he says. This unfortunate raid was remembered for one of those ghastly ironies of war, a result of a foul-up in communication between the services. Instead of the incendiaries requested by Brian Horrocks, the army commander on the ground, the RAF bombed with high explosive, turning the once-exquisite town of Cleves, birthplace of the fourth wife of Henry VIII, into an impassable sea of rubble, thereby defeating the entire purpose of the operation. It was not one of the RAF's finest hours.

Harvey's crew soon found themselves the most senior on the squadron, one with a reputation for hard work and reliability. They were given a brand new Lancaster, with the designation P-Peter. Leave would come around every few weeks, but that, says Harvey, was a double-edged sword. 'You'd come back to the base and you'd look around the mess and see many familiar faces gone. It was harder than when we were operating with them. There was the guilt, you see – we'd been on leave while all this had happened.'

There was, he says, a strange sense of 'persona non grata' surrounding those men who had failed to return. It simply didn't do to dwell on their fate, lest it reflect too much on your own. By the next day, the men of the air force 'Committee of Adjustments' had done their ghoulish work – clearing out the personal belongings of the dead airman and stripping the sheets from his bed, ready for his replacement who would often arrive within hours. It was as if they had never existed. The friendships formed within the aircraft were often timeless, but rarely did they extend to other crews. There didn't seem to be much point.

'*Number 20. Dresden.*' My meeting with Max Durham came back into my mind. Harvey's entry for this infamous night is a grim study in understatement: '*The target was left burning.*' The men were told they were attacking railway transport centres used to rally German troops for an offensive against the Russians, and had no sense it was to be anything out of the ordinary. Approaching the target, however, Harvey had a feeling that this one was indeed different. 'We were part of the second wave,' he tells me. 'I could see the target glowing on the horizon from about eighty miles away.' Passing over the inferno, rising heat from the blazing city buffeted the Lancaster, and below, like in a mirage, Harvey saw aircraft shimmer in the man-made heat haze. 'I'd never seen anything like it – just one mass of molten orange and red. There's no film or picture that captures what it was like,' he says. 'You just had to see it to believe it.'

The next day Harvey had off and, according to the diary, he attended a dance. Here, the perfunctory entry is revealing: *'Had a few beers. Did not dance.'*

'Yes,' he says, reflecting thoughtfully, 'perhaps it did have an effect on us.'

Gelsenkirchen . . . Hannover . . . Hanau – then number 29, Dortmund, the trip that should have been his penultimate, 24 March 1945, just a few weeks before the end of the war. What happened that day is described in a single sentence in his logbook, another epic of understatement. *'Hit by flak at 1632. Abandoned aircraft over target.'*

Just to set the scene, I look it up in my invaluable and much-thumbed tome, *The Bomber Command War Diaries*. Its description too is cold and cursory: '173 Lancaster and 12 Mosquitos of 1, 6 and 8 Groups attacked the Harpenerweg plant at Dortmund and the Mathias Stinnes plant at Bottrop. 3 Lancasters were lost on the Dortmund raid.'

'Yes,' he says, as I read, 'I watched those other two go down. Actually, they just exploded.' A couple of days later, he would chance upon one of their crew, lying dead in a field. 'He was an RAF bloke. His parachute hadn't opened. I suspect he was blown out of the aircraft.' But let's stick to the timeline, just as Harvey prefers.

Dortmund was a 'hot' target – highly industrial and heavily defended, and the attack was carried out in daylight. Turning into the bombing run at 18 000 feet, the smoke rising from the ground made the aiming point clearly visible. Then, says Harvey, from underneath the aircraft came 'a tremendous flash' which lifted them as if from a giant hammer-blow. Two of the engines were immediately set on fire, and the Lancaster began to shudder violently, going into a steep descent. Harvey could see the two wrecked motors. 'I can see it, Phil!' he said over the intercom. 'I know, and I can't hold her any longer,' came the reply. Harvey is pretty sure the rear gunner, Jim Griffin, had already been killed in the explosion.

With no sense of panic, the six remaining men were able to bale out, but Harvey nearly didn't make it. In order for him to be able to leave his turret, his guns needed to be facing forward, but the hydraulics which controlled his turret were powered by one of the knocked-out engines. He was stuck, two metres above the floor of the fuselage with his guns pointing sideways. Precious seconds were expended manually winding the turret round to the escape position as the aircraft went down. Then he became tangled in oxygen and radio leads. 'I had to fight my way out of the darned thing,' he says. He can't remember just how it happened, but in the violently lurching aeroplane, he fell to the aircraft's floor and broke his femur just below the hip.

In what must have been incredible pain, he was just able to reach his stowed parachute, clip it on and start crawling towards the open rear hatch which, in the plummeting nose-down attitude of the aeroplane, was above him. 'For the life of me I don't know how I did it,' he says.

He rolled out into the sky, counted three and pulled the cord. There was a jolt, and then, away from the screaming aircraft, an overwhelming sense of peace and calm. At 16000 feet, he watched the other Lancasters passing high above. 'It was then the enormity of the situation struck me,' says Harvey. 'I can still remember the sense of isolation and loneliness as I watched those aircraft disappear in the distance.' (Without exception, every aircrew I spoke to who had baled out similarly remembered this same forlorn sensation.)

His mind however, was calm and clear, his only thoughts being the dreaded telegram his parents would soon be receiving back home, and the RAF issue Smith and Wesson revolver he had tucked behind his Mae West life preserver. 'In the situation I was about to face, I thought it might be a liability,' he says. He pulled it out and let it drop.

For Harvey, the last few hundred feet arrived too soon. Initially, he drifted slowly and thought he would come down among roofs and buildings, but then he saw what appeared to be an old sports field – now growing vegetables – rushing up to meet him. He could also see people converging, silently watching his slow, inexorable descent, clutching rakes, hoes and shovels.

'I landed very badly. My leg had been windmilling up in the air.' At first the crowd fell back, but when he did not move, they guessed he was unarmed and rushed him. Amid the kicks, spits and blows, they stood on his hands stretched above his head and grabbed at his harness to take his flying clothes. 'The worst part was having the women fighting over my parachute silk and pulling my boots off. I was not,' he says, 'having a very good time.'

I can see that telling this is not easy for Harvey. At several points he stops, pauses and with shaky hands takes a sip of lukewarm tea. But he's determined to finish it. Ignoring his emotion, I prompt him with minor questions of detail. This seems to refocus him a little, but it's hard.

One can only imagine the state he was in, lying in agony with his shattered leg, being beaten by a mob. Despite the blood in his eyes, though, he can still today picture the little man who pushed his way through the malevolent crowd, clutching an old gangster-style Tommy gun. He was a Volksturm, an old soldier from the Great War and now in the German Home Guard. He came and stood over Harvey and cocked his weapon. The crowd fell back.

'He saved my life,' Harvey says. Both of us are finding it hard to keep it together. I suggest a break, but he prefers to go on.

A second Volksturm man appeared, this one pushing a wheelbarrow. Harvey was lifted into it and he remembers the sound of the wheels as they rattled over the cobblestones. Shrieking 'Schweinhund Flieger!' the crowd spat on him but, guarded by the two men, he came to no further harm.

He was then taken to a building that appeared to be a military barracks and deposited onto a concrete floor. As much as he could, he thanked his two old saviours. They left, and he never saw them again. Lying there without a blanket, his leg began to swell up terribly, almost bursting the seam of his trouser leg. In the evening he was interrogated by a Luftwaffe officer. Among a sheaf of identity cards in the officer's hand, he saw one for his bomb aimer, Jim Gillies. He showed no recognition, but at least knew that he too had survived.

The next day, after a night spent on a freezing concrete floor, with only the electric light above him to give his mind some kind of company, he was handed a bowl of porridge and taken to a cell. A short time later, Jim Gillies was brought in, his bloodied head wrapped in crepe paper. 'We chose not to recognise each other,' says Harvey.

Jim, he later discovered, had had a similar experience. Bashed about the head, he too was saved by one of the old men of the Volksturm.

It is with some trepidation I now ask, 'What happened to the others?' Harvey says nothing but pulls out a copy of an old typed document headed 'War Crimes Group (North West Europe)' dated 21 April 1947. It refers to case WGG/15228/2/C.1190, 'Ill-treatment and murder of Allied airmen who baled out of an aircraft over Dortmund. 24 March 1945'. Slowly, hesitantly and through an occasionally breaking voice, Harvey reads me the terrible story of the four remaining survivors of No. 150 Squadron Lancaster 'P-Peter'.

One came down near a policeman who struck him on the head. A crowd soon gathered and beat him to death with a hammer.

Another was captured, then protected by some Wehrmacht soldiers until the local Nazi Party leader forced them to hand him over. He was subsequently beaten and shot. A similar fate befell the last two. The document states that two men, including the local Nazi, were condemned to death by the War Crimes Tribunal after the war, and several others were given prison sentences of varying lengths.

At war's end, the Americans undertook the investigation, exhuming the bodies of the men and, with the evidence of their only witness, an extremely brave and noble woman, put the cases together and prosecuted.

With effort, Harvey reads the document in its entirety, then seems to recover somewhat. Next he hands me an old, yellowing envelope. It is the telegram he so dreaded his parents receiving as he floated to his fate above the town. I unfold it and read. 'Regret to inform you that your son 419835 Harvey Hayward Bawden missing as a result air operations 24 March 1945 STOP Known details are that he was a member of Lancaster aircraft detailed to attack enemy target which failed to return to base as a result enemy action STOP . . .' etc.

Harvey's ordeal continued throughout the final, surreal weeks of the war in Europe. He and Jim were put on a truck and taken out of the city. On the way, they stopped by a field to retrieve the body of the RAF airman whose aircraft he had seen explode over the target shortly before his own was shot down. He was taken to a three-storey military hospital in nearby Kirchlinde, and was there witness to the terrible endgame of Nazi Germany played out violently around him. He was caught in what became known as the 'Ruhr Pocket', where the foul-mouthed, pro-Nazi General Model pointlessly held out against the encircling Americans until almost the end of the war. Then, rather than surrender to face war crime prosecution, he walked into a forest and shot himself.

In the prisoner-of-war hospital, Harvey received some rudimentary medical attention but his broken leg had fused, shortening it considerably. I ask him about the pain. All he says is, 'It wasn't a happy time.'

In a basement as the floors above him were steadily obliterated, he listened to the chaos and the bombing outside. Next to the hospital an 88 battery, similar to the one that had claimed his own aircraft, fired constantly. He met a blind English soldier, an American GI and a wounded young German called Helmut whom he befriended and told stories about life in Australia. Helmut was fascinated, but Harvey doubts whether he survived. At one stage, a deranged SS soldier wandered in and held a Luger to his face, leering. He still gets a slight shudder thinking about it.

At last, the Americans arrived. He was lashed to the front of a jeep and taken to a US army field hospital. His femur would have to be re-broken and reset. On a nice sunny morning, Harvey was loaded into a Dakota and flown back to England, landing in Swindon.

A few weeks later, in his hospital bed, he listened to the church bells pealing for the first time in years, and the massive victory celebrations on the radio. He shared little of the joy around him. 'There really wasn't any great feelings of joyousness where I was.' His thoughts were with all the young men who had contributed to the victory but were not there to see it.

A buxom English matron brought in two bottles of hospital

brandy under each arm, apologising that she had nothing better to offer. That was how Harvey finished his war.

For all the unhappy memories still alive in Harvey's head, he is thankful for his time in the air force and is surprisingly magnanimous to the people who so tormented him on that terrible afternoon after he parachuted into the city he helped destroy. 'They were quite justified. I understood that. We knew in Bomber Command that if you had to bale out over the target your chances of survival could sometimes be small. It was an absolute miracle that I was spared.'

Harvey remains firm friends with his fellow survivor, Jim Gillies, who came home to have a long career as a dentist. The two still speak every week or so. Perhaps Harvey thinks himself lucky after all.

Before I go, he hands me some type-written sheets briefly summarising the events we have spoken of. The last sheet ends simply with a list of his crew:

Phil Morris, pilot
Kevin Kee, navigator
Joe Davis, flight engineer
Bob Masters, wireless operator
Jim Griffin, gunner
Jim Gillies, bomb aimer

And Harvey Bawden, mid-upper gunner.

ABOVE David Roberts with pilot Allan Tutt and crew, Gould, 1944.

TOP David Roberts, wireless/air gunner, in the nose section of his 1 Squadron Beaufort.

BOTTOM American Bostons, in New Guinea, snapped by David Roberts from the window of his Beaufort.

ABOVE A 100 Squadron Beaufort somewhere along the New Guinea coast.

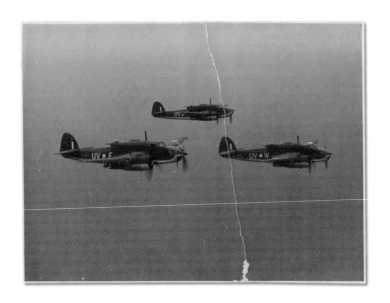

TOP A flight of 8 Squadron Beauforts head out from their base at Aitape, New Guinea, late 1944.

BOTTOM The form reporting Max Durham's low-flying misdemeanour. He tore it from the book and possibly saved his career.

LEFT You have to start somewhere. A de Havilland 89 Tiger Moth – the standard trainer for all new RAAF pilots.

ABOVE A Lancaster rear-gunner with his four 303 machine guns for defence. Their rate of fire was high, but their range short.

ABOVE Max Durham at the cockpit of 'Easy Does It', his 115 Squadron Lancaster at Witchford near Ely.

ABOVE A fresh-faced Max Durham. By the end of his tour as a bomber pilot, he would be wearing the ribbon of the Distinguished Flying Cross under his pilot's wings.

LEFT At their base in Witchford, Max Durham poses with his crew in front of their 115 Squadron Lancaster. Already a veteran of 45 trips, it was a lucky kite, and remained so for them.

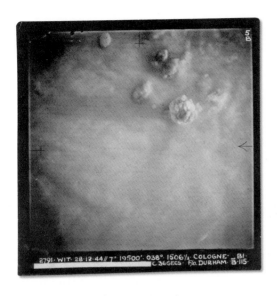

2791·WIT· 28·12·44// 7" 19500'· 038°· 1506/4· COLOGNE· _BI·
C.36SECS· F/o. DURHAM· B·115·

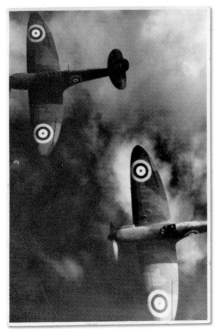

ABOVE A camera flash target photo taken of a cloudy Cologne from Max Durham's 115 Squadron Lancaster, December 1944.

LEFT James Coward's amazing shot of two pre-war 19 Squadron Spitfires, Duxford, 1938.

TOP Sea mines and incendiary canisters wait to be loaded into the cavernous bomb bay of a Lancaster.

BOTTOM Harvey Bawden snapped this 150 Squadron Lancaster coming in to Hemswell, Lincolnshire, after a raid.

ABOVE Harvey Bawden stands with his crew under their 150 Squadron Lancaster PB853P, 'P Peter' at Hemswell, 1944. L to R: Joe Davis, Bob Masters, Kevin Kee, Phil Morris, Harvey Bawden, Jim Griffin, Jim Gillies. Harvey and Jim Gillies would remain friends for the rest of their lives. The others were less fortunate.

LEFT Harvey Bawden next to the mid-upper turret from which he barely escaped alive.

TOP 3 Squadron Tomahawk pilots in the Western Desert. Seeming happy-go-lucky here, they formed the deadliest Australian fighter unit of the war.

BOTTOM 3 Squadron Tomahawks set out on a sortie with 250-pound bombs strapped underneath the fuselage.

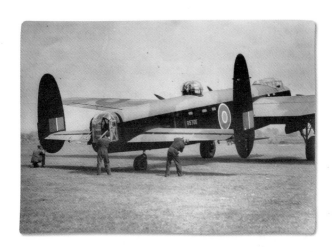

TOP An early Lancaster, straight from the factory and still without its squadron markings, is checked out on arrival by the fitters.

BOTTOM A bomber pilot's 'office' – Lancaster cockpit with the bomb aimer's position visible, lower right.

LEFT A fine study of the RAF's first four-engine bomber, the chronically hampered Stirling.

BELOW 71 Squadron Avro Anson at Lowood, Queensland. In training, many bomber pilots cut their teeth on these slow but reliable aircraft.

ABOVE An unmistakably Australian Lancaster is adorned with the mug of 'Mo'.

LEFT A young Alistair Smith, formerly ground staff, in his new uniform as flight engineer.

LEFT Jean Smith – front row, second from left – poses with some airmen and WAAF mates.

BELOW Alistair and Jean Smith on their wedding day.

Sunderland K - 461

Machine-gun U-boat attack - Sql. Sam Woods DFC, 10 Squadron

TOP A 461 Squadron RAAF Sunderland over the Atlantic. When Dudley Marrows first saw one, he hardly believed it could fly.

BOTTOM U-boat under attack by 10 Squadron RAAF Sunderland, Bay of Biscay.

Eddystone lighthouse Plymouth

ABOVE A 10 Squadron Sunderland banks over Eddystone Lighthouse, Plymouth.

LEFT The power of a Mark VII depth charge exploding in the Atlantic.

ROY RIDDEL

Pilot, RAAF

After two years, Roy Riddel had had enough. Slogging his heavy rifle and pack across the paddocks of southern Queensland on route marches with two or three hundred other bods from his University Regiment was, he decided that afternoon, not for him. So, together with a couple of mates, he hatched a plan.

Somewhere near the site of the present day Route 2 Motorway, along which cars speed between Brisbane and Ipswich in minutes, the trio of miscreants quietly dropped back to the rear of the column, and waited till the little railway station at Goodna came into view. It's all wall-to-wall suburbs now, but in 1940 it was a quiet little staging-post between the two towns.

A glance to see they were in the clear, and the three men walked into the office. 'Look after these,' said Roy, passing his rifle and kit to a surprised stationmaster, 'we'll be back tonight.' As the column continued on without them, the boys boarded the next train into Brisbane, signed up at the nearest RAAF recruiting office, then headed back to collect their packs a few hours later.

Thus, Roy deserted one branch of His Majesty's Armed Forces for another, destined not to march over wartime forests and jungles but to soar above them as a fighter pilot.

A few months later at Archerfield in Queensland, he was part of the very early course 5 at No. 2 Elementary Flying Training School. At the same time the pilots of the RAF were slogging out the Battle of Britain, Roy was getting the feel of a Tiger Moth.

'I went solo at six-and-a-half hours,' he says, sitting today in his living room in subtropical Coffs Harbour. Roy and his wife Judy, also a pilot ('She's got 2000 hours of her own, you know,' he tells me with pride), have lived in this lush setting since 1951. He had a long flying career, giving it away only four years ago. It all started in 1932 as a twelve-year-old with a joy-flight with his dad in a Genairco biplane. The Sydney Harbour Bridge had just opened and Roy Senior was keen to get a first-class view of the wondrous span. It was Roy's first time in an aeroplane, and a decade later, he was astonishing his instructors with his uncanny natural aptitude in the air.

'Gee, I can't cope with you,' his rattled ex-civil instructor remarked. 'I'm going to get the flight commander.'

The officer took the precocious young man aloft to gauge this raw talent for himself. 'Yep. You're alright,' was all he muttered. The next time Roy flew, he was on his own.

He soon proceeded to advanced training at Amberley. Shortly after arriving at the newly constructed aerodrome, Roy was sitting in the flight hut, waiting for his turn in a Wirraway. 'About from here to the house over the road,' he tells me, pointing across a large and exotic flowering vine, 'I saw my instructor collide with another aircraft and burst into flame. That was my introduction to war: a great big bonfire of two Wirraways and four blokes.'

Despite this ghastly overture, Roy speaks of the Wirraway with affection. 'People say dreadful things about them, but I thought they were marvellous. I thought all the aircraft I flew were marvellous.'

Having again impressed the instructors, Roy headed out on one of the final phases of his fighter pilot education, a long cross-country navigation exercise across southern Queensland. But flying on your own has its advantages. 'Luckily they hadn't removed the names of the stations on the train lines,' he says. 'If you got a bit lost, you just came down low and saw where you were.'

With the rare distinction 'above average' written in his log-book, Roy collected his pilot's wings and sergeant's stripes and, in early 1941, headed to England.

What is it about these old fighter boys? As I sit across from him, sharing a joke, enjoying the tea, cake and hospitality supplied by Judy, I can't help noticing the same uncanny confidence common to them all. Almost without exception, you can still see the golden boy in every man who once flew a Hurricane, Spitfire or Kittyhawk: the top footballer or leg-spin bowler; the professional or successful executive – the same flash of individuality that charmed and conquered, and equipped a young man with the unique mettle needed to work as a team and hunt as a maverick. Such a contrast to the quieter, steadied demeanour of the bomber men whose talents could only ever be realised as part of a whole, enmeshed among the personalities of others.

It was at his Operational Training Unit at Harden in England's north that Roy first got his hands on a Spitfire – a clapped-out Mark I Battle of Britain veteran, but a Spitfire all the same. A new pilot's introduction to this 1000-horsepower machine was rudimentary to say the least. 'You just sat in the cockpit and learned the layout. Then they put a blindfold on you, and you put your hand on the instruments as the instructor called them out.' Again, Roy passed with flying colours, and he was off.

On only his second flight over the city of Crewe, the engine of his worn-out warhorse started to cough. 'I steered back to

Harden, and on the downwind leg, it just stopped,' he says. Roy looked anxiously at the crowded English landscape below and saw a series of 'bloody great church spires'. Coming in on a glide, he managed to pass over a hangar and felt that he was going to make the runway – then spotted a row of electric wires dead in front. 'I held it off a bit longer, then the thing stalled,' he says. With a bone-numbing 'thump', the Spitfire flopped hard onto the grass. 'The right wheel leg came up through the top of the wing, the other made a big bulge.' The aircraft was a wreck.

Observing Roy's travails was none other than James 'Ginger' Lacy, Britain's second-highest-scoring Battle of Britain ace, nine times shot down, a man who once brought his Hurricane back to earth riddled with 87 German bullet holes, and despite having risen through the ranks in an extremely class-conscious society, a virtual national hero. He also happened to be Roy's boss, and the first on the scene of his inglorious landing.

'Gawd, I'll be sent home in chains, like our forebears,' Roy thought as Lacy wandered up to the sorry scene. 'You alright?' he enquired.

'Yes, I . . . I'm feeling good, thanks,' said a shaky Roy despite a soreness in the lower back. 'Oh that's good,' replied Lacy, languidly surveying the broken aeroplane. 'It's about time this thing stopped for keeps. It's been giving us trouble.' And at that, he turned and walked away. Nothing more was said.

This was but one encounter with the intriguing nature of the British temperament. In training, Roy had to contend with his early Spitfire's antiquated manual 'hand-pump' undercarriage system. As soon as his wheels left the ground, the pilot selected 'up' from a small switch on the dash, and with his right hand on the control stick, vigorously pumped a large L-shaped lever with his left to bring up the wheels. 'You try flying an aeroplane pumping with your left hand, while not making your right hand swing like this,' he says, showing how he inadvertently slewed the aircraft sideways one morning, collecting his instructor's wingtip with a nasty bump. It wasn't serious, but soon the weary voice of Squadron Leader Farnes was in his ears. 'I don't mind flying with you, Riddel,' he said calmly, 'but please don't hit me again.'

'He was a lovely man,' says Roy. 'We used to go to the pub. He had a car – a little Singer Le Mans – and offered it to me at a good price. He went through France and the Battle of Britain and then after all that, ended up being torpedoed on the way to the Middle East. Terribly sad.'

Roy speaks quietly, occasionally giving out a deep laugh. He tells me when it comes to the war, it's the amusing things he prefers to think about, and for good reason.

'There were four pilots that knocked around with me when I first got to England: Arthur Corser, Bill Norman, Norm Mullett and Tommy Enright,' he says, rattling off the names with ease. 'One of them had done law. One had a commission. Within six months they were all dead. That's why I laugh at the war. If I think about all the other stuff, I get all churned up.'

Roy joined No. 66 Squadron, an RAF unit that had seen action in the Battle of Britain but was now stationed at England's relatively quiet southwest corner at Perranporth in Cornwall.

Despite being one of the most instantly recognisable aircraft of all time, the Spitfire throughout its long and illustrious career was made to perform some curious roles for which it was wholly unsuited and for which its famously graceful outline was outrageously defiled. It had, at various stages, its wings stretched and tapered, then clipped off at the ends, and its tail and engine grotesquely enlarged to increase performance. It was made to carry drop-tanks, bombs and rockets, forced into the roles of dive-bomber and ground-attack, and even to fly off aircraft carriers to perform extended patrols over deserts and jungles, all tasks for which R. J. Mitchell's elegant short-range interceptor was never designed.

But the particular round hole into which Roy's Spitfires were shoved was that of long-range maritime escort. 'We had a 40-gallon tank stuck under the port wing which couldn't be thrown off,' he says. This not only looked ridiculous, but drastically affected the performance of the delicately weighted aircraft. On one occasion, the squadron had to escort some twin-engine Whirlwind fighters on a rocket-firing operation into France. Catching up to them in their strangely lopsided Spitfires, the smart alec Whirlwind leader called up his 'escorts' on the radio/telephone. 'Well, hello there. It's a pity we had to throttle back so you could keep up with us.' The jibe was greeted with silence.

Three German battleships, the *Scharnhorst*, *Gneisenau* and *Prinz Eugen*, were, in mid-1941, harboured in the French port of Brest, being harassed by bombers of the RAF before their daring 'dash' up the Channel to safety. The Luftwaffe did their best to protect them, which included attacks on British airfields, and one day Roy was a witness to one of them. 'This Junkers 88 came hurtling over and bombed the airstrip,' he remembers. His mate, fellow Australian Bill Norman, instantly dived into a slimy gutter, but Roy was intrigued. 'I was fascinated by the thing,' he says. Part of the airfield defence was a series of rockets on wires which, at the press of a button in the control tower, shot skywards to entangle in the propellers of hostile aircraft. 'He was too late on the button,' says Roy. He watched them fire harmlessly into the air, the Junkers got away, and Bill Norman was covered in muck. A little while later, Bill was dead, killed in a collision attempting to chase down just such a German raider.

Roy operated with Fighter Command at one of its quietest periods of the war, after the initial battles of France and Britain, but before the fury of Normandy and the Second Front. With the Continent occupied, all that could be done was to fly over the German airfields, drop a few bombs here and there, and generally make a nuisance of yourself. These oddly codenamed 'rhubarb' and 'ramrod' raids were, according to Roy, 'pretty ineffectual', with not many sightings of enemy aircraft to be had. Nonetheless, the squadron lost eight Spitfires in the time Roy was with it – almost half its pilot strength. On several occasions, he nearly added his own name to the ledger.

His obvious skill evident to all, Roy was soon leading formations. Coming back across the Channel in bad weather, he was not too sure just how close he was to the English coast. Then, looking out, he saw that he and the squadron were flying through a forest of barrage balloons, tethered to the ground by strong, steel cables which could shear through an aircraft's wing like paper. Amazingly, the Spitfires continued through them unharmed. They later realised they had crossed the coast over the heavily defended port of Southampton. 'Good,' he said to the rest over the radio. 'Looks like we've found England.'

Later, he went through an uncanny replay of his earlier engine-failure episode, with near-dire consequences. 'I think I got hit by ground fire,' he tells me. With a damaged oil-cooler, Roy made it back across the Channel to his new base at Portreath on Cornwall's rocky tip, just before his oil-deprived engine began to seize. The prop windmilled for a while and then stopped dead as the cliffs loomed ahead with the aerodrome just beyond. 'I couldn't tell if I was going to make it to the 'drome,' he says. Looking about, he noticed a soft strip of beach right below him and prepared to turn in for a belly landing, but a snap decision made him think he might just make it home. On a long glide, with only the sound of the wind flowing over the aircraft, Roy managed to put his wheels down on the grass at the end of the runway.

Later that night in the pub, a local soldier approached the RAF pilots as they enjoyed their pints. 'Who was that fella today whose engine stopped when he was coming in to land?' he asked. 'Someone pointed to me,' says Roy. 'Oh I wasn't too worried,' he announced to the soldier, 'I was going to just put it down on the beach.'

'I'm glad you didn't,' replied the soldier. 'We'd just finished laying mines on it.'

'I don't know what they were more worried about,' says Roy. 'Me blowing up, or them having to come and get me.'

Even relatively mundane flying duties could have their moments of drama. At 20000 feet one day, Roy was flying back and forth across Plymouth facilitating a radar check exercise for the operators to test their skills and equipment. The advantage of the Spitfire IIa was the range afforded by its additional fuel tank, but only if it actually functioned. 'The clouds were getting a bit thick. When I changed over onto the extra tank, it refused to feed,' he says and, once again, his engine began to splutter and die.

Deciding now was a fine time to head down through the clouds to Mother Earth, Roy noticed a couple of bright yellow painted Tiger Moth trainers in the sky ahead of him. 'I was surprised to see them that close to the south coast,' he says, but he thought that he could squeeze past them to their training airfield below. The trainee pilots would no doubt have been surprised to see a spluttering Spitfire fly down between them, but not as surprised as Roy when he realised that there were a good many more of them, which he had failed to spot in their drab green camouflage paint.

'Suddenly there were Tiger Moths everywhere – landing, and

taking off. I hadn't seen them,' he says. In the alarm of weaving his way through the trainers without power, he forgot the last part of the landing procedure – 'undercarriage-mixture-pitch-fuel-*flaps*' – and came hurtling along the trainer airfield at high speed. 'A stone wall pulled me up faster than any flaps,' says Roy, and he hurtled into it. Just another in the growing collection of very bent aeroplanes Roy was becoming responsible for.

When at last he was issued with the improved Spitfire V, he was more than pleased with his new mount. I asked him if he encountered enemy fighters. 'I had a shot at a few,' he tells me, 'but I don't think I bothered anyone. I got better at it in New Guinea.'

Roy's war, relatively quiet so far, was about to take a very dramatic turn.

'When we heard the stories of the army blokes being tied to coconut trees and used for bayonet practice, we hated the Japanese. We wanted to kill them all, I think.'

With his homeland in peril, Roy was posted back to Australia, to join the ranks of perhaps the most famous fighter unit in the RAAF, No. 75 Squadron. Thrown together in Townsville in March 1942, its pilots were sent into battle with just a few weeks' training, and proceeded to write themselves into the history books. In an extraordinary six-week defence of Port Moresby, they stood alone against the continuous Japanese aerial assault for 44 legendary days. Although its heavy P-40 Kittyhawks were no match for the nimble Japanese Zeros in a fight, No. 75 Squadron nonetheless accounted for thirty-four enemy aircraft destroyed – the first being chalked up just hours after its arrival at Seven Mile Strip – but virtually wiped itself out in the process. When time came for it to be stood down, there was almost no one left to be sent home. Only one serviceable aircraft remained out of the original twenty-five. Twelve pilots had been killed, and many more wounded.

In July 1942 Roy, now a junior officer, became part of No. 75 Squadron's most recent incarnation, just in time to be sent back into another maelstrom, the Battle of Milne Bay.

Historians, as well as veterans of this campaign, constantly bemoan the poor status Milne Bay holds in the pantheon of our military achievements. They're probably right. Turning back a 2000-odd strong force of elite Japanese marines, preventing them from gaining the vital aerodromes and outflanking Port Moresby was an astonishing feat of daring, quick thinking and courage which cost the lives of 161 Australians, but many times more of the enemy. It was also the first real occasion the air force fought alongside the army, each winning the undying respect of the other. For the Japanese, it was an unmitigated disaster, their first defeat on land, ending in an ignominious, previously unthinkable, withdrawal.

In stark contrast to the fields and stone walls of Cornwall, Roy's new home was a clearing in a coconut plantation on the eastern tip of New Guinea – wedged between the mountains and the sea – where perforated metal 'Marsden Matting' had been laid down over mud to form a runway. 'It rained every day,' says Roy, 'but it was quite a good strip. I enjoyed landing on it.'

Not long after arriving, Roy and some of the pilots were sitting about as the intelligence officer explained the situation. 'The Japanese fleet is currently in the China Straits,' he said. No one paid much attention. 'The China Straits,' he reiterated with a little more urgency, 'are not in China. They lie between us and Goodenough Island – just around the corner!' Early next morning, 25 August, the Japanese landed just a few miles down the track.

'People decry the Kittyhawks,' says Roy. (He's right, and I'm one of them, though I resist the urge to do so now.) 'But they were perfect for Milne Bay.' Indeed, photographs of the jungle after heavy strafing by the Kittyhawk's six half-inch machine guns show it looking like it had been done over by a giant scythe.

'We were up before dawn,' says Roy. 'We stuck to our leader and just strafed the hell out of things. We destroyed their barges, destroyed their food and petrol and hopefully destroyed them.'

The Kittyhawks got to grips with the enemy that morning even before the soldiers of the 2/10 Infantry Battalion did so on the ground. Roy shows me the photograph of his own aircraft, inscribed with the word 'Orace' on the nose. 'My father was Horace – it was named for him,' he tells me.

The Japanese brought in their men and supplies along the narrow, twenty-mile wide bay not on large ships, but as a flotilla of small boats and barges. Many were of light construction and were shredded by the tremendous firepower of the low-flying Kittyhawks. An army officer six miles away on the other side of the bay described the sound of their guns not as a chatter but as a roar.

For the next few weeks, Roy and the men of Nos 75 and 76 Squadrons underwent a daily ritual of taking off and blasting the Japanese as they attempted to fight their way towards the airstrips. One day in August, he is reminded by Judy, he was up four times.

The Japanese advanced but failed to break through. The defending Australians (and some rather terrified Americans from an engineering company) were reminded of the Western Front a quarter of a century earlier, as successive waves of bunched-together Japanese marines attempted to charge over open ground and were mown down in piles.

As sure as they attempted to resupply by night, the Kittyhawks would appear at dawn roaring in low over the coconut fronds and blasting everything the pilots could cram into their gunsights. One of the most famous photographs taken not only of Milne Bay but of the entire New Guinea campaign is that of a lean, exhausted

Australian soldier standing next to a damaged Japanese Type-95 light tank they had managed to get ashore. For a while its commander had guided it along the narrow jungle track until shot by an Australian sniper. The vehicle slewed off and became bogged, blocking the way for others behind. It was still there long after the battle had ended.

'We all had a shot at that tank,' Roy remembers, bringing the fragment of history to life. 'It was painted yellow.'

It was at Milne Bay that Roy, for the first time, properly encountered enemy fighters. Flying in their Zeroes from Lae and Rabaul, the Japanese desperately tried to gain control of the air and prevent the pitiless extermination of their people on the ground. For Roy, it was an exciting time, but a dark one.

The simplicity and brutality of the war on the ground was in some ways mirrored in the air. Roy tells of 'head-on' encounters with Japanese aircraft, flying towards them at high speed, each daring the other to pull away in a grim game of 'chicken'. On one of these occasions, he was number two to his close friend Stuart Munro. The two Queenslanders knew each other from home, Munro's parents owning a cane property close to his own. 'We'd both flown together in England, even both been hit over there,' he says. Stuart had survived several such encounters, but this time, Roy saw him emerge, 'trailing smoke, and he was shot down and killed', he says.

A little while later, Roy recognised the aircraft of the same Japanese pilot who had claimed his friend, and at 700 feet over the base, locked into another head-on charge. 'Stuart was dead,' says Roy. 'He was my friend and I felt pretty strongly about it. We must have been closing at about 600 miles an hour. He was the more experienced pilot, so I just kept shooting.' Perhaps the Japanese pilot sensed the resolve in the man he was approaching, perhaps it was the thought of the six guns in his wings.

As the two aircraft closed, the Zero began to pull away. 'Luckily, I didn't,' says Roy. 'I lifted the nose a bit and blasted a great big hole in his starboard wing, and he went in.'

I ask Roy whether there was a point that he himself was prepared to pull away. He ponders the question. 'I don't know,' he says in a curiously abstract tone. 'You get so engrossed in it, you see.'

Later, people who had witnessed the overhead duel remarked to him in awe, 'Jeez, we thought you were going to collide.'

But the day was not over yet. His friend gone, and a bitter taste in his mouth, Roy looked around and hooked up with the squadron CO, Les Jackson, whose own number two was nowhere to be seen.

At the end of the bay, a Japanese Zero was lying in clear, shallow water near the beach, a recent victim of the guns of an American B-26 Marauder. As they approached the scene, two companion Zeros were attempting to strafe the stricken aircraft of their leader and destroy it before it could be captured and evaluated.

Les Jackson was only the squadron's second Commanding Officer, having been handed the job when his legendary predecessor, a man whose qualities as a leader exemplified the spirit of No. 75's small band of tenacious airmen, was killed over Port Moresby back in April. It was in his honour that No. 75's aerodrome had been renamed Jackson Field. For Les, they were considerable shoes to fill, even more so as they belonged to those of his older brother, John. A more melancholy duty can hardly be imagined.

But one thing the younger Jackson had learned was that their E model Kittyhawk, excellent gun platform though it was, was no match for the highly manoeuvrable Zero in a one-on-one fight. The one, indeed the only advantage that could be brought to bear was height, and, on this particular day, here they were poised above two unsuspecting Zeros.

'Les and I were up at about 1500 feet,' says Roy. 'The Japanese were just above the water.' The two pilots looked down, then swooped. 'Les picked on one, I picked on the other.' The Japanese, caught at the top of their climb, were hit from behind at 300 miles an hour. 'They were so busy trying to demolish the plane below they didn't see us. I hit him from about fifty yards, and he got the lot. They both went straight into the water. We were lucky.' The nimble but badly protected Zeros crumpled under direct hits and crashed into the sea. 'I'd been shot at myself over the last few days,' says Roy. 'I remember hitting the button and letting out a great yell of delight.'

Two kills in one day. It had been an eventful one and the day he earned a name for himself in the squadron. Quite simply, 'Shit Hot'.

The air war became something of a strafing campaign. The Australians would attack the beaches and jungles; the Zeros would strafe their airstrips. If alerted early enough, the Kittyhawk pilots would attempt to climb above the Japanese before they appeared.

'One day,' says Roy, 'we were trying to get above them but couldn't do so.' Over their own airfield, he found himself in the highly dangerous position of being right in amongst the Zeros. 'There were about ten of us. I was flying another bloke's aircraft that day, and I knew it always swung strongly to the left. Above me I saw one Zero turn around and so I did what any law-abiding hero would do in a Kitty – I dived.' But before he could get anywhere they were on his tail. Immediately, Roy felt thumps all over his aircraft and watched a line of cannon shells and bullets rip along his tail and left wing, amazingly, straddling either side of the full ammunition boxes. 'If those had been hit I wouldn't be chatting to you now,' he says. 'We lost four aircraft and pilots straightaway.'

In one of those moments in which time slows to a stop, and

casts itself indelibly on the memory, Roy recalls the strange smell as the Japanese shells hit his aircraft. 'I was going down flat out at about four or five hundred miles an hour,' he continues, 'and noticed I was skidding through the air sideways to the left.' His tailplane had also been hit, and a hinge on the rudder jammed, refusing to move to the right. 'I could only turn left. The Japanese pilot must have felt very frustrated,' he says.

Staggering down towards the airfield, Roy managed to line up, put it down and pull up, continuing his tradition of surviving rough landings. 'When I eventually landed, Les Winter, the man who usually flew the aircraft, came out of the flight tent. "Christ, Riddel," he said. "Look what you've done to my plane!" I thought he might have been pleased to see me.'

'How on earth did you manage to fly it?' I ask with a certain incredulity. With that same air of bewilderment, he tells me he isn't quite sure, but as he walked around the aircraft, pale-faced, inspecting the chaos of holes of varying sizes in wings and fuselage, he no doubt asked himself the same question.

Milne Bay was a short, sharp and extremely nasty campaign, which brought home to the Australians the true nature of their enemy, as well as the type of war they were fighting. After Milne Bay, it is said, no quarter was given or expected from either side. Having lost the gamble, the Japanese were made to suffer the new humiliation of evacuating their remaining troops one night by sea, shooting their own wounded rather than allowing them to be captured.

Roy clocked up 800 hours on Kittyhawks, then came home to do a stint as a test pilot. Here, without an enemy in sight, he came closest to his demise when his brakes, badly adjusted, flipped his aircraft over on landing, breaking his neck and sending him to hospital for five months. He has suffered for it ever since. 'You can put a cigarette into my right leg and I can hardly feel it,' he says today.

He flew again later in the war, in Moratai, but by this time it was hard to see the point of harassing the already-defeated Japanese.

'I could see the uselessness of it all. The things we were bombing and strafing were of no value at all – pockmarked airstrips that you couldn't have landed anything on anyway. They were just getting rid of the ordnance. Blokes were dying from useless trips.'

Apart from being one of the few pilots I had met who had engaged enemies on both sides of the world, Roy was unique in another way. He was the only pilot who refused to show me his logbook. It was there, next to him on the table, for the whole of our discussion, but remained closed. 'It's a very personal thing, a logbook,' was the only reference to it he made, glancing at its cover. I ponder this afterwards. Roy could remember the name of every pilot he knew who had been killed both in Europe and the Pacific. Perhaps he was happy for some of the memories to remain locked within its pages. A stranger poring over it, pulling at something here, rattling off a name there, was perhaps more than he was prepared to endure.

Outside, as I re-entered the world of the present, the sweet air mixed headily with the smells of the sea. Almost as an aside before I go, there on the lush manicured grass he tells me one last story.

After the war, he sought out the names of the two Zero pilots he and Les shot down that day over Milne Bay. 'They were good pilots,' he says. 'One had twelve kills, the other fourteen.' He also discovered the identity of the downed man whose aeroplane they were attempting to destroy. It belonged to another ace, one Petty Officer Second Class Enji Kakimoto of the Imperial Japanese Navy Air Service – a farmer's son, twenty-two years old and already with five kills to his credit, two in a single day over Guadalcanal. Having ditched his Zero and swum to shore, he had watched in dismay from the shelter of the trees as his two flight companions first strafed his stricken aircraft, then fell to Roy's and Les's guns. For three days Kakimoto was cared for by Papuan natives who led him to believe they would reunite him with his own, before handing him over to a lone Australian signaller, who marched him into an astonished RAAF camp nearby. The notes from his interrogation state little other than that he was able to neatly print his name in English: E. KAKIMOTO.

One of the few Zero pilots to be taken prisoner, Kakimoto, in August 1943, threw a rope over a beam in his prison hut in Cowra and hanged himself on the night of the breakout.

'I visited Cowra one time and found his brass plate,' says Roy. 'I put a bit of flowering gum on it,' he says. 'He was quite a warrior.' From one warrior to another, it was some gesture.

HARRY
Air Gunner, RAAF

'Who gave you this number?' is the abrupt greeting I receive when I ring Harry for the first time. I am taken aback, but I suppose I should have been expecting it at some stage or other. Tracking down elderly people from just about every conceivable source, then ringing them out of the blue to pry into difficult events sixty years in their past, it was almost certain I was going to come up against one who wasn't pleased as punch to hear from me.

'*Who gave you this number?*' he repeats with slightly more agitation. The truth is, I don't actually know, and this just infuriates him further. It could have come from anyone. His was simply a name in a Spirex notepad I had jotted down sometime in the recent past. Organisation not being one of my more shining qualities, I had never quite managed to establish a central repository for the large number of names of former aircrew people had passed on to me at random. Friends, wives, acquaintances, old employees, neighbours and a variety of others with connections both strong and tenuous had telephoned, emailed and buttonholed me, thrusting scribbled names on the backs of business cards and torn diary pages, all of which formed part of an increasingly daunting pile in an out-tray on my desk. Occasionally I would manage to work my way to the bottom, but others would soon take their place. Once I pulled out a paper napkin, handed to me a few weeks previously by someone's long-estranged daughter-in-law. Beside a name and number, 'Air Force?' had been written in smudged eyebrow pencil. When I rang, a cold female voice told me the man had died the year before. I made up a story about where I had found the number, apologised and rang off.

It was what was written next to Harry's name that made me perhaps a little more persistent than I would otherwise have been – 'Nuremberg'. I looked at it for a while, intrigued. Most times I had at least managed to scribble the source on the back, but the identity of this contributor was a mystery. Certainly it was someone aware of the importance of the great medieval Bavarian city and its tragic twentieth century history, but who? I had no idea, and neither – much to his annoyance – does Harry.

He is gruff and combative. 'What do you want to know about all that stuff for?' In my politest voice, I explain the nature of my enquiry but assure him that if he chooses not to participate, I will trouble him no further. At this, he makes a kind of a 'humph', which I hope might be a softening, so I fire a question to try and keep him a little off balance, and to let him know that I know my stuff. 'So, you were in the Nuremberg raid?'

This really gets him going. 'How the hell do you know that?' he barks again. I begin to sense I am going to get nowhere with the grumpy old coot and decide to cut my losses. Perhaps he hears the resignation in my voice. 'Hang on, hang on. Yeah, I was on the Nuremberg raid. So what?'

I had made it a rule never to conduct an interview over the phone and say so, but because he's the only one I have met who was on the Nuremberg disaster, and recalling something about the bird in the bush, I ask him to tell me about it. There is a pause.

Then, just as abruptly he says, 'Alright, son, I'll tell you over lunch. Naval and Military Club. Next Wednesday. One o'clock. Wear a tie and don't be late,' and hangs up.

And so I find myself running down Little Collins Street six days later, a couple of books and my tape recorder thumping awkwardly around inside a bag, sweating under an unfamiliar collar and tie. A clock somewhere says 1:01. I see him about fifty metres off, looking anxiously at his watch and throwing glances up and down the street. He is a stocky man, wearing a reefer jacket and grey pressed trousers. Despite the heat of the November afternoon, not a drop adorns his brow. 'You're late,' he tells me as I stand panting before him. Before an apology can be offered, he has turned on his heels and entered the building.

Despite my lifelong obsession with things military, and being a former inmate of a school to which the Naval and Military Club is a virtual old boys' association, I have never previously darkened its door. I am a little disappointed. I had expected something like a Mayfair Club: plenty of Chesterfields, wood panelling and an ageing retainer called Bernard who greets you by name at the front door. In truth, the retrofitted cafe where I had just been catching up with a friend and lost track of time fitted the bill far more than this airy, contemporary setting. A few framed portraits, a cabinet full of medals, a couple of old swords banged up on the wall, but apart from that, it could be one of dozens of modern-ish establishments within the same square kilometre. But I'm not here for the setting, or the food. I'm here to speak to Harry, and I suspect it isn't going to be easy.

As we sit at the table, we size each other up properly. His face is more youthful than I had expected, with pale sharp eyes that dart everywhere then fix you with a gaze. I put my small tape recorder on the table. 'What's that?' he says suspiciously. I explain that I need to record him, but he will have none of it. 'Turn it off. We'll talk first.' I pretend to fiddle around with it, pushing it to one side to hide the little plastic window where the tape goes around. 'What's that red light?' he says, and I know I am foiled. With great reluctance, and a rising annoyance of my own, I switch it off and take out my notebook.

As soon as the tape recorder is gone, he calls over a waitress and orders a bottle of red. Without looking at the menu, he asks for a steak – rare. I order the duck. He pours me a generous glass, but as I'm virtually incapable of drinking anything in the daytime, let alone red, without falling into a soporific heap, I sip daintily and watch Harry take to it with gusto. 'Not bad eh?' he says holding the glass. He is nuggetty, and highly alert. The perfect rear gunner.

'So, what are you on about anyway?' he asks. He remains suspicious at my claims of innocence as to the identity of his nominator, and runs through a list of suspects in his head, grumbling lowly to himself. 'Well, anyway,' he says at last, 'we're here now, I suppose.' Then suddenly reversing his earlier reticence, he tells me he's always been 'a bit of a loner'.

'Been married four times,' he says. 'You?' I tell him that's four more than I have. He then asks if I have children, and my answer quells a momentary look of alarm.

'I'm from the bush,' he tells me without revealing where. 'I was always a good shot.' He tells me that on his gunnery course, he was noted for his proficiency, as well as his enthusiasm. I can well believe it.

Sent to an Operational Training Unit in England, he remembers one night flying low enough to smell the smoke from a chimney stack they had just over-flown. Then, there was a posting to an RAF squadron in Lincolnshire.

Gradually, Harry starts to loosen up. Whatever suspicions he had seem to evaporate with the wine. The waitress, pretty and with an accent, arrives with the meals. Harry's steak is so pink that I quip that the chef probably showed it the hotplate rather than placed it on it. He points to it with his fork. 'Shush. He heard that.' It's the first funny thing he's said, and I start to wonder whether all the gruffness has been a ruse. He looks at my duck curiously, not sure why anyone would want to eat such a thing.

Within five days of arriving on base, Harry's crew was posted on the battle order for their first trip, and a more dramatic debut cannot be imagined – 30 March 1944: Nuremberg. It was a distant target, and undertaken at a time when operations were usually suspended due to a bright moon. But an early meteorological report that day stated that a high layer of cloud would conceal the bomber stream and that the target would be clear.

A terrible alignment of events brought disaster to the bombers that night. Because of the length of the trip, it was boldly decided to abandon the usual series of doglegs and fly an almost direct route to the target. This, it was hoped, would not only save fuel, but baffle the Germans with an unfamiliar tactic. The Luftwaffe night fighter controllers were not so easily duped. They correctly ignored the diversionary raids and assembled their 200-odd aircraft around two radio beacons code-named Ida and Otto, which in a terrible coincidence, lay directly across the bombers' flight path. The German pilots couldn't believe their luck. Instead of having to hunt for the 800 Lancasters and Halifaxes, they simply appeared around them, clogging their radar screens. The bomber crews fought a 750-mile running battle from the Belgian border to the target, with aircraft going down at the rate of one per minute. Pilots reported the ground below looking like a battlefield with the wrecks of flaming aircraft dotted all the way to Nuremberg.

The meteorologists had got it dreadfully wrong. The protective cloud cover did not eventuate, and the light of the half-moon was so bright, one pilot reported being able to clearly read the squadron identification letters on the Lancaster beside him. Clear white condensation trails caught the moonlight and acted as fingers pointing the way for the German pilots. An astonishing ninety-six bombers were shot down in the massacre and another ten crashed in England. A massive 745 aircrew were killed or wounded and nearly 160 taken prisoner. It was, and has been known since as, the blackest night in the history of the Royal Air Force.

Harry, sitting in his perspex capsule at the rear of his Lancaster, saw it all.

'They got onto us as soon as we crossed over into France,' he says. 'You could see for miles. It was like daylight. You saw them when they opened fire with their tracers. I saw aircraft going down all over the place,' he says. Nothing was spoken about it on the intercom to the rest of the crew. They watched the unfolding carnage around them in stunned silence.

Harry was not himself attacked that night, but what he saw shocked him to the core, and forged his attitude to the remainder of his tour. Not for him to simply sit and wait for catastrophe to come knocking. He instead made a few personal modifications to even up the odds. He had the armourer remove the tracer bullets from his ammunition so as not to give away his position, and in a trade of range for firepower, his four Browning machine guns were realigned to converge at just 300 yards. 'That's about as far as you could see in the dark anyway,' he says. With the guns firing a combined eighty rounds a second, it was, he hoped, a deadly punch for anything that got in their way. He also liked to keep moving. 'I spoke to some German pilots after the war,' he tells me. 'They told me if the turret wasn't moving and active, they reckoned they were either asleep or not very interested so they'd attack them.'

But those guns still had to work. One of his most vivid memories (all Harry's memories, I realise, are vivid) was of a Junkers 88 looming suddenly out of the dark immediately behind him. 'About twice the distance from that wall behind us,' he says, turning around and pointing. Just as the German looked about to fire, Harry yelled 'Go' to his pilot, who put the aircraft into a dive. 'I fired my guns for about ten seconds. That's a terrific time to have all of them firing.' But then three of them jammed, and the other fired only erratically. The German pilot stuck his tail into the dive but backed off a little, no doubt intimidated by Harry's initial aggression, and eventually broke away. He tells me he still sees the metal and perspex lattice nose of the Junkers pursuing him in the darkness. 'We didn't have to use the guns again that night, thank God,' he says, then pauses. 'Oh well, I'm still alive. Are you learning anything?' I assure him I most certainly am.

He goes silent for quite a while, and I can tell that the memories are bubbling up inside.

'I did one trip where my oxygen came undone. I don't know how, Flak or something. I did the whole trip without oxygen at 20000 feet.' From someone else, it would be almost hard to believe. 'And searchlights. When you're coned, you don't know if you're upside down; you don't know which way you are,' he says.

With all the men I speak to, I at least try to extract from them something of the atmosphere in which they fought and flew. I want to hear about the informalities, the asides, the distractions and the small forgotten scraps of conversation that brings it all to life. But he assures me an operational bomber was no place for chit-chat. 'You don't turn on your intercom unless you have something to say,' he tells me in the vivid present tense. Occasionally members of the crew would forget to switch theirs off with the switch located on the oxygen mask. 'You could hear them breathing,' says Harry. 'If anyone leaves one on, you say, "Turn that bloody mike off!" I can remember that.' This for some reason sticks in my imagination for some time.

Unlike some bomber crews I had spoken to who flew near the war's end, Harry served when the prospect of surviving the obligatory thirty trips was at its nadir. 'Three weeks on, one week off. You lived from day to day. Every penny you had, you spent because you weren't there tomorrow. That's the way we lived,' he tells me.

By this time, he has relaxed sufficiently to begin flirting with the waitress who's young enough to be my daughter, let alone his. She's tallish with short dark hair. 'Where do you reckon she's from?' he asks. I guess France but he disagrees. 'I don't act like I'm in my eighties, do I?' I just have to laugh at this one.

Harry no longer has his logbook, so some of the details he gives me are imprecise. He reckons it must have around his twentieth trip when he received a minor leg wound from a piece of flak. Hospitalised for a short time for a minor reason, he was given a brief spell on the ground while his crew carried on their tour with a substitute gunner. One day he was summoned by the CO. 'What have I done wrong now?' he thought to himself as he walked into the big office. But as he stood before him, the officer's mood was conciliatory. 'How are you?' he asked.

'I'm alright. Well, I will be when I get back to the boys,' said Harry. The CO looked at him and said directly, 'They didn't come back last night.' Harry says he simply turned his head in the other direction. 'I couldn't believe it. I just couldn't believe it. You were so close to your crew. You did everything together.' He becomes silent again at this point and finishes his meal.

Their fate was never discovered. 'They were mine-laying in the Kattegatt and just disappeared,' he says.

The air force didn't like to give you too much time to reflect. Two days later, he was tagged up with a new crew and flying again. They were Canadians, and, still green, looked to Harry as an old hand. 'They were always asking my advice. "What do you think of this, what do you think of that?"'

At this point he takes some papers out of a bag beside his chair. He slides across the slightly yellowing photocopied pages of some documents. I begin to read. It is a citation for the awarding of the Distinguished Flying Medal, something about scoring hits on an enemy aircraft. I look at Harry and detect just the slightest of smirks. This was one he'd been keeping from me. He ignores me as I read and returns to the waitress who, inured by countless afternoons of being chatted up by old men, is surprisingly charming. 'Now where are you from?' he asks. 'France,' she replies. 'Hmm,' he says to me a little miffed, 'you were right.'

Highly respected but rarely awarded, the Distinguished Flying Medal was the 'other ranks' equivalent of the Distinguished Flying Cross. But whereas nearly 20 000 RAF and Commonwealth air force officers were awarded the DFC for acts of bravery in the face of the enemy during World War II, the sergeant-only recipients of the DFM numbered fewer than 7000. Ordinary airmen, it seems, needed to be three times as brave to win a medal. Harry was full of surprises.

He recounts the incident. 'There's a Lanc up there,' he heard the mid-upper gunner say over the intercom. 'That's no bloody Lanc,' he replied peering up from his turret. The aircraft, probably a Messerschmitt 110, swooped down in a curve towards them. 'They get in and get their nose ahead of you and make you fly into their cannon fire,' says Harry. 'He was only two or three hundred yards away.' Harry saw the German drop his starboard wing slightly, and knew he was about to open up. 'I got a burst into him and he dropped away.' I hadn't finished reading the citation before I asked him to tell it to me in his own words. I'd assumed I was reading about him simply damaging an enemy aircraft. 'You mean, you shot him down?' I ask, rather stupidly. 'Yeah, of course I shot him down!' he retorts. The other members of the crew saw the aircraft trailing to the ground, and Harry was officially credited with a kill, as well as a Distinguished Flying Medal.

'Look, why are you interested in all this?' he asks me again, resuming his old line of enquiry. It's not the conversation I feel like having and I push the topic back onto himself.

'Do I act like I'm eighty?' he asks me again. This time I assure him he most certainly does not, although what exactly an eighty-year-old is supposed to act like I don't really know anymore. 'I don't believe in any religion. Mum was a Methodist, but I think it's the greatest bullshit there is. I've never prayed. If anyone should've prayed it's me.' Surely, I suggest, there must have been times in his turret over a burning city with tracer bullets firing towards him out of the darkness when he must have come close. 'Nah,' he says dismissively. 'Never thought about it. Never had the time. You had to think straight, you see, or you were dead.' I ask him if he thought he was going to survive his tour. 'No,' he repeats calmly. 'We lived day to day. Three weeks on, one week off.' Then he reflects a little more on his own luck. 'I didn't give a bugger about anything. Been married four times. Did I tell you that? My fault. I just could never settle down.'

His appetite undiminished, Harry calls the French girl over again and orders the bread and butter pudding. 'It's delicious. You have to have it,' he tells me.

Harry completed an amazing fifty-six operational trips with

Bomber Command, his second tour being flown with a Pathfinder squadron, once flying six trips in five days. 'I was nineteen. Can you believe it? Would you give a gun turret in an aeroplane to a nineteen-year-old today? I wouldn't give them a bike!' he says. 'Yeah, bit of a loner. Always have been. Suited me.'

During the course of our conversation, he alludes to several other instances but refuses to elaborate. He bombed on D-Day but soon after his Lancaster was shot down, he says, by American 'friendly fire' in Normandy. (Such incidents are becoming familiar to me.) He baled out and walked to the American lines, for the second time being the only one of his crew to survive. The experience gave him a dislike for Americans that endures to this day. Try as I may to get him to expand, though, he won't budge. 'Why do you want to know about all this? It was sixty years ago!' he exclaims again.

Then, abruptly as it started, it's over. 'I've talked enough. I'll shut up now,' he says and drinks the extra-strong coffee he has ordered. When some chocolates arrive, he makes sure he gets his rightful share, and a few more.

We split the bill and talk about other things for a while. We discover that we follow the same football club and talk about meeting up at a game sometime. We walk outside and say goodbye. It's still hot, and I immediately find a quiet spot in a nearby park, take out my recorder and record into it everything I can remember. His last words to me are, 'Have I been any use to you?' but I think he knows he has.

My meeting with Harry, who still didn't want me to use his real name, stayed in my head for a long time afterwards. For all his initial gruffness, he opened up to me, not just in terms of his extraordinary war, but in revealing himself in ways that many men of his generation would be incapable of, even if it would occur to them to do so. In some ways, alarmingly, he reminded me a little of myself.

I found Harry a strangely timeless figure, neither young nor old, isolated but not lonely, a man who has run very much his own, slightly disconnected race, and an absolute one of a kind. The perfect rear gunner.

BOB MOLESWORTH
Pilot, RAAF

As beginnings to days go, it had not been a good one. It had been a slow morning to start with, and when I finally got into the car to leisurely open the map to check just where Bob Molesworth lived, I let out a short, sharp scream. Having contented myself that he resided somewhere vaguely on the edge of town, I suddenly realised I had a country drive ahead of me and that I was going to be late. Very late.

Still, a quick call to explain my predicament should suffice, and Bob, according to his son John, had no plans to go anywhere that day.

An hour or so later, hurtling out along the Western Highway in an old white Ford station wagon with a ravenous addiction to petrol (I had bought it in a hurry as an 'in-between' car; that was two years ago), I was beginning to enjoy the beautiful spring day and the comforting hum of the six big cylinders working away beneath the slightly dented bonnet. Then, my eyes flicked routinely down to the temperature gauge and I let out another short sharp scream. It was into the red. Actually, it was beyond the red, the needle having vanished beyond some threshold where temperature needles are never meant to go. Suddenly, everything started to shudder violently. I pulled off onto a side road, stopped abruptly and, cursing, waited an eternity for the needle to reappear. This, I thought, is definitely not the way to endear yourself to a ninety-four-year-old who piloted Bristol Blenheims in Europe and North Africa.

Another phone call to John. Country gent that he was, he offered to come to my rescue, or at least tow me to a wrecker. But after a long wait I opened the cap of the bone-dry radiator, filled up from a nearby garden tap, and to my amazement, managed to start it up. Perhaps I'd got away with it. After yet another phone call to clarify directions, I stopped, hours after my appointed time, at the beginning of an impressive dirt lane lined with sugar gums.

This was a driveway unlike any I had seen, long enough to warrant its own route number. I drove tentatively up through working paddocks and livestock, all well kept and, drought notwithstanding, surprisingly healthy. Everything had that well-ordered, rural blue-blood feel, the home of serious landed gentry. A modest house appeared in view, at which point I was intercepted by a man on a small motorbike who waved and indicated I should follow him to yet another part of the estate. At this point I noticed the car settle into a permanent, disturbed grating sound, like someone trying to saw their way out from under the bonnet. Whatever was causing it, it didn't sound cheap.

At last I came to an old and elegant Victorian-era house, surrounded by ancient azaleas and established trees, the centrepiece of a 4000-acre property that has remained in the family since the 1850s. I was shown in and walked past cabinets full of Victorian cut glass and admired an old framed etching of a Viscount Molesworth that went back to the seventeenth century. The whole place dripped of pedigree.

Bob was wearing overalls and reading with his feet up in the library room, stacked to the ceiling with volumes ancient and modern of every conceivable size. He looked up vaguely and extended his hand. To reach it I had to step over an enormous labrador who had comfortably stretched out – as labradors do – in the most inconvenient place possible. Short of a forklift, this mutt wasn't moving. 'Hello, puppy,' I said cheerily, trying not to sound ironic.

Bob is by far the oldest flyer I have spoken to. So much so that when he joined up in early 1941, he had to *lower* his age to get in. 'All my friends in the Western District were going into the army, but I thought, "If I can get into the air force, I will,"' he says in a slow but very deliberate voice. 'Twenty-eight was the limit. I was just on the borderline. I think it was an advantage being a little older. I had an excellent instructor – a Flying Doctor in fact.'

I settle into an elegant old couch in the elegant old book-lined study. I hand Bob my prized and indispensable *Bomber Squadrons of the RAF*. He takes it and begins reading quietly to himself. There is a long pause that stretches into an extended silence as he surveys the pages pertaining to his old squadron, No. 114. I sit there quietly as he turns the pages. Perhaps he's forgotten I am in the room.

'Yes,' he says at last, pointing to a photograph. 'This is after they brought in the long-nose Blenheims.' Time, I realise, isn't something to which Bob feels any particular deference, so I just relax. Besides, after today's performance, I'm in no position to rush anybody.

He tells me about his training at Somers, learning to fly Tiger Moths at Essendon Airport and receiving his wings at Wagga, thereby avoiding a long and chilly sojourn in Canada. Embarking from Sydney, he set foot in a very battered England in October 1941.

It's a slow, measured afternoon with Bob, not just on account of his age but, I suspect, the legacy of a life on the land. If I am to find gold in his story, I am going to have to dig for it.

The twin-engine Bristol Blenheim, never one of the most auspicious aircraft in the RAF's arsenal, had a crew of three.

'We got together at the local pub,' he tells me, describing the day he met his crew. It's a complicated tale involving a missed train, a remark on a platform, and a conversation around pints of ale. At the end of it, he had found Bill Burberry, his cockney wireless/air gunner, and Tim Denny, his navigator who still resides in Tasmania.

Despite their poor reputation, Bob enjoyed flying the Blenheim, and his squadron was the first to be equipped with this somewhat ignominious type. 'The trouble is, they were already outmoded,' he says. Indeed the Bristol Blenheim, developed amazingly enough as a quick twin-motor fighter in the early thirties, was initially ahead of its time, arising out of a millionaire's private venture and blessed with high speed and long range. But that was ten long years before the war, and by the time the shooting started, it had been well eclipsed by rapid developments in single-engine fighters. Initial losses were dreadful.

He remembers his first trip well – 8 March 1942. 'They sent us over at night to bomb the docks at Ostend. Only two of us went.' Then, as if remembering something important for the first time in years, 'The other bloke didn't come back. They never found out what happened to him.'

I scan the pages of his logbook and come across a curious list of early-war targets I have not seen before: Harlingen, Soesterberg and Schiphol aerodrome near Amsterdam, today the site of one of Europe's largest airports. These operations were the beginning of the RAF's 'Intruder' raids – small packets of aircraft attacking

German bomber and fighter stations in occupied France and Holland. Sometimes they were effective, mostly they gave little more than nuisance value. But it was the genesis of a tactic the RAF would employ for the rest of the war.

Bob began operations way before the development of electronic aids that would later be able to pinpoint a target in a city thousands of blacked-out miles away. All he and his crew had to rely on was good intelligence, a thorough briefing and a compass. 'And they weren't much good,' he says.

It was a time when losses from German fighters were heavy. I ask him if he encountered them. 'Oh . . . yes,' he says vaguely then goes into another tantalising pause. 'They were very good, the German pilots. Much better than the Italians,' he says, still flicking through the pages of the book. 'What did you do when you met one?' I ask. Another pause. 'Well, we'd turn towards them,' he says, not looking up. This perplexes me completely. I decide to just wait. At last he resumes. 'We'd turn towards them, and then go underneath them. Oh, yes, we lost a few.' I'll bet they did.

I prompt Bob by asking him the basics, such as how often he flew after becoming operational. He leans forward and places his old logbook on his lap, turning the pages with the same hand that more than sixty years previously filled it so meticulously with entries in ink: targets, bomb loads and flight durations. There is another long pause, then he notices something and reads aloud. 'Oh yes – *"badly shot up by a night fighter"* – lucky to get back to England that time.' More silence. It's all becoming a kind of torture. I'm beginning to fear I'll barely have anything to write about. Perhaps he's getting back at me for my lack of punctuality after all.

'What, er, happened on this occasion, Bob?' I ask tentatively.

It was 26 April 1942. He tells me it was another 'Intruder' trip:

duck over to Eindhoven at night, drop a few bombs and cause as much mayhem as possible then get back home fast. 'Yes, we caught up with a German,' Bob says. 'Or rather, he caught up with us.'

At this point, Bob pauses again, but this time I can tell something has occurred to him. 'Actually,' he says, and without completing the sentence, gets up and goes to the bookshelf.

'I don't think we were supposed to do it,' he says, rummaging for something in the stacks. He pulls down an old, thin volume and, still standing, opens it. 'I used to write it all up.'

'Write it all up?' I ask.

'Yes. Write it all up. After the trips.' He hands me the volume. It is an old exercise book, red-covered and with an old-fashioned gummed label on the front reading 'On His Majesty's Service' and 'Robert Molesworth' in ink. 'No, we definitely weren't supposed to do it.'

Inside, every page is covered in Bob's tidy, old-fashioned hand-writing. Blinking, I realise it is his own, personal diary of every operational trip he ever flew. 'My goodness,' is all I can say. I open the first page. The handwriting is clear and legible and I begin to read:

8.3.42 HIGH LEVEL ATTACK ON DOCKS AT OSTEND.
A/C BLENHEIM IV V.5645 R for ROBERT. BASE – ALDEBURGH –
OSTEND – SOUTHWOLD – BASE. 4x250lb G.P. BOMBS.

This was our first operational trip so of course we were somewhat
nervous and excited. The aerodrome was in a frightful state with
melting snow and wind, however we were rather lucky to get off
as eighteen a/c were taking off that night, and as we discovered
later, several of them got bogged and were unable to go . . .

I turn from page to page. It is like the opening of a floodgate. Reading, I can at last hear Bob's voice loud and clear. Each trip is here vividly described, written only hours after it had been completed and with the excitement and freshness of youth leaping off the page. A little like the diaries kept by Harvey Bawden, but in much longer form. Almost an essay has been written for each operation. I flip through it. Keeping such a journal during wartime was a security risk and a strict no-no in the RAF. Had it been discovered he would have been in some trouble and definitely lost it. If I had been looking for gold, here it was in my hands.

I ask Bob whether he had ever shown it to anyone, or given it to the newspapers. 'I don't think so. No,' he says, as I turn the pages carefully.

Bob's journal could be the subject of a book on its own and it is beyond the scope of this one to reproduce it fully. For the next few hours I take in the story of his tour as he tells it, complementing it with what he wrote just hours after he landed. The journal fills in what Bob, by way of memory or modesty, omits. It's an extraordinary, time-shrinking journey.

But back to the night they met the German night fighter. I read that even before they encountered it, they were already defenceless:

> After crossing the English coast at 2000 feet Billy Burberry on testing his guns discovered that they were unserviceable. I asked him to try to fix them. Bill told me the 'fire' and 'safe' units were missing so it was impossible . . . I decided to carry on to the target and told Bill to keep a special look out as it was a bright moonlit night.

'Those nights were rare,' says Bob, 'but we were grateful for it later.' They found the target, bombed without incident and headed home.

About thirty miles from the coast, Bill asked me if he could reel out the aerial and get a wireless fix. Thinking we were out of night fighter range, I told him to do so. Just as I heard the aerial reeling out, a stream of tracer seemed to blind me, there was a sickening explosion and the old kite was completely filled with black smoke and the smell of cordite . . . I realised we were up against a night fighter and had been badly hit . . . I then saw it climb over the top of us having given us another burst. Two bullets whipped past my head like wasps, and made two neat holes in the perspex in front of my face.

It was, says Bob, a very fast, very deadly Junkers 88, but he knew it would only follow them thirty or so miles out to sea. 'I dived and flew back at about twenty feet above the sea, keeping it between ourselves and the moon until it lost us,' he says. Limping back towards England, Bob had no desire to come down in the Channel. 'You couldn't ditch a Blenheim,' he says. 'It would go straight down like a stone.'

Bob now took stock of the damage. I read aloud some of his own words describing the scene:

A bullet had hit Bill's hand and a shell had exploded right beside his shoulder. The floor of the aircraft had been torn away by cannon fire, Bill's parachute having fallen out into the sea. The wireless had been hit, the instrument panel was shot away, the hydraulic system destroyed and the electric circuit ceased to function, so we had no lights whatever as we approached the English coast.

At this Bob chuckles a little. 'Sounds like we were in trouble, doesn't it?' They gained height, and made landfall over East Anglia.

'We crossed the coast at 700 feet, which was a great relief,' he says, 'but then I noticed the starboard engine losing power. I tried all sorts of things to keep it going but then it just stopped.' As he tells me this, I look down to the journal.

> Immediately I tried to trim the aircraft to fly on one engine but discovered the rudder trimming gear to be completely jammed from a shell-burst . . . I told Tim we were losing height and would have to land just where we were.

'We let a flare off at about 250 feet and that's when we were grateful for the bright night because we spotted an airstrip still under construction in the moonlight,' says Bob. 'I turned and went in. The wheels wouldn't come down so we made a belly landing.'

> . . . we came in downwind without flaps and must have touched down at about 120 mph. We bumped and crashed along the ground until we came to a sudden stop . . . then there was a flash of flame and we knew we were in for more trouble.

'Actually,' he tells me, 'the sudden stop was us hitting a bulldozer they were using to make the airfield. We slammed straight into it. That's when the engine caught fire.'

> I shouted to Tim to get out quickly but he needed no encouragement. I climbed out onto the starboard wing and shouted to Bill that we were on fire and not to waste any time. A muffled voice from inside told us he could not move the hatch.

However Tim pushed it from the outside and to my relief, out
came Bill's head. We then shook hands on our amazing escape
and climbed into a large ditch where we lay for about twenty
minutes while the petrol tanks, oxygen bottles and ammunition
exploded in a sheet of flame . . .

I am now full of questions for Bob that I try to get into some
kind of order while he gets up and heads for the bathroom, nego-
tiating the prone mass of dog with surprising agility.

I sit there alone for a while in the strange but impressive room,
trying to read as much of the journal as possible before his return.
The dog snores at my feet.

'You must have been shaken up by this?' I suggest later. Bob
answers, again vaguely. 'Oh, I dunno whether I was really.' It's no
boast, just a simple statement.

It was 1.30 in the morning when they crash-landed near, they
later discovered, the little Norfolk village of Dickleburgh. The
crew was taken to a farmhouse, given a meal and later that morning picked up and flown back to base. On the way they circled the
wreck of their aircraft, 'Q for Queenie'. 'All that was left were two
wingtips and the tail,' Bob tells me.

A few weeks later, one of the true turning points in the direction of the European air war took place, the so-called 'Thousand
Plan', the first 1000-aircraft raid on Germany.

New Bomber Command chief Arthur Harris had enjoyed
recent success in a series of attacks along the Baltic coast, virtually
wiping out the old Hanseatic League towns of Lubeck and Rostock
in the first flexings of his indiscriminate 'area bombing' policy.

Harris now pressed Churchill for an all-out attack, pulling together everything he could get into the air for a one-night
show against a big city. Always conscious of the power of a strong

headline, Harris pressed for the magic total of 1000 aircraft to be made available. Crews and machines were brought in from everywhere: Coastal Command, Fighter Command and even Training Command, who supplied forty-nine aircraft flown by student pilots.

Nothing like it had ever been seen before. For the first time, aircraft were coordinated to fly at particular heights and intervals to avoid the possibility of collision, and hopefully, overwhelm the defences and fire services. Cologne was chosen for the attack, and big parts of Germany's third-largest city were destroyed.

Some 1047 aircraft of various types took part in the first 'Thousand Plan'. Among the 12 840 buildings destroyed or damaged, 486 people killed and thousands more injured or made homeless, only one military installation is mentioned as being hit, a solitary flak barracks.

Churchill had stated he was prepared to lose a hundred aircraft in the attack, but in fact only sacrificed forty-one. The 'Thousand Plan' was considered a great success and set the pattern for the next three years.

Bob was in the air that night too, with the squadron, keeping the German night fighters busy with raids on their aerodrome at Bonn. 'The searchlights were the brightest I had seen, and very accurate. They sort of just passed us on from one to the other,' he says. 'It was so bright I had put my head on the instrument panel to avoid the glare, and escaped to the south.' Despite this, he managed to find the target, laying a stick of bombs across the aerodrome. In the journal, he writes of looking to the north and witnessing:

an amazing sight. The 'heavies' were arriving over Cologne at
a rate of 12 a minute. There were the most terrific flashes from

the ground as the four and eight thousand-pounders burst with terrific flashes. A cone of searchlights completely encircled the city in an endeavour to blind the bomb aimers. As we watched we could see a Wellington held by thirty or more searchlights, but he seemed completely unperturbed.

Harris quickly followed up the Cologne raid with two more, to Essen and Bremen. I return to Bob's logbook for the Essen attack, 1 June 1942. Here he has departed from his usual neat entries and written, '*Crossed Heligoland*' in large writing followed by two large exclamation marks. 'Oh yes,' he says, peering at it and ruminating for a good while. 'Bit of a mistake all that.'

Today, Heligoland and the Fresian Islands in northern Germany are frequented by sea birds and tourists who come over from the mainland on weekend packages to enjoy their relatively warm and allergy-free climate. In the early 1940s, they formed a natural platform for anti-aircraft batteries protecting the approaches to the Ruhr, and were studded with guns. The RAF always tried to avoid them.

'Actually, we didn't intend to fly over them at all,' says Bob. It was always going to be a difficult trip, relying on precise navigation by dead reckoning to a turning point sixty miles out in the North Sea. The meteorologists had warned that it was a dark and overcast night without much visibility.

'There was a strong wind that night,' he says. Tim Denny the navigator began making corrections to the course. 'Lay off another five degrees,' then a little later, 'Lay off another ten degrees.'

'We can't be drifting that much!' replied a concerned Bob, but Tim was adamant. 'Well, we are. This is a hell of a strong wind.' God knows where they were.

According to Bob, some of the squadron never even found

their target – the German airfield at Vechta near Bremen – running out of fuel and just disappearing into the sea en route. I read what he says in the journal for that night:

> We flew through some very bad weather – rain and thunder which gave us a fairly rough trip. The first sign of life was a shower of flak curling up at us when we thought we were still miles north of Germany; this turned out to be Heligoland which we all knew was very heavily defended. We had overshot our turning point by quite a distance.

'We were out over the coast, the next thing we were over the island,' Bob says. He gave up on the target and gave Tim permission to bomb 'anything which looked suspicious'.

> Tim sighted something and we started our usual run-up. After 'bombs gone', I hardly took any evasive action as things were so quiet, but a few seconds later absolute hell was let loose. It was the most concentrated flak I had ever seen with several searchlights lending a hand. It seemed impossible to get away without being hit. Bill shouted that the heavy flak was dangerously close and to get down a bit. We were twisting and diving, but the ack-ack gunners followed us everywhere, finally at about 800 feet we got away to the east.

'It turned out we bombed Borkum, one of the Frisian Islands and one of the most heavily defended places in the whole of Germany,' says Bob, still slightly bemused by his foolhardiness in stirring up the hornet's nest. 'They probably wouldn't have even bothered us if we'd just flown by.'

I can see he is tiring and I ask whether I can somehow get a copy of his quite extraordinary document. 'I don't see why not,' he answers.

I read a little more as we drink some tea in the stately old room. As the journal goes on, I notice Bob's writing become more confident. At the end of June 1942, he describes a trip across the North Sea to attack a German aerodrome at Herdla in Norway.

> I was most interested in my first sight of Norway as we came skimming in from the sea; we roared over several little fishing boats and could clearly see the Norwegians waving to us. One old chap asleep in the back of a little coastal boat got quite a fright as he saw 12 RAF planes go over his skiff at mast height.

Locating the airfield only after several attempts, which sufficiently alerted the German night fighters, the operation was promptly abandoned and the squadron returned to England with their bombs. However, a few weeks later on 25 July they made another trip to attack the base of one of the most famous German night fighter squadrons in the Luftwaffe, Nachtjagdgeschwader 1 at St Trond in Belgium. This deadly unit was commanded by none other than Heinz-Wolfgang Schnaufer, the top-scoring German night fighter ace of the war with 121 victories to his credit – nearly all multi-engine bombers – and dubbed 'The ghost of St Trond'. It's estimated that he single-handedly accounted for the deaths of nearly a thousand RAF aircrew (he survived the war, only to die in a bizarre road accident in 1950, when a gas bottle fell on his head after his open-top sports car hit a truck).

As Bob recounts in his journal, it was a ghostly night for No. 114 Squadron also. *'This was the worst night the squadron had to date while I had been with them, as out of eight crews who set out, we lost three.'*

Bob defied the odds and continued to fly trip after trip. As the squadron's casualty rate mounted, his experience saw him rise quickly through the ranks. 'I went from Pilot Officer to Squadron Leader in about four weeks because of the casualty rate,' he says. 'One time we flew up the Elbe River at water level. Practically the height of the cranes,' he says, shaking his head at the memory of it.

Once, I read, the German searchlights actually helped him over a target:

> The searchlights lit up a single-engine Hun last night – a night
> fighter after us probably – the pilot must have been cursing
> searchlight operators below.

The journal continues for forty-three handwritten pages. Large chunks are left unchronicled, such as '*August to November. The squadron did 293 night intruder sorties losing thirty crews*.' Then, as it says, they received their orders for the Middle East.

Several pages read like a travel book describing the 1200-mile flight from Cornwall to Gibraltar through terrible weather:

> We were bumping about like a cork just below the cloud base
> at about 1800 feet. The Bay of Biscay looked very rough and
> forbidding.

Eventually it cleared to a peaceful trip along the Portuguese coast, passing small ships in the bright azure sea which '*took very little interest in us. It seemed hard to imagine we were at war*'.

Eight hours after leaving England, Bob touched down in Gibraltar. They had been loaded up with as much fuel as the old Blenheim could carry, with barely any margin for error allowed.

'It was touch-and-go whether they could do the distance,' he says. 'You usually circled a new airfield when coming into it but we were told we wouldn't have the petrol; we just had to go straight in and land.' All four fuel tanks were showing empty as Bob came in to Gibraltar. 'Two of our blokes never got there. We never found out what happened to them.'

Bob's war continued. In Tunisia and Algeria, he battled cold, trigger-happy Americans and the danger of mountains to attack aerodromes, docks and troop concentrations, usually at low level. In May 1943, he led an attack against gun positions in which eleven out of the twelve aircraft in the formation were hit.

Eventually he would lead squadrons in attacks across the water from Africa to Italy, and hunt submarines in the Mediterranean. Not before time, the Blenheims were withdrawn in favour of the faster, better-armed Douglas Boston. 'There was no conversion course,' says Bob. 'We just read some of the manual and took off. Lucky they were easy to fly.'

Bob completed an amazing seventy-four operations in Europe and the Middle East and was more than happy to receive the news that he was being sent home en route to flying again in the Pacific. Upon his return, however, the Commanding Officer at Essendon looked at his record and the DFC ribbon on his tunic. 'You've done enough,' he said. 'If you like you can go home.'

'My son was two years old and I hadn't even seen him,' he says. 'I couldn't jump at it quick enough.'

Bob went back to his beloved farm with the long row of sugar gums and never left it.

We have come to the end of a long day, and, again, I am exhausted. I say goodbye to Bob who happily takes his place on the couch in his beloved library next to his big dog and resumes his book as if it he had put it down just minutes ago. John, his son, in that quiet unspoken way of country hospitality, brings me over to his house across the way for a meal, which I devour before heading out on my way home.

True to his word, I am permitted to borrow the precious journal and there's just time enough to make the local newsagent where I can photocopy it. 'Don't bother bringing it back,' I am told. 'Just leave it behind the counter and I'll pick it up tomorrow. They know me there.'

On the way, I glance down at the old exercise book sitting on the passenger seat beside me like it's gold bullion. The car, although sounding decidedly sick, seems to understand the gravity of the occasion and gets me to the newsagent without incident. Next day it's a different story, and a week later I'm forking out for a replacement engine.

The woman at the local newsagents wants to close up but is happy to wait when I explain what it is I am doing. As I work the machine, I notice something I had missed. The only variation from the pages of compact handwriting are four small newspaper cuttings which he has pasted in. One is from the old *Argus* dated from the time Bob brought his Blenheim in for a belly landing after the Eindhoven raid. I read the article which begins:

Victorian Airman Wins DFC – Danger Disregarded in Raid. Completely disregarding danger, though his guns were out of action, Pilot Officer John Robert Nassau Molesworth, an Australian pilot attached to an RAF bomber squadron, pressed home his attacks on targets at Eindoven, Holland. He has been awarded the DFC . . .

But it's not this heroic citation that moves me the most, or the fact that Bob hadn't even bothered to mention it. On the very last page, in small handwriting, a fellow airman has penned a farewell on the occasion of his return to Australia. For me, its tone seems to capture the amazing wartime career of this very quiet, very dignified man. 'Cheerio, Bob. Sorry I can't see you off. Good luck and keep ducking. Very good shooting. – Wing Cdr J. O. Thompson.'

Some months after I conducted my interview with Bob Molesworth, his son John telephoned to tell me his father had passed away. He had outlived his beloved labrador, whose name I discovered was Ollie, by just three days.

JAMES COWARD

Pilot, RAF

I have had in my possession, for a time longer than I can remember, a blue, cloth-bound little book titled *The True Story of the Battle of Britain*. It's a smallish, sombre-looking volume, published in England in the early 1950s. I can't remember how I even came by it – a gift from an older person, I suspect, curious at the interest I had shown in the period, and probably just as happy to offload the dowdy little thing, still unread after all these years and just cluttering up the bookshelf.

I devoured its pages when I was a youngster, but looking at it now, it's hard to get very excited about it. It was put out by the British government to mark the tenth anniversary of the Battle, and while it gives a good enough sketch of the events of that legendary summer – from the daylight attacks in August to the beginning of the Blitz later in the year – it's a pretty dry work when all's said and done. It does, however, have one very interesting appendix, to which I have returned many times: a list of every Allied pilot – British, Polish, American, Canadian, Australian and many other nationalities – who took part in this monumentally important fifteen-week engagement. The list runs for twenty-two pages and includes nearly 3000 names, starting with 'Adair, H.

213 Squadron. British. Killed' and ending with 'Zurakowski, J. 234 Squadron. Polish', who, presumably, survived.

On several occasions over the years, people kind enough to feel a need to engage with my interest have mentioned that their father, or uncle, or next door neighbour, or former maths teacher, or greengrocer, or whoever, was a Battle of Britain pilot. Admittedly, some of these people were a little vague on details, some even a little uncertain as to what the Battle of Britain actually was, when it was fought, or (amazingly) even where. Others, though, were well informed and quite insistent about this personal connection they had with the epic aerial battle, fought in the war's early stages, still with a faint residue of chivalry and which, in the glorious summer skies above Kent, by the narrowest of margins saved Britain from invasion.

As a kid, I had planned to make this list a record of my own personal collection of all the Battle of Britain pilots I had encountered. As the vast bulk of them were British, it would be unlikely I would meet many myself, but one degree of separation, I decided, would suffice. I would rule a pencil under the name, then make a little annotation about where I had met them, or via whom.

So, whenever someone told me about their old Uncle Bernard's Spitfire heroics, I would race home to look it up in the book to underline it. I was always, however, disappointed to find the name was never on the list. Not even once.

It dawned on me eventually that people, despite the best of intentions, simply got things wrong. Maybe Bernard had just missed out on the actual battle itself (the dates of its parameters are quite specific), or had in fact flown bombers, or flying boats, or was in the army Pays Corps for six years or had just made the whole thing up to impress the grandchildren. Whatever the reason, the list in the back of the little blue book remained undefiled, with not a single underline to be seen.

But the name James Coward *was* there: 'Coward, J. B. 19 Squadron. British'. Needless to say, it lacked the sombre addendum 'killed', and one freezing but fine morning in mid-2007, I pulled up outside his house in suburban Canberra, a rapidly disintegrating tape recorder in hand, ready to meet my first ever Battle of Britain pilot. To top it off, he flew Spitfires. I was terribly excited.

First, though, I had to get him to stop telling jokes. Not that they weren't funny; in fact I could have sat there and listened to them all day – that was the trouble. James has dozens of stories, usually centred around the eccentricities of upper-class English behaviour. Take, for instance, the one about meeting the Duke of Edinburgh and being asked the name of the place where he was stationed. 'Oh, yes, I passed right by there yesterday,' said the Duke. 'Where do you live?'

'The married quarters,' replied James. 'Well don't complain to me!' snapped the Duke. 'I have to too, you know!'

Or what about the skinny little man in striped trousers and morning coat spotted next to the enormous figure of the Queen of Tonga in the dignitaries' box at Her Majesty's Coronation? 'Who's that man next to the Queen of Tonga?' someone enquired. 'Her lunch,' was the reply.

He even had one about Winston Churchill going for a pee in the House of Commons loo after the war just as Attlee, the new Labour PM, stepped up to the urinal beside him. Churchill immediately moved three paces away. 'I say, Winston, you're very standoffish this morning,' said an affronted Atlee. 'I know,' said Winston (with James supplying the appropriate Churchillian drawl). 'You socialists. Every time you see something big with good prospects of quick growth, you want to nationalise it!'

And this was all before we had even sat down.

I had caught an early morning flight to Canberra one chilly Sunday, then a taxi ride that seemed to take me halfway home again. As we sped through what appeared to be vast tracts of bush, I had forgotten how deceptively wide is the national capital's spread. The address James gave me seemed to take me up a path that wound through some native shrubbery, until a weathervane in the shape of, what else, a Spitfire told me I had arrived.

The tall immaculately dressed figure of James greeted me at the door and ushered me inside. He spoke so quickly with such a delightful accent that I suggested he must surely be related to his namesake, Noel. He assures me his origins are far humbler, but much of the afternoon that followed was like a P. G. Woodhouse novel sprung to life.

'I left school at fifteen without any qualifications to do anything,' he tells me as we take our positions on the couch. Then out of the blue in class one day, the young James received a phone call from his father, a businessman who had been knocked back by the army in the Great War because, of all things, "abnormal toes". 'Your mother's left, and I'm taking you out of school,' was the abrupt message. His father subsequently lost everything in the divorce settlement, and James was sent to work in his office. He hated it, yearning instead to be a pilot in the RAF.

'I refuse to give permission for you to go and get yourself killed,' were his father's stern words, 'and he was jolly nearly right,' says James today. But when he turned twenty-one, James was free to make up his own mind, and in 1936 he stood before three Group Captains at a selection committee in the Air Ministry in Whitehall. After looking him up and down a bit, the one in the middle asked, 'What games do you play?'

'Er, rugby and cricket, sir,' James replied.

'Right. Down the corridor and see the doctor.'

'And that was it,' he says. 'I was in.'

If nothing else, this is turning out to be the most amusing interview I've yet conducted, but I wonder if this incident is typical of the Royal Air Force in the years before the war. 'Oh, it was tremendous fun,' he says in his rapid-fire way. 'Just think – I'd gone from working in an office in London to being woken up in the morning by a batman who pours you a cup of tea and runs you a bath; then going down to a splendid breakfast, and dinners in the mess four nights a week – it was a wonderful life!' However, the notion that it was the exclusive domain of the Oxbridge establishment is, says James, a myth. 'Where I was at Duxford we had a terrific mixture: people from Australia, New Zealand, South Africa, English, Scots, Welsh.'

It all sounds disappointingly egalitarian, but at least there was Lord Dudley. 'Ah yes, Lord Dudley,' says James, slowing down a little for the first time. 'He was posted to us in disgrace – court-martialled for bringing a dog on an aeroplane. But he beat the charge by proving it wasn't a dog, but a hound.' Ah, those magnificent men and their flying machines.

'Actually,' says James, suddenly sounding rather like Hugh Grant, 'I wasn't even sure that I was going to get through the course. I had one or two shaky dos in training, you see.' Almost decapitating a Squadron Leader would indeed have put a dampener on one's career.

'Right, your engine's on fire,' said the officer one afternoon in the air when testing James's readiness to go solo. He was used to the emergency drill by now and turned the Avro Tutor towards a nearby paddock for an emergency landing. Just as he was coming in, however, the officer abruptly announced, 'I have control,' and gave the engine a burst of power. Then, it abruptly stopped.

'I'd already turned the fuel off,' says James, 'which is actually what you're supposed to do in an engine fire.'

They came down roughly in a field. The day wasn't going too well, and the Squadron Leader wasn't hiding his annoyance. To restart the engine, they needed to manually 'swing' the prop – something James had never done before. Cursing even more, the Squadron Leader grabbed the propeller in both hands while James remained in the cockpit. 'He swung and swung and nothing happened,' says James. Then he realised the fuel was still off. Just as the officer was in mid-swing, James switched it back on, and it immediately roared into life in his hands. 'Amazingly, it didn't hit him, but you've never heard such language in your life,' he says. 'I thought, "That's it, I've had it."'

Another 'shakey do' was an unscheduled landing in heavy fog at an unfamiliar training field. Walking into the hut, the other pilots were astounded he had managed to get down at all, but not as surprised as the woman who rushed in saying, 'Who's that bloody fool I just saw fly *under* the high tension cables?'

'I hadn't even seen them,' says James. 'Got away with that one, too.'

James joined one of Fighter Command's true pedigree squadrons, No. 19, based at the famous Duxford aerodrome in Cambridgeshire, cutting his teeth on slow but steady biplanes such as the Gauntlet and Demon. But one day in 1938, they began to hear about a very new aeroplane which their squadron was to be the first to receive. A few days later, a small sleek monoplane appeared over the aerodrome, put on an impromptu aerobatic display before the slack-jawed pilots and landed. The Spitfire had arrived. 'I became about the fourth person in the RAF to fly one,' James tells me. Not that he had much in the way of an introduction. 'You read the handbook, found out what the stalling speed was and then you flew it,' he says.

These were indeed the halcyon days, but they were not to last. 'We all knew the war was coming but we weren't particularly worried about it. We were having such a lovely time,' says James.

On the very first day of World War II, No. 19 Squadron was on standby. James remembers he and the other pilots sleeping on camp stretchers under the wings of their Spitfires in case anything happened quickly. It didn't. In fact, not much happened at all in the first few months of the so-called 'Phoney War' while the Germans quietly gathered strength for their attack in the west, and the atmosphere was much like peacetime. James flew mainly on convoy escort patrols. 'Yes, that was exciting,' he tells me. 'As soon as you approached them, the ships started shooting at you with everything they had!'

When the Germans attacked in May 1940, James was spared the disaster of France as it was only the Hurricane squadrons that were sent over to be largely annihilated. His first encounter with the enemy was in June, above Dunkirk.

There seems to be something particular to the Anglo-Saxon temperament that makes us celebrate our defeats as fervently as we do our victories. Perhaps this gives a clue as to why the British have been so rarely conquered throughout history. Australia has its Gallipoli, America its Alamo, but the almost mystical 'miracle of Dunkirk' has implanted itself into the most noble aspects of the British character like few other events. And to think it was all a catastrophe.

In three short weeks, the combined French and British armies – victorious over this same enemy barely two decades earlier – were whipped by the highly mobile, new-look Germans who, compensating for their lack of numbers, threw away the military rulebook and employed a deadly combination of speed, bluff and utter ruthlessness. Armoured attacks through supposedly

impenetrable forests, sirens fitted to bombs to terrorise the population and clog the roads, then strafing them as they fled to cause
further panic: the Germans did every ghastly thing imaginable.
The morose, half-sozzled French and woefully ill-equipped British
hardly knew what hit them until they were lining up for kilometres
along a beach praying for a boat to spirit them back to England.
But spirited they were, and in incredible numbers.

With hardly a rifle between them, the army was saved by vessels of the navy, merchant services, fishing boats, pleasure ferries
and every other thing that could float. This ragtag rescue fleet,
under constant bombardment, brought over 300 000 weapon-less
soldiers home to fight another day. The Germans, bewildered as
to how easy it had all been, just looked on. People in Britain were
so ecstatic that Churchill had to remind them, 'This is not a victory. Wars are not won by evacuations.'

Flying above all this in a Spitfire, James Coward fired off his
first shots in an odd, scrappy engagement.

'Follow me, chaps' was all that Squadron Leader Hunnard
said as his pilots took off from Martlesham Heath in Suffolk.
James didn't think much of his CO – inexperienced, a poor flyer
and a bad leader – an opinion reinforced by the fact that, on this
day, nobody had the slightest idea of where they were going, or
why. 'We followed him as he turned and took us out over the sea.
We thought he'd gone mad,' James says. 'Then he put us into
a full-power climb. He didn't even know the proper climbing
speed – our engines were all boiling.'

Flying along the coast of Belgium straight into the sun –
another serious no-no – James could see columns of thick black
smoke coming up from the destroyed oil reserves, and a jumbled
flotilla moving in and out, braving air attacks to get the men off
the beaches.

Suddenly, he looked up and saw a descending stream of Messerschmitt 109s about to surprise a Spitfire squadron some 5000 feet below. With little faith that his boss knew what was going on, James called 'Tally-ho' and led his flight into an attack. 'They saw us coming and broke away and ran,' he says. 'I got a bead on one and fired but I couldn't get in range.' At the very least, he had broken up their attack.

On landing, however, he had strips torn off him, with his CO accusing him of deserting him in battle. A report was put in, and James had to front the Group Captain for another tongue-lashing. He feels his treatment was distinctly unfair, but 'fairness' has never been one of the military's overriding considerations, especially in wartime. Later, though, he feels he was exonerated when this same officer was himself the subject of a complaint. After his logbook was inspected, it was found he'd hardly flown at all. He was sacked soon after, but James's black mark remained.

Most fighter pilots of the Battle of Britain were single and lived within the confines of their usually crowded base. James, however, was – and still is – married to the woman now preparing our lunch, the very elegant Cynthia. In 1940, they lived in a house a couple of miles away from Duxford in an ostensibly normal domestic arrangement. 'Cynthia used to get me breakfast in bed,' he tells me. 'We'd say, "Bye-bye, darling, have a lovely day," etc., and I'd drive to work like I was heading off to the office. Half an hour later I'd be up at 30000 feet in the middle of a great battle. It was an extraordinary way to live.'

James's combat experience in the Battle of Britain was brief, but sensational. According to the records, 31 July was a relatively quiet day, with only three RAF pilots being shot down. Unfortunately for James, he was one of them.

This cloudless morning, he was scrambled, and encountered

the enemy close to Duxford. No. 19 was being led that day by a New Zealand officer, as their CO had been killed a couple of days before and his replacement was yet to arrive. 'I saw them first,' says James, 'I had wonderful eyesight in those days' – a formation of Dornier 215 bombers with a large escort of sixty-five Messerschmitt 110 and 109s above. James was ordered into a 'number one' attack – line astern, each aircraft forming up behind their respective bomber. He manoeuvred to attack just as the German fighters pounced from above. 'I went turning round to take the chap on the far side and my number two pulled out,' he says.

No. 19 Squadron had just received the new Spitfire1b, the first to be armed with 20-millimetre cannons in the wings, and this engagement was one of their earliest tests in combat. Some of the bugs, it seems, had yet to be worked out. The black-crossed and splinter-green camouflage pattern of the German bomber filled James's windscreen as he moved to within fifty yards and pressed the firing button. It clicked, and . . . nothing. His two cannons and four machine guns had jammed. Cursing, he pulled his now unarmed and useless aircraft away.

The rapid-firing 7.9-millimetre gun in the hands of the Dornier's rear gunner, however, functioned perfectly. Just as he turned, he felt what he describes as a 'hard kick on the shin – like you'd get in a rugby scrum.' He almost didn't even look down, but when he did he was astonished to see his bare foot sitting on the rudder bar. Two bullets had ripped through both bones in James's lower right leg, almost severing it. His flying boot had simply blown off.

His elevator controls were also gone – 'I pulled the controls back and nothing happened' – his aircraft was plummeting straight down in a steep dive at 480 knots. 'I didn't have much time to think about things,' he says. There was only one thought required: to get out. Unstrapping and releasing the hood at such high speed, he was almost sucked straight out of the cockpit, but became pinned as his parachute caught on the rear wall. 'I was trapped there. My arms were thrown back by the slipstream, my gloves blew off and my foot, hanging by just some ligaments, was thrashing up against my knee.' Then, like a ball out of a cannon, he was free, and tumbling head over heels in the air.

His first thought was to fall to a lower height before opening the parachute, lest he be carried for miles, but the pain of the rushing wind twisting his leg was unbearable, and he pulled the ripcord at about 20 000 feet.

Then, all was peaceful. 'Suddenly, there wasn't a sound or a sight of an aircraft anywhere,' he says. The pain had vanished as well, and James was completely alone in the sky. 'It was a marvellous feeling. I could see this wonderful view of the Cambridgeshire countryside stretching for hundreds of miles.'

He also saw that he was losing a lot of blood very quickly. 'I was swinging on the end of the parachute and I could see blood pumping out of me in brilliant red blobs,' he says. He was also soaked in petrol from the central fuel tank located immediately behind the instrument panel which had also been hit, and which fortunately had not ignited. He still had his helmet with the attached radio/telephone cord, so wound this around his shattered leg as a tourniquet, doing his best to tuck it under and stop the bleeding. The rest, surreally, seems to have been rather pleasant: a gentle journey back to earth. 'I could hear cows mooing and dogs barking. It was quite marvellous,' he says. 'A couple of Spitfires heading home circled around me and gave me a wave.'

Looking back, sixty-seven years later, it seems that he was in the air forever, but he reckons it would have been no more than about twenty minutes. 'I finally came down with a thump in the middle of a stubbled field,' he says.

Close by, farm workers were stacking big sheaves of corn. James moved himself to keep his bloodied leg out of the dirt, when a couple of them came rushing up with pitchforks. 'This made me absolutely furious,' he says indignantly. 'It had taken all that to get down in one piece and now some bloody fool wanted to stick a pitchfork in me!

'Piss off and get me an ambulance!' he barked at the men who had obviously taken him to be a German. 'They sped off like startled hares.'

He was in no pain at this stage, but his leg was numb. The first car the farmhand stopped was, amazingly, an army doctor on his way to Duxford for breakfast. Soon, James was in hospital in Cambridge. When he came to, his heavily pregnant wife was sitting beside him. 'Our first born was due any minute,' he says, and he knew how lucky he was to be around to see it.

James's leg was amputated below the knee, a prosthetic fitted, and his flying days were over. At least for a while.

The funny stories are on hold as James relates his death-defying exit from his Spitfire, drenched in petrol with a shattered, bleeding leg. But they soon start up as he goes on to tell me about the rest of his very active war. For a while he was part of Winston Churchill's personal staff, assessing the risk to the PM from air attack during the Blitz, and later flying again as an instructor, eventually commanding an Operational Training Unit in Scotland. Here, one day, a young Typhoon pilot came up to him. 'Do you remember me, sir?' James looked blankly at the young man. 'I'm the one that found you when you were shot down,' he resumed. It was the same lad who had rushed him with a pitchfork three years earlier. 'Well, I hope you're better at recognising the enemy these days,' was James's retort.

James stayed in the RAF till well after the war, having a fine life flying some of the thoroughbreds of the early jet age such as the Hunter and the Meteor, then as air attaché in places like Norway and Australia, where he settled with Cynthia and their children, eventually reaching the lofty rank of Air Commodore.

It could easily have been so very different. One of a dozen sets of circumstances could have conspired that day in the Cambridgeshire sky in 1940 to snuff out James's young life, as it did with thousands of others, denying him these sixty-seven productive years.

Cynthia, who lived through it all herself, actively contributes to James's story. I look at them, and as the wine flows over lunch, I see what a dashing couple they still make. They talk of their skiing days, and I picture them instantly on the slopes of Grindelwald and Gstaad in the stylish fifties and sixties.

We sit around the table enjoying the generous meal Cynthia has prepared. Unlike all of the wives of the other men I have spoken to, she was there with her husband, sharing much of the experience, and they sit recalling the names of the pilots they both knew – the ones who survived, and those who did not.

They speak of Carl Withall, the only child of elderly parents in Canberra, and one of the first Australians Cynthia ever met. 'He was twenty-seven and the younger pilots called him "Granny". They'd tease him – offer to carry his parachute and so on,' she says. One afternoon in his Spitfire, he was attempting to chase down a fast-moving Junkers 88 at sea level off the Isle of Wight. 'He was going flat out and got a bullet in the radiator and his engine suddenly seized,' says James. He radioed that he was about to ditch, but he was unable to free himself in time, and went down in his aircraft.

'When I was posted here in 1960,' says James, 'his father rang me up and asked me around. He wanted to know all about his son. There was so little I could tell him.'

Then there was 'Ace' Pace (neither can now recall his actual name). Nineteen years old and the only Roman Catholic on the squadron, he was so badly disfigured by burns after being shot down that mirrors were kept out of his reach in hospital. When a visitor unintentionally left one by his bedside table, he tried to cut his throat with it after seeing his reflection. Eventually he flew again but was killed soon after.

Or Stevenson, another Australian, the son of an admiral. 'He was in my flight,' says James. 'He'd been jackarooing in Western Australia – a really delightful character.'

'It's so sad,' says Cynthia, the man's face back in her mind. 'He would have made a wonderful husband and father.' He was last seen flying into the middle of a melee with a large number of German fighters in a high-altitude engagement over the south coast.

My time with James and Cynthia has been for me the fulfilment of a decades-long wish. By the time the cab arrives to take me away, we are all exhausted. James was all and more than I'd expected from a Battle of Britain pilot: immensely charming, funny, and sharp as a tack. In a way he's still fighting the battle – these days with the Australian War Memorial, whose lack of adequate recognition for the fourteen Australian pilots killed in the engagement still irks him, and for whom, he says, there is no fitting memorial. 'One of them up there told me that the Battle of Britain wasn't important, and that the Americans would have saved us anyway! Can you believe it?' he fumes.

He is, in his advanced years, still a man of enormous vigour and energy, and even as I am leaving, he still has volumes of anecdotes about Eton, the King of Norway and Lady Astor that have me chuckling in the taxi. It's another long ride back to the airport and I try one out on the driver, but it falls flat and we continue to the airport in silence.

Later that evening, I arrive back home in Melbourne. In true RAF style, I mix myself a very stiff gin and tonic. Glass in hand, I go to the bookshelf and pick out my old battered copy of *The True Story of the Battle of Britain* and turn to its much-thumbed index at the back. Now at last I can claim to have met a genuine Battle of Britain pilot. But in the end it's not one but four names I underline carefully in lead pencil: 'Withall, L. C. 152 Squadron. Australian. Killed'; 'Pace, A. C. 19 Squadron. British. Killed'; 'Stevenson, P. C. F. 19 Squadron. Australian. Killed' and 'Coward, J. B. 19 Squadron. British' – survived.

DUDLEY MARROWS

Pilot, RAAF

'I turned ninety the other day,' Dudley tells me as we sit for a chat. 'You've got to do it sometime or other.' He seems a little bemused to have reached such a milestone, but I'm awfully glad he did, because it was Dudley upon whom I was relying to fill a significant blank in my quest. For this reason, I had travelled to the edge of the desert to meet a man who had flown – and fought – over the endless expanse of the ocean.

His aircraft – the magnificent four-engine Sunderland flying boat – also happens to be the only type with which I can claim some kind of personal connection. Up until 1974, you could still see them, slipping free of the flat blue surface of Sydney Harbour and pulling into the air before wheeling to the left and heading out across the Pacific towards Lord Howe Island. Ansett Airlines of Australia were the last in the world to operate them. The vision of this enormous old aeroplane throbbing through the warm Sydney sky in its elegant airline livery remains one of the most memorable of my childhood, yet it was only by chance I even got to see it, thanks to one of my father's failed business ventures.

After a couple of uncharacteristically good years in the early 1970s, Dad convinced himself the world was ripe for the taking,

and, against every bit of sound advice (which he never took anyway), decided to open up an office of his one-man PR company
in Sydney. It was doomed from the start. A man with a big heart
and big ideas, my father possessed not a skerrick of the panache
needed to succeed in the fast lanes of the Emerald City.

I remember the first trip I made up there, with my mother, as
a thirteen-year-old, a few weeks into his foray to set it all up. As
long as I could remember, Dad had always worked from home,
staking out the front room of the house for his office. Late into the
night I would hear from my adjacent bedroom the soft thudding
of the keys of his antiquated typewriter as he sat in his dressing
gown, bashing out the draft of a yet another brochure for the fenc-
ing industry or an annual report. Resentful as one is at that age of
the eccentricities of one's parents, I had always hankered for the
respectability of a father who, like all other fathers I knew, went
off to work every day in a suit with a briefcase. Although it was odd
him not being around at this time, the house was decidedly more
peaceful, and I remember the pride I felt as I pictured him striding
into the foyer of a big Sydney skyscraper to start his day's work.

I was, of course, to be terribly disappointed. Ever the small-
town man with little concept of false economy, Dad's new 'office'
turned out to be a cheap and rather ordinary flat he had found in a
residential part of Double Bay with a desk in one room and a roll-
out bed in the other. Walking up the concrete stairs for the first
time in silence with my mother, I still wince at the shame I felt at
the sounds of kids' television blaring through a flyscreen door and
the smell of someone cooking their evening meal. Any potential
clients would have fled in a minute.

For most of that first trip, I sulked around, swearing to make
it my last. Then, one afternoon with little else to do but watch
my father's rising consternation at his obstinately silent telephone,

I set off down the street past gardens with their blazing jacarandas towards the sparkling water of Sydney Harbour. The unmistakable roar of big propeller engines somewhere ahead rose over the muffled sound of the traffic, riveting me to the spot. Then, looming over the rooftops, there appeared the tremendous sight of a four-motor flying boat, low and banking steeply, showing off its upper wing and fuselage.

I watched it wheel around, slow and majestic, then vanish towards the east. I bolted back up the hill. Dad was on the phone and did not appreciate the interruption. 'They're the Sunderlands,' he said, covering up the mouthpiece and waving me out. 'They take off from Rose Bay. Go!'

I headed back down to the harbour, determined to find this Rose Bay and its flying boats, and watched expectantly for the next one to appear.

My father's Sydney expedition lasted just a few months and cost him a packet. Inside half a year he was back home on familiar turf, still blithely unaware of the reasons for his failure, and already making plans to expand somewhere else. A stern word from my dour but realistic mother was enough to bury the dream forever. One of mine, though, had been planted.

If the Sunderland wasn't the finest flying boat of World War II, it was certainly the most famous. It was built by Short Brothers in Belfast, the same people who made the superbly engineered but compromised Stirling. The Sunderland, however, was permitted to fulfil the potential of its design. It arose out of the graceful 'Empire' flying boat, itself a staggering leap forward from the biplane and wire types Short had produced throughout the 1920s, and was built to cash in on the decision made by the British Postmaster General that all First Class overseas mail must henceforth be carried by air.

From the mid-1930s, the sleek all-metal Empires ferried passengers and mail in indulgent comfort all around the globe. Poignantly, though, as the war approached, they came to symbolise the decline of the very empire from which they took their name. The Sunderland was its military variant and, in the grey-green waters of the Bay of Biscay, came to represent the terrible, unbending struggle against the German U-boats that raged the entire war. It was in the midst of this effort that, on a July afternoon in 1943, Dudley Marrows played an extraordinary, history-making part.

I visit Dudley and his wife Sylvia at a busy time. After many decades, they have recently moved from their large citrus property on the outskirts of Mildura into a modest unit in the middle of town. Large wood and leather chairs – unused to such confines – line up awkwardly in the living room, and boxes of documents wait in piles to be sorted – a task neither of them relish.

Like the wives of many of the men I had spoken to, Sylvia proves as rich a source of information – and inspiration – as Dudley himself. 'My ancestors are German,' she tells me – a little proudly – as she takes my arm and directs me to a cabinet filled with family memorabilia. In her pale blue eyes, there's still a trace of the film star good looks she sported as a young woman, and my indelicate gaze returns repeatedly to a framed photograph of her – a stunning blonde in an off-the-shoulder white satin creation – taken more years ago than she can probably bear to remember. Sylvia became a schoolteacher and speaks several languages. 'I gave a lecture last week on Lutheranism,' she tells me. 'Just to keep my hand in.'

Decades after the events, it was Sylvia's skill in German that enabled her to her play her own part in a moving epilogue to Dudley's war.

Outside, even at nine in the morning, it's hot. Dudley seems a little nervous to begin with, and wants to place some important facts on the table.

'I'm going to try and get you into the picture as I see it after surveying it for sixty years or more,' he says to me earnestly, as if addressing a youth he suspects in danger of going off the rails. 'People think of an aircraft going down as just one entity, but with a Sunderland, it was twelve people who were lost. And the U-boats. When they sank, sixty-five men died. I don't think people always realise that.' If anyone's qualified to make the observation, it is Dudley, as I will discover.

'I was born in Bendigo – a long time ago,' he says. Dudley joined the air force in 1940 after four part-time years in the militia. In the meantime, he'd completed a degree in accounting and with his mother dead and father absent, lived with an older brother – surviving, as he puts it, 'on my own resources'. He does not care to elaborate, and I suspect his was not the warmest of upbringings. He looks at me sagely. 'At your age you could never comprehend the severity of the Great Depression.'

At Initial Training School, Dudley was selected to be an observer, but after topping every subject his instructors could throw at him, he convinced them to re-muster him for pilot training – a rare occurrence indeed. It became apparent that the young Marrows was no ordinary student, and the powers-that-be began to think his talents might be better suited to more demanding roles. With the almost unheard-of distinction 'exceptional' stamped in his logbook, Dudley found himself on his way to South Africa to complete the highly specialised General Reconnaissance and Navigation Course, flying Harvards over the tourist sites of Victoria Falls and the Zambezi River.

From his cockpit, he watched vast herds of wildlife scatter

before the sound of his engine across the wide African plains. He's keen, though, not to romanticise it. 'Training was one of the most stressful periods of my life,' he tells me. Accidents, as always, were common. Going over on the ship, the men had taken bets as to which among them would be the first to go solo. Dudley remembers the gifted young pilot who eventually won the distinction – as he was also the first to be killed. 'A complete natural,' he says. 'That was his problem. He thought he was *too* good.'

A few weeks later under a leaden sky, Dudley stepped off the old liner *Empress of India* into a bleak Scottish midwinter, as a newly commissioned Pilot Officer. In a sense, though, he would never really leave the water, because he had been earmarked to perform one of the most demanding and important jobs in the RAF – piloting the long-range flying boats deep into the Atlantic Ocean, protecting the very arteries of Britain's war effort, her sea lanes.

'The only thing that every really frightened me was the U-boat peril,' wrote Churchill in his history of the Second World War. He had very good reason. The Battle of the Atlantic was fought on every single day of the six-year conflict – a brutal, terrifying cat-and-mouse struggle between ship, aircraft and submarine ranging over thousands of square miles of largely empty ocean. It was like a battle fought in slow motion, with countless hours of tedium spent on all sides, then moments sudden, violent and terribly cruel. I can envisage few deaths more ghastly than being trapped inside a sinking vessel or helplessly watching the surface of the great grey sea looming from the cockpit of a doomed aircraft.

Britain was like a baby, needing to be spoon-fed just about everything for its very survival. Oil, steel, food, clothing and war matériel were needed every day and by the ton. The only way in was via fleets of small merchant ships – up to sixty at a time – sailing in convoys from the Americas. If the Germans could cut the supply line they could starve Britain and win the war, and they knew it. One of the weapons used to counter this very real threat was, therefore, the long-range, depth-charge-armed flying-boat.

Dudley remembers seeing a Sunderland for the first time, moored on the water. Compared to what he had flown before, it towered over him, a huge, camouflage-painted hybrid of ship and aeroplane.

'When we first walked into them, with their twin-decks, proper toilet, sleeping and cooking facilities, we wondered how in the hell they could fly,' he says.

Part mariner, part aviator, the flying-boat captain too had to deal with the vagaries of currents, swells and wind. 'When you hit a big wave,' Dudley says, 'it's like hitting a brick wall.' He also had to relearn some of the basics, such as landing on water. 'It could be that rough that you could bash the hull in,' he says. Smooth water also presented problems. When too calm on take-off, the sea would create its own suction, adhering to the hull, requiring the pilot to 'rock' the aircraft back and forth to break free. 'Sometimes fully loaded, we could take well over a mile to get off,' he tells me.

In recognition of the importance of the struggle against the U-boats, the RAF established several new squadrons dedicated to the task. One of them, No. 461, was an all-Australian outfit. It came into existence on Anzac Day 1942, and hence was known as the 'Anzac Squadron'. Dudley was one of its original members.

Unlike those assigned a Bomber Command tour, whose duration was determined by individual operations, the Sunderland crews were indentured to fly no less than 800 operational hours: 800 hours flying low over the almost empty ocean escorting convoys, or tracing the lines of a vast grid on a map; 800 hours watching the featureless slate-green surface of the Atlantic pass beneath, all the time fighting the soporific lull of monotony, red-rimmed eyes constantly anticipating a dark shape on the horizon that might be the conning tower of a submarine, or the tiny yellow speck that signified the dinghy of a downed airman. 'We saturated the Bay of Biscay, day and night, irrespective of weather,' he says.

Sightings of U-boats by flying-boat crews were in fact rare. It was, according to Dudley, 'like hoping to find a needle in a haystack'. But their mere presence was often enough. As they were told when briefed, it was considered important merely to keep the U-boats under the water. A submarine in 1943 travelled fast on the surface – around seventeen knots – but this dropped back to around seven knots when submerged. At this slow speed, it was difficult for the U-boats to reach the convoy areas from their bases in France and they expended far more fuel in doing so. For the Admiralty, preventing them from causing havoc among the convoys was a tactical victory, and people like Dudley spending twelve hours at a stretch in the air had their part to play, as monotonous as it was.

It was hoped to catch the German submarines close to their French bases of St Nazaire and La Rochelle, and the Bay of Biscay became a vast hunting ground. On three separate occasions, Dudley spotted U-boats on the surface, but by the time he reached them they had submerged. 'You had to get there quick,' he tells me. 'Never had I got there quick enough.'

Some days, though, you just get lucky. The day of 30 July 1943 began as a normal patrol: pick up the Scilly Isles, fly a straight course to Spain, crawl along the coast, then another straight line back to the Scillies, then home to their base at Mount Batten in Portsmouth. It was similar to the dozens of assignments Dudley and his crew had already carried out in nine months of operational flying, usually without incident. Peter Jensen, the wireless operator, has written his own account of the day's events: 'It was a beautiful day,' he says. 'Just outside the three-mile limit of Spain we could see people on the beaches; the water was sparkling and blue. How we envied them.' Even in the aircraft it was warm. Jackets were off and Jensen was in shirtsleeves. Then, just before midday, he picked up a signal from another aircraft reporting a sighting: 'Grid coordinates FKJE2020' – it was nearby.

They implemented the standard 'square' search but saw nothing. Then, another signal, directing them to another spot. Dudley started to get a creeping feeling that this day was not to be an ordinary one. 'As we were approaching – I'll always remember this – I heard my second pilot, Jimmy Leigh, say, "There's some destroyers ahead."' As they reached the scene, it became clear that the low, dark shapes in the water were not destroyers, but a formation of three U-boats running in a tight V formation on the surface.

It was an amazing sight, 'a circus', says Dudley. Several aircraft were already on the scene providing the Germans with some company – two B-24 Liberators and a Coastal Command Halifax from No. 502 Squadron which were attempting (very ineffectually, according to Dudley) to bomb them from high altitude.

The trio of German submarines, brazenly defying the accepted practice of diving at the first opportunity, were sailing at speed, electing to fight it out on the surface. Dudley didn't know it, but this remarkable tactic was the result of a recent directive from the U-boat commander, Admiral Doenitz. By mid-1943, the policy of slowing down U-boats had proven highly effective, and their attacks on convoys had begun to drop off. Doenitz insisted they now move at speed on the surface. For protection, he made them travel in groups, and armed them to the teeth. This last fact is one Dudley is keen to emphasise.

'You're not going in to sink a poor defenceless thing, you

know,' he says. The submarines he attacked had each been armed with twenty-seven anti-aircraft guns of various calibre including two or three batteries of 20-millimetre cannons. 'They put up a firepower as fierce as any fortified position,' says Dudley. He watched one Liberator go in for an attack, then break it off as if hitting a brick wall. A myriad thoughts ran through his mind: should he attack? If so, from which direction, and what were the intentions of the other aircraft?

Further back in the Sunderland, Peter Jensen – with some apprehension – heard the sound of the klaxon ordering the depth charges to be run out onto their racks for dropping. Then, over the intercom came the voice of Dudley, discussing the situation with his number two. 'Right, we'll take the port one, Jimmy. Get ready to take over if I'm hit.' Jimmy Leigh, the second pilot, apparently suggested they attempt a diagonal attack to try and take out the lot. 'My God,' thought Jensen. 'We haven't got one maniac on board, we've got two!'

Dudley tried a standard attack, but was instantly subjected to intense fire from all three U-boats. Shrapnel rattled against the hull, with the occasional loud bang as bigger pieces were picked up by the props and hurled against the fuselage. 'It was too thick even for Dudley,' says Jensen, and the skipper broke off to port.

'Skip, we're low on fuel,' said the voice of his Irish engineer, Paddy Watson. Much had already been expended on the fruitless grid search earlier. Dudley knew he could only afford one more run.

'You don't have long to think,' he says. But for Dudley – the strategist, the course dux – thinking was something he was very good at indeed. He looked down and considered the situation like a chessboard, and noticed the swell that rocked the submarines slightly from side to side as they pushed through the water.

'I wanted that sub to be rolling a bit,' he says, 'to be side-on to the swell so its guns would be hard to aim!'

Ahead of him, one of the Liberators made another run. Dudley saw his chance, and swung in behind the attacking bomber. It was soon hit, and began trailing smoke.

This time, Dudley's attack was low. So low that his hull skimmed the wave-tops. He approached from side on, gambling that the guns of only one U-boat could be brought to bear, the remaining two risking firing on each other. 'As it was, we had enough coming up at us from just the one,' he says.

In the Sunderland's nose, the front gunner, 'Bubbles' Pearce, watched the grey shapes enlarge in his gunsight, but hung off until just 400 yards before raking the deck of the nearest sub with every one of the hundred rounds from his single Vickers machine gun. Then, they flashed underneath.

'I was so low,' says Dudley, 'I had to lift the aircraft up to clear the conning tower.' Rarely was it an exact science. 'Feeling' the submarine beneath him, Dudley pushed a button on the dash, and seven 450-pound, Mark VII depth charges fell from the racks slung under the wings. His immediate concern was not for his enemy's destruction, however, but his own safety. His aeroplane was now revealed to the other U-boats, and Dudley swung hard left to avoid their combined firepower.

Here he pauses momentarily. 'This part,' he says, 'will always stick in my memory.' It was the voice of his navigator Jock Rolland saying calmly, quietly and 'in a very odd voice, "You've got him."' The way Dudley recounts it is almost eerie.

Jock was hanging out a rear-facing hatch, holding on, reckons Dudley, 'with his toes and fingernails'. He had a perfect view of the sub below, and even managed to take a photo. A series of massive plumes straddled the U-boat, ripping off the stern and throwing up towers of scummy, oily water. The Germans in the conning tower and on the deck were thrown – or leaped – into the water. Those inside were simply carried to the bottom, probably crushed to death by the weight of the water before they could drown.

Still partially disbelieving of what had just occurred, Dudley turned the Sunderland around. Where there had just been three boats, now there were two. Any jubilation the crew may have felt, however, was soon dampened by the dismal sight that greeted them. 'Here were these poor blokes, shaking their fists at us in the water.' The intercom was silent. Then, Dudley made a snap decision, the implications of which would continue to echo down the decades of his long life. 'I suppose it was on the spur of the moment. I dropped them a dinghy.' Again, Dudley's aim was on the money, and it landed right amongst them. A handful of German sailors managed to clamber onto it.

In a coincidence that almost defies belief, Dudley's aircraft – Sunderland 'U' of 461 Squadron – bore the exact same number of the submarine it had attacked and sunk – *U-461* – and this boat had a story of its own.

Korvettenkapitan Wolf-Harro Stiebler had taken command of the brand-new *U-461* on 22 April 1942, just three days before the formation of the RAAF squadron that would eventually cause its demise. Stiebler was a career sailor, having started off as an apprentice on merchant ships that regularly rounded Cape Horn. *U-461* was a type XIV 'milk cow' supply submarine servicing the hunter U-boats of the Wolf Packs. At a predetermined dot in the ocean, they would rendezvous and transfer vital diesel oil, food and water from their generous holds, enabling the hunters to continue their deadly work. Only ten of these 'queen bee' vessels were ever built by the Germans, and their destruction was greatly valued by the Royal Navy.

Stiebler had already completed six patrols, sailing out of the big concrete Keroman U-boat base at Lorient and stationing himself around the Azores. Up until now, he had been blessed with good luck, his crew suffering no casualties either from operations or accidents, and although attacked by Canadian Wellingtons in April, no real damage had been done. He had even shown mercy at sea when, the previous December, he had come across some lifeboats from the British cargo vessel *Teesbank*, torpedoed by a U-boat a few days before. In the spirit of the painted emblem of the she-wolf suckling Romulus and Remus that adorned his conning tower, he took the captain prisoner and gave food to the rest. All sixty men were later picked up safely by the Americans.

Out of all the services in all the fronts in all the armies of World War II, there was no more certain way of getting oneself killed than by volunteering for the U-boat service of the German Kriegsmarine. During the war, 743 boats were sunk killing an estimated 28 000 seamen and offering the truly pitiful survival rate of just one chance in four. The bravery of these young German sailors as they shut the hatches on their enormous grey metal monsters and set out from their bases in France on six-week patrols – knowing it was odds-on they would never be coming back – can scarcely be comprehended. It is a statistic of which Dudley is acutely aware.

Just fifteen of Stiebler's crew made it to Dudley's life raft that day after their submarine had been blown out from under them, and were taken prisoner. The remaining fifty-three perished.

The second boat in the group of three, *U-504*, dived, leaving *U-462* to battle it out on the surface alone. With one depth charge left, Dudley thought he may as well put it to good use and turned to attack his second submarine for the day. As he approached, however, great splashes appeared in the water around it, announcing the arrival of none other than the most famous sub-hunter of all time, Captain F. J. 'Johnny' Walker of the Royal Navy. The story of this remarkable modest man, and how he developed the tactics of using small sloops to break up the Wolf Pack attacks, was devoured by schoolboys in the 1950s in the book, *Walker, R.N.* Half a century on, it remains a classic of the navy, and although the man himself died of exhaustion before war's end, his image, in bronze, today looks out over Liverpool Harbour, the finishing line for so many of the ships he protected over three arduous years.

High above the battle, Peter Jensen watched as the guns from the little ships of Walker's 2nd Support Group – HMS *Kite*, *Woodpecker*, *Wren* and *Wild Goose* – opened on *U-462*. Like a great crippled shark, Peter saw it begin to billow smoke and start sailing drunkenly in circles before sinking. The crew took to the water and, inflating their yellow one-man dinghies, they resembled 'a mass of flowers bursting into bloom'. Over the radio, Dudley signalled there were German survivors in the water, and all but one were picked up and taken prisoner.

The already submerged *U-504* was not so lucky. Walker's flotilla soon gave chase. A few hours later, the depth charges found and destroyed her – two years to the day after she was launched – with all fifty-three hands.

With all three German submarines sunk, the day's action passed into history as the biggest single engagement between submarine, ships and aircraft, and remains so to this day.

And for Dudley, it was not yet over. Having fought the battle with his fuel mixture rich, he and his engineer did some quick calculations and realised there was not sufficient to get them back to base. As they discussed the alternatives on the way home, an excited voice called out in the intercom, 'Skipper, there's a submarine below us!' And there it was, incredibly, the fourth U-boat of the day again travelling defiantly on the surface.

Thinking quick, and hoping to catch it unawares, Dudley pushed the stick forward and went to attack, but this time, it was not to be. This one was waiting for him, and sent up a blast of fire. 'By God it was frightening,' he says today, a half-eaten Anzac biscuit in his hand, his focus fixed on a patch of floor that could be a mile away.

In the dive, he'd unknowingly knocked the lever that engaged the automatic pilot, and the controls of the big aeroplane froze. 'When I went to level out, I found I couldn't,' he says. He and Jimmy Leigh used all their strength to overcome the mechanism as the aircraft took several hits from the U-boat's 20-millimetre cannon. 'A fire started somewhere behind me and bits were coming off the spar,' he says. A later inspection would reveal that a few inches higher and the shell would have ignited a petrol tank. An extinguisher doused the flames, but this round went squarely to the Germans. Dudley did not risk another.

Levelling out at last, he jettisoned the remaining depth charge and made course for the Scilly Isles. Every moveable object was hurled out to save height and fuel. They arrived without further incident, but 'with about a pint of fuel left in the tanks'. They had been in the air thirteen hours, fifty-five minutes.

A day like this would be enough for anyone's war, but a few weeks later, Dudley and his crew outdid themselves again. It is another long story, involving an attack in the same patch of ocean by six Junkers 88s, being forced down after a forty-minute running air battle, landing on top of a seventy-foot swell, and the entire crew of eleven taking to the sole undamaged dinghy designed to hold a quarter that number. Then a miserable night spent in the open before being sighted by a Catalina, and another encounter with Captain Walker who, on the southern extremity of his range, turned around to pick them up. When word got around the flotilla that these were the men who had sunk *U-461*, an almighty cheer went up, and in the finest traditions of the navy, a whooping chorus of klaxons sounded out over the waves.

Dudley Marrows, to his considerable surprise, became the most highly decorated Sunderland pilot of the war. 'As I understand it,' he tells me with a laugh, 'I got the DFC for the sub, and the DSO for the air battle.' Quite a haul.

Another first – my one and only recipient of the Distinguished Service Order, an award second only to the Victoria Cross, and rarely awarded to an officer holding so lowly a rank as Flight Lieutenant.

As we talk, Dudley's wife, Sylvia, prompts him to reveal some other aspects of the story he has omitted, such as his swimming around the sinking Sunderland collecting his men – some wounded – and pulling them towards the dinghy, or the baritone of the rigger who kept the rest of the crew's spirits up during the long, uncertain night with a fine rendition of 'A life on the Ocean Waves'.

'It's nearly 2008,' says Dudley, who I have questioned and pummelled and drawn out over a very long afternoon. 'You'll have to excuse my memory.'

After sinking a submarine, being shot down in the sea and rescued, Dudley's tour was considered well and truly completed. He undertook some further training, then taught, then had the honour of flying himself back to Australia – in a Sunderland.

But for the final chapter of the story, I turn to Sylvia.

'I just love languages,' she tells me, and she speaks several excellently, although even she isn't quite sure of the origins of it all. A long time after the war, an address was somehow located for one Wolf Stiebler. By then, the former master of the *U-461* was working for an oil company setting up petrol stations across

Europe. With Sylvia's help, a correspondence was started, which lasted many years.

Then, accompanied by Peter Jensen, former wireless operator of Sunderland 'U' of 461 Squadron, the two of them made a trip to Regensburg in Germany to meet the remaining survivors of *U-461* and their families. With Sylvia translating, they talked and shared stories and reflected on how odd it was that such decent people as themselves had once been mortal enemies. Both Peter and Sylvia were treated like honoured friends. At one stage when Sylvia was leaving, a widow of one of the Germans took her aside. 'Please thank your husband,' the woman said earnestly. 'What he did gave me forty years of happy married life.' It was a remark Sylvia couldn't wait to pass on to Dudley.

Then one day a year or so later, a small party waited anxiously at the international arrivals terminal of Melbourne Airport, and Wolf Stiebler emerged to meet the man who was both his nemesis and his saviour. He stayed with them at their big citrus property at Buronga near Mildura, where for a week or two they talked about times both before and since the war, posed for photographs of Wolf wearing his new gift of a big Australian hat, and reflected on the terrible, dramatic events in the middle of the ocean that changed both their lives.

'Fifty-three dead. That doesn't sit too well on you at times,' says Dudley as he looks at the photo of him and Wolf, sitting together in a living room, smiling like old mates. 'Not that I worry about it too often.' It's the only thing he has said all day that I suspect might not be completely true.

Tiring of the war and, I believe, wanting to leave me with an idea of him more expansive than simply his years flying and fighting, Dudley shows me a proud collection of Aboriginal grinding stones discovered on his property, turned up by ploughs over the course of many years. 'You'd hear a "tink" against the metal and go and investigate.' He rubs his old hands over the old round stones, savouring their smoothness with his fingertips, and speaking of them reverently, as one would sacred objects of art.

My dad was half right when he told me the big aeroplanes flying out of Rose Bay were Sunderlands. Actually they were Sandringhams, the Sunderland's civilian incarnation with turrets, armour plate, depth-charge racks and every other vestige of their wartime career removed. In place of the sombre green and grey camouflage which concealed their outline against the deep and murky Atlantic was a handsome red and white livery which welcomed passengers for a pleasant jaunt across to an island in the Pacific – a far happier cargo than in their former days.

But as I watched them as a child pulling up off the water and heard the change in pitch in their big radial engines as they banked, then levelled out towards the east, it was the power, even the terror that I heard of a time before my own – so recent yet so different – when a dreadful struggle consumed the far corners of the globe; when the lives of millions were shattered against a mighty anvil, and young men like Dudley, and Arthur, and Max and Nevin, and even Peter and Heinz embarked on a terrible crusade which shaped their lives and changed the world.

Now, heading into the final laps of their long lives, each of them had permitted me to delve and prod and question, to stir up the solid layers of memory – sometimes decades dormant – to hear and record the deeds of their long-departed youth.

For some, the few years spent wearing the blue uniform – a brief moment in the context of their eight decades or more – has continued to tower over the landscape of their lives. Some still seem to be fighting the war, reliving the stresses and the visions which, to their astonishment, have returned with the years rather than diminished. For others, it was simply a blip, forgotten but for the persistence of a curious stranger half their age with a tape recorder.

As close as I could come to what I set out to achieve – understanding what they did, seeing what they saw – bringing to the table a lifetime's fascination which eased open the heavy gates of reticence, I remained with my four-and-a-half decades spent in luxuriant peace but little the wiser. The fires, the fears, the youthful faces long dead are traumas which I and millions more have been mercifully spared.

For their time given both sixty years ago, as well as in long afternoons with me in their homes, I am both honoured and grateful.

ACKNOWLEDGEMENTS

Putting together a book about the airmen of the Second World War was in reality a labour of love for me, and I am indebted to the people at Penguin Australia not only for believing such a project to be a worthwhile one, but for allowing me to write it, then with patience and good grace, standing by as I blithely ignored a series of deadlines before delaying them further with endless, last-minute finessing and fiddling. Thank you particularly to my ever-encouraging editors, Kirsten Abbott and Anne Rogan, and also to Louise Ryan for being an early champion of the book.

I have received great co-operation from many people over the course of the project, particularly those who contacted me with the names and numbers of former airmen, who I would otherwise have never met. I would especially like to thank Charles Palliser, Lisa Louden, Murray Glegg, Ian Spiers, Dick Levy and Les Gordon. Your enthusiasm made my job so much easier.

I am particularly grateful for the patience and support of wives, partners and children, who allowed me to pick and prod at the memories of their loved ones, poring over log books, raiding private photo albums, and stirring up goodness knows what demons to be dealt with long after I had departed the scene. Over the course of many hours and many afternoons, you kept both spirits and blood sugar levels from flagging with sandwiches, cakes and encouragement.

Most importantly, I am indebted to the men themselves who allowed a complete stranger into their homes to wrench open the often difficult past with a trust and openness that both humbled and inspired me.

Many of those I interviewed for this book have had to wait a long time to see it appear. For some, sadly, it has been too long, and a number have passed away before they could see their stories published. I hope, for their families and all those interested, I have done their memories justice, and that the effort and the courage they showed in revealing to me their part in a great conflict has been a worthwhile one.

PHOTOGRAPHY CREDITS

P 1: Jock McAuley, private collection

P 2: Jock McAuley, private collection

P 3: top – Jock McAuley, private collection;
bottom – Barney Barnett, private collection

P 4: Barney Barnett, private collection

P 5: Ralph Proctor, private collection

P 6: Ralph Proctor, private collection

P 7: Ralph Proctor, private collection

P 8: top – Ralph Proctor, private collection;
bottom – Bob Molesworth, private collection

P 9: Bob Molesworth, private collection

PP 10–11: Bob Molesworth, private collection

P 12: Bob Molesworth, private collection

P 13: Roy Riddel, private collection

P 14: Roy Riddel, private collection

P 15: Roy Riddel, private collection

P 16: Arthur Cundall, private collection

P 17: David Roberts, private collection

P 18: David Roberts, private collection

P 19: David Roberts, private collection

P 20: top – David Roberts, private collection;
bottom – Max Durham, private collection

P 21: Max Durham, private collection

P 22: Max Durham, private collection

P 23: top – Max Durham, private collection;
bottom – James Coward, private collection

P 24: Harvey Bawden, private collection

P 25: Harvey Bawden, private collection

P 26: Tom Trimble, private collection

P 27: Michael Veitch, private collection

P 28: top – wikipedia.com; bottom – Ian Spiers, private collection

P 29: top – Michael Veitch, private collection;
bottom – Alistair Smith, private collection

P 30: Alistair Smith, private collection

P 31: Ian Spiers, private collection

P 32: top – Ian Spiers, private collection;
bottom – Dudley Marrow, private collection

Also from Penguin

INVADING AUSTRALIA
Japan and the Battle for Australia, 1942

Peter Stanley

1942 was a key year in Australia's history. As its people had so long feared, White Australia, an outpost of empire, seemed about to be invaded by the Japanese. In that one year, Darwin was bombed, submarines torpedoed ships in Sydney Harbour and Australian Militiamen died on the Kokoda Trail.

Each year, more and more Australians celebrate Anzac Day and honour the lives of those who fought for their country. There is even a push to create a new public holiday, in remembrance and celebration of the 'Battle for Australia'. But was there ever really such a battle, and how close did Australia actually come to being invaded?

Invading Australia provides a comprehensive, thorough and well-argued examination of these and other pertinent questions. Peter Stanley writes compellingly about Australian attitudes to Japan before, during and after World War II, and uses archival sources to discuss Japan's war plans early in 1942. He also shows that rather than a 'Battle for Australia' there was a worldwide fight for freedom and democracy that has allowed the West to enjoy great prosperity in the decades since 1945.

BEATEN BY A BLOW

Dennis McIntosh

One man's story of life as a shearer, a tearaway and a young father trying to make ends meet.

Dennis McIntosh was always determined not to get stuck in a factory like his father, but it's only once he takes a job as a roustabout that he discovers what he really wants to be: a shearer. Travelling from station to station, he revels in the smell and feel of the sheds, and the freedom of being answerable to no man except his mates.

And it's a thrilling time to be in this legendary occupation. There's a fight on: the union is defending its workers against scab labourers' use of the wide comb. But while shearing's a fine life for a nineteen-year-old, it's a hard one for a man. As the added weight of adulthood settles on Dennis's shoulders, the sheds take their unforgiving toll.

Beaten by a Blow shows us the reality behind the romance of the shearer. Most of all, it tells the story of a boy full of hope crashing headlong into life – into work, into drink, into responsibilities he isn't ready for, which come closer to breaking his back than shearing ever did.

Subscribe to receive *read more*, your monthly newsletter from Penguin Australia. As a *read more* subscriber you'll receive sneak peeks of new books, be kept up to date with what's hot, have the opportunity to meet your favourite authors, download reading guides for your book club, receive special offers, be in the running to win exclusive subscriber-only prizes, plus much more.

Visit penguin.com.au to subscribe.